CHOOSING
A
CLASSIC
CAR

FOREWORD BY STIRLING MOSS

Foulis

A FOULIS Motoring Book

First published 1986
© Lindsay Porter, Graham Robson, Jeremy
Coulter, John Williams, Jonathan Wood, L.J.K.
Setright, Peter Williams, Paul Skilleter, Ian
Ward, F. Wilson McComb, Mike McCarthy,
Paul Clark, Robin Wager and Haynes
Publishing Group 1986

Published by
Haynes Publishing Group
Sparkford, Near Yeovil, Somerset
BA22 7JJ, England

Haynes Publications Inc,
861 Lawrence Drive, Newbury Park,
California 91320 USA

Library of Congress Catalog Card Number
86-82329

British Library Cataloguing in Publication Data

Choosing a classic car.
  1. Automobiles
  I. Porter, Lindsay
  629.2'222   TL145
  ISBN 0-85429-564-X

Page layout: Mike King & Chris Hull

Printed in England by
J.H. Haynes & Co. Ltd

Foreword by
Stirling Moss

Although my name is usually associated with motor racing, vehicles of all sorts have always fascinated me. Not only have cars and driving given me a lifetime of pleasure, but they have also been the basis of my professional existence for just on forty years. I still seem to spend much of my time hopping from one driving seat to another!

My involvement with the automotive industry and motor sport, has taken me all round the world and so I know there are many people less privileged than ourselves. It therefore seems very appropriate that this book will give much pleasure to fellow motor enthusiasts, and more importantly, should provide practical help to those in real need in the world's underdeveloped countries.

I hope that readers of this book will be encouraged to become involved in the thriving classic car scene. Not only are these cars great fun, mainly well built and quite beautiful, but each and every one of them is helping to preserve our automotive heritage.

I thank you for the help you have given Intermediate Technology through your purchase and hope that you will enjoy this book.

Introduction and Acknowledgements

Although it seems a long time ago now, I don't suppose I shall ever forget watching the "Live Aid" concert on TV! To start off with, I thought it would be just an extraordinary piece of razzmatazz but as the event went on, it seemed to create its own sort of magic ... All those rock stars, and all those millions of people around the world, giving something of themselves to help people they had never seen and would never see; simply because they had been made aware of their suffering. It was an event, a phenomenon, to show cynics that there *is* more to folk than simple self interest!

It was during the transmission of that concert that I had the idea for this book. After all, if rock stars can do it, why not, in their humble way, a bunch of motoring writers and editors? The idea for a guide to classic cars came simply because I couldn't think of anything else that most motoring writers who are involved in the classic car scene would have in common! In the event, when I contacted Jonathan Wood, Paul Skilleter and Graham Robson to try the idea out, all were enthusiastic about it and couldn't wait to get started. Similarly, every other writer I was able to get hold of was delighted to contribute and I'm sure that we could easily have filled this book twice over. If your favourite motoring writer doesn't appear here (and most of those in the classic field *are* here) it's simply because they couldn't be contacted at the time the book was being produced – no-one who was asked said "No!"

In the same spirit, my wife Shan, neighbour 'Terry' Johnson and Judith St Clair-Pedroza at Haynes were all thoroughly involved in typing and preparing the work for typesetting while others at Haynes and in particular Rod Grainger and Mansur Darlington have also given freely of their valuable time. Jeremy Coulter, Deputy Editor at "Classic Cars" magazine, carried out some picture research as did Paul Skilleter, Managing Editor at "Practical Classics" magazine while the National Motor Museum researched and donated the use of a number of other prints that couldn't be found elsewhere. Stirling Moss has kindly contributed a foreword. Mel Smith at Tandy helped to get out the original mail shot to other writers and Grahame Butterworth at Impact PR has agreed to assist Murray Corfield of Haynes in promoting this book.

When I approached John Haynes with the concept for the book, he also readily agreed to it and it must be appreciated that the Haynes Publishing Group has brought its usual high level of expertise to bear in this good cause. In fact, it was John Haynes who suggested that the author royalties and publisher's profits should go to the charity "Intermediate Technology" – and when you read in the next section about all IT has to offer, I think you'll see why ... After all, they are the sort of organisation that doesn't attempt to swim against the tide of technology, but instead, they seek to adapt technology and to make it suitable for people's needs in areas of the world where greed for 'consumerist' technology in the West has contributed strongly to poverty and suffering. A fine irony!

Naturally, everyone involved with the book is delighted that you have contributed to Intermediate Technology through your purchase (or if the book is borrowed, the address for sending your donation to is shown at the end of the next section). Aside from the good the book will do, I hope you *enjoy* what may have turned out to be a unique compilation of information on some of the best loved of classic cars.

Lindsay Porter
Upper Sapey,
County of Hereford and Worcester

Contents

Foreword by Stirling Moss   3

Introduction and Acknowledgements   4

Intermediate Technology by Steve Bonnist   6

Why Buy a Classic? by Lindsay Porter   8

Super Spider – Alfa's 1750 & 2000 Spider by Graham Robson   10

Armstrong Siddeley – the Sapphire by Jeremy Coulter   16

Austin Seven – the Baby Austin by John Williams   22

Buying a Bentley – the MkVI & R-type by John Williams   36

Citroën Traction Avant – French f-w-d by Jonathan Wood   46

Citroën SM – M for Maserati by L.J.K. Setright   50

Top of the Pops – Ford's ubiquitous sidevalve by Jonathan Wood   54

Hawk, Super Snipe, Imperial – the 'Series' Humbers by Peter Williams   60

An XK for Restoration – Jaguar XK120, 140 & 150 by Paul Skilleter   66

An E-Type for Restoration – the Jaguar XKE by Paul Skilleter   76

S-Type – the alternative Jaguar saloon by Paul Skilleter   84

Jaguar XJS – a realistic option? By Jeremy Coulter   94

Healey Hunting – the Jensen-Healey by Lindsay Porter   102

Jowett Javelin – the car from Yorkshire by Jonathan Wood   110

A Dash of Elan – the legendary Lotus by Ian Ward   114

Super Cooper – Mini magic by Graham Robson   122

MG T-Series – a development profile by F. Wilson McComb   130

MGA – the story of MG's first modern sports car by F. Wilson McComb   134

Living With a Midget – a look at the small MG by Lindsay Porter   140

B for Buying – MG's B, C and V8 by Lindsay Porter   146

Mercedes-Benz 300SL – the story of the Gullwing by L.J.K. Setright   156

Porsche 356 – a portrait of the original Porsche by Mike McCarthy   164

Porsche 911 – a sting in the tail? By Mike McCarthy   174

924 – everyman's Porsche? Paul Clark   184

Buying a Rover – P4 quality? By John Williams   190

Second-hand Supercars – the car you've always promised yourself ... By Ian Ward   200

An Alpine ... or Tiger – the Rootes roadsters. By John Williams   204

TR 4A, 5 & 6 – a Triumph? By Jeremy Coulter   214

GT6 – Triumph's sports tourer. By Graham Robson   222

Buying a VW Beetle – der Käfer. By Robin Wager   230

DRIVE AID

Driving Towards the Future

An introduction to Intermediate Technology & its aims by Press Officer, Steve Bonnist

Many of the cars featured in this book were conceived and built with tender loving care, by teams of men and women who cared about their work, what they were producing and for whom they were producing it. And the fact that you are reading about their achievements shows that they were right ... you care because they cared!

It's difficult to imagine people feeling the same about today's models in 20 or 30 years' time. Cars built by robots with built-in obsolescence simply do not have the same allure, do they? And look at the complexity! The late Fritz Schumacher, the man who wrote the book "Small Is Beautiful" and founded the charity Intermediate Technology, used to tell a story about a friend who had a splendid Mercedes which had developed an electrical fault. All the windows were stuck open in different positions, and he had to drive all winter, from garage to garage, trying to find someone who could penetrate the system. Finally, in the spring, he found someone who could repair it – for $300! Schumacher asked, "Was it worth $300 so he didn't have to turn a handle?"

The sheer size of modern production methods also bothered Schumacher. In a speech given just before his death in 1977, he noted that the Ford Motor Company was founded with just $30,000. Today, even accounting for the change in value in the dollar, you couldn't change a screw in a new model for less than $100,000. "When Ford started, it was uncertain whether the steam engine wasn't better than the petrol engine; he could have switched from a petrol engine to a steam engine in the shortest possible time without disturbing anybody, and for very little money. Can't we look back in that direction?"

Complexity, size and automation were issues that, to Schumacher, needed to be tackled if the Third World in particular was going to make technological progress appropriate to the resources and needs of its people. His argument was that in countries with a highly dispersed population, very little foreign exchange, a poor – to nonexistant – communications infrastructure, and millions of people unemployed or underemployed it makes no sense to install large scale, expensive automated factories in the cities. The rich would get richer, and the poor would sink lower into poverty.

Schumacher's solution to this was to develop a range of intermediate-level technologies which could be made and used in the areas that needed them most: the rural areas, where over 90% of the population lives in Third World Countries. This intermediate range would be more productive than traditional tools, but of lower cost, simpler and more labour-intensive than the large-scale equipment used in industrialised countries. He started the British-based charity Intermediate Technology in 1965 to challenge the prevailing "Big is Beautiful" approach to development, by showing that Small is not only beautiful, but possible.

Since then Intermediate Technology has indeed shown that small scale production is not just possible, but powerful. Experience in

Intermediate Technology-designed "Oxtrike". Manufactured and used in Nairobi, Kenya. (Courtesy Intermediate Technology).

over 60 developing countries has shown that, given the means to get on with the job, the poor can really work themselves out of poverty. Rural workshops can turn out an astonishing range of goods desperately needed by villagers to improve their lives: fishing boats, spinning and weaving equipment, agricultural tools, bricks, roofing tiles, windpumps, crop processing equipment, wood-saving stoves – the list of what makes simple technology work for people is endless.

The challenge of providing the right kind of help to the Third World is very exciting. The task of helping to identify what people need, what they want, what skills and resources they have and what they are willing to do is not easy. But once the ingredients have been mixed together, the result can be terrific! Patience and sensitivity combined with ingenuity and perseverance can open up new avenues for millions of people who want a hand up and out of poverty, rather than just a handout.

The charity Intermediate Technology, which pioneered this approach to "development as if people matter", is now considered one of the world's leading organisations of its kind. Band Aid, Oxfam, Christian Aid and dozens of other charities all draw upon its resources in planning and implementing their projects. Governments, U.N. Agencies, and the World Bank turn to Intermediate Technology for advice and assistance. Thousands of volunteers, missionaries, extension agents and local

Built in Kenya, and known as the "Kijito" (Swahili for stream of water) this wind-powered water pump is another I.T. design. (Courtesy Intermediate Technology).

individuals and organisations use their free technical enquiry service every year. Hundreds of manuals, bibliographies, DIY books, technical briefs and case studies have been published by the charity, to help guide those in the field.

Intermediate Technology's development of windpumps and low-cost electronic controllers for tiny village hydro-electric systems have recently won a prestigious international award for helping to solve global social and economic problems. Their designs for efficient cooking stoves, workshop equipment, fishing boats and dozens of other pieces of useful, practical technology are now used in tens of thousands of villages. The need now is to spread these and so many other techniques and methods to *millions* of villages.

Live Aid helped to save many lives. The next crucial step is to create livelihoods which will provide lasting relief from poverty and hunger for hundreds of millions of people. That is Intermediate Technology's aim, and we are pleased that the authors, editors and the publishers of this book have chosen to help us and out collaborators overseas in meeting this challenge.

Read on. Enjoy the Book. And thank you, too, for your support!

Intermediate Technology Development
Group Ltd
9 King Street
London WC2E 8HW

Bob Geldof is shown how to make low-cost roofing tiles the Intermediate Techno-logy way at the "Design for Need" Exhibition. (Courtesy Design Council).

DRIVE AID

Why Buy a Classic?

Lindsay Porter looks at some of the reasons for wanting to buy a classic motor car.

Once upon a time, all those vehicles known as classic cars were very ancient pieces of machinery indeed. Many of them looked like converted horse carriages, some were steered by tillers and all their owners were considered cranks. All other old cars were thought of as, well, old cars; things to buy if you couldn't afford anything better. Mind you, some people had a 'feeling' for even moderately old motor cars even then, it's just that they didn't 'come out' and talk about it unless they were *very* sure of their company, lest they were also thought of as a bit of a crank. Nowadays, it's not only acceptable to like older cars (and to think of them as classics), it's even seen as a good thing! Classic cars are anti-waste where resources are concerned, they're anti- the throw-away society and everyone believes they actually appreciate in value rather than depreciating. And, of course, They Don't Make Them Like They Used To!.

In fact, there *are* sound reasons for running or owning a classic car, but they're not necessarily the ones of popular myth. So why buy a classic? Firstly, what about the idea that classic cars are anti-waste. Very largely, this is true, and although exhaust emissions from most of them are something of an ecologist's nightmare (although this is not true of all; look at the beautifully designed, clean burning Lotus engine used also in the Jensen-Healey for instance), the small numbers of classic cars still in daily use make that insignificant and, in any case, the ecological 'pros' are much greater than the 'cons'. Once a car is built, that's it as far as using up resources like steel and aluminium, plastics and power are concerned apart, of course, from the inevitable maintenance needs. But there's a human side to the increase in interest in classic cars too: modern car manufacturers boast of their robotically operated factories and the lack of humanity that goes into their cars for all the world as though they were virtues! Personally, I'd rather be in a car that human hands have touched and wrought any day, faults and all. And all classic cars have not only that attribute but also the one that says that since they are old, almost by definition they will need extra maintenance. And maintenance means people doing satisfying, paid work instead of sitting at home listening to the hum of the robots working in the factory next door.

The fact that people made classic cars – and more to the point-that people designed them, means that they have been built in such a way that human hands can take them apart and put them together again. It also means that they have almost invariably been overdesigned, because without the calculations of a computer to design a car's structure down to the thinnest, cheapest, nastiest level the maker can get away with, human designers built in safety margins that don't necessarily make the parts last longer (although in the case of engines, that usually *is* what it means) but that do make them repairable. Because, unlike CAD (Computer Aided Design) built cars, there's always something left to repair, even after wear has taken place: for instance, there's invariably enough 'meat' around corroded body and chassis parts to allow repairs to be grafted in when chassis and monocoques have been designed in the traditional way.

But what about the third good reason for running a classic rather than a modern car? That is the belief that classic cars invariably appreciate in value. Well, I've got a special interest in classic car values because, as my first project in motoring journalism and working with my wife, Shan, I developed the first regular guide to classic car values for *Practical Classics* magazine, research having begun some six months before the magazine's launch in early 1980. We still produce the *Price Guide* and so we've had the chance to become as close as anyone to changes in classic car values. And I can state quite categorically that of all the hundreds of classics we've studied over this period, only a tiny handful have appreciated in value *after* inflation has been taken into account.

It's true that many older cars, once their 'natural' depreciation is over, start to increase in paper value while almost all of the others cease to lose 'value', but in almost every case, the value of money falls quicker than the value of old cars increases. On the other hand, unless you're considering the purchase of a classic as an alternative to an old master (the picture rail may never take the strain!), this is irrelevant. If you're considering the purchase of a classic as an alternative to a modern car, however, this piece of information is highly relevant: new cars depreciate so quickly that their loss in value is the most expensive part of keeping such cars on the road for each of the first few years of their life. A typical 2-litre saloon loses an average of well over £1,500 per annum, according to the AA, while a Triumph GT6, bought ten years ago for around £425 and worth about £1,350 today, obviously won't have suffered the same sort of fate. In point of fact, it won't have gained in value either, despite the fact that it is now worth more in purely cash terms; the rate of inflation means that the value of the GT6 is today virtually the same as it was ten years ago after the effects of inflation are taken into account, but you could imagine how much, say, a 1975 Cortina would be worth now even if it had been as well looked after as the Triumph. A few odd-balls have actually appreciated in real money terms, among them the VW Beetle Cabriolet and the muscular AC Cobra while other putative classics such as many Fords and most Vauxhalls have depreciated right down to a sort of 'old banger' level. On the other hand, virtually every car produced by the old BMC set-up is now achieving some sort of following.

Of course, classic cars can be a lot more troublesome than their new counterparts to keep mobile (although not more so than *some* new cars that one comes across!), but there are increasing numbers of specialist manufacturers and suppliers making it easier to keep classics like the MGB and Midget, the MkII Jaguar and the Morris Minor on the road than some nearly new cars considered by their makers to be 'obsolete'. And, in any case, this is one of the undeniable penalties – challenges, as some would have it – of owning something with character.

Now, what about the sigh, the shake of the head and the assertion that 'They don't make them like they used to' from Mr and Mrs Maestro Owner whenever they park next to a classic? They're not generally referring to technical virtuosity or innovation, but to the elusive 'character' that you can't define, although everyone knows it's there. Some examples: older Jaguars were fitted with engine camshaft covers made out of polished aluminium and had window frames made from chromium plated drawn brass, (and I'm talking about cars as recent as some E-types and the MkII Saloon!). M.G. saloons had twin-carb aluminium inlet manifolds with an 'M.G.' motif cast proudly and prominently into

them, and cars as everyday and ordinary as the Morris Minor, the Austin Cambridge and the MGB were fitted with real leather seats. Even the early Mini had brass door hinges and a beautiful brass heater tap on the engine. And so many perfectly mundane, inexpensive motor cars had fixtures and fittings built into them that would today be prohibitively, impossibly, expensive. That's not all there is to the 'character' of these cars – more still comes from the nostalgia that enables us to forgive and even enjoy features that would be criticised in a new car. But the way an early VW Beetle door shuts still makes a modern mid-price car sound like a tin can by comparison.

For perfectly understandable reasons of economy, of course, modern manufacturers have, in their race not to win the wooden spoon in a contest where there are too many contestants and where somebody must fail, made refinement superficial. As a result, style has become something that is self-adhesive and durability lasts the shortest decent time beyond the warranty period – if you're lucky.

By contrast, most classic cars are things of beauty in their own right, especially those that were well built and well designed in the first place. Choosing a good one is never easy – over the passage of time there have been too many opportunities for maltreatment for most cars not to have suffered to some degree. But a well planned search, a realistic acceptance of values allied to a determination *never* to be won over by external appearances, should mean that classic car motoring, whether you wish it to be in a humble Ford Popular, a wind-in-the-hair MGB, or an early, opulent XJS, can be within your grasp.

Super Spider

Graham Robson looks at the Alfa Romeo convertible – the Spider 1750 and 2000

'They don't make them like that anymore. What a pity!', was one remark we heard recently when driving an Alfa Romeo 2000 Spider. Wrong! They do, they do – if only for export to the USA, for the Spider, in a way, is Alfa Romeo's MGB – timeless, popular, and still selling, still being made. A few reach Britain for conversion to right-hand-drive.

Somehow, though, it's always been much more glamorous (and faster) than an MGB. And so it should be, with a 130bhp twin overhead camshaft engine, and styling by Pininfarina!

No question, it was a 'classic' when launched, and it is still a 'classic' today. It was merely the latest (and, as it happens, the last)

of a whole series of Alfa Romeo Spiders. It was also the definitive statement on the Giulietta/Giulia theme. Yet, in terms of numbers built, the Spider has always been overshadowed by the Coupes.

In theory, too, the Spider is several Alfa Romeo generations out of date (the Alfetta arrived in the early 1970s, after all), but that could never make it look ordinary. Now that there are so very few new Spiders of any type on the market, the Alfa Romeo deserves further study, for it has a twin-cam alloy engine, taut handling, and timeless looks to its 'classic' credentials.

The choice

This could be a very long article, so right away we'd better say that most of the analysis will be of the 1750 and 2000 models. Even so, the body shell itself has appeared in two distinctly different forms, and with four different engine sizes.

The story really started with the new Giulia generation of 1962, where the basic Giulietta theme was enlarged, the engine size settled at 1,570cc, complete with twin overhead camshafts, and the five-speed transmis-

The 1974 Spider had a classically attractive shape, sadly, few will have survived as well as this one without considerable pampering or major surgery. (Courtesy Philip Young/"Sporting Cars" magazine.)

sion was standard. All types had four-wheel disc brakes, coil spring independent front suspension and worm and sector steering, with the complex location of a rigid rear axle.

The first sporting Giulia was the Sprint GT, on a shorter version of the Giulia's floorpan, announced in 1963, with 106bhp, the lightweight 115bhp GTA 'homologation special' followed, but it was not until 1966 that GT became GT Veloce (with 109bhp), and the original Spider, sharing the same running gear, was announced.

This had an even shorter wheelbase (88.6in, compared with 92.5in for the GT Veloce, and 98.8in for the saloons) of the same basic floorpan, and a rounded body style by Pininfarina. There were only two seats, a long tail, body shell construction was at the Pininfarina works in Turin, and final assembly was at Alfa's Milan factory. Like all other Giulias of the day, it had 15in wheels. Its official title was 1600 Duetto Spider.

Next, late in 1967, came the 1,799cc/ 118bhp version, simply called 1750 Spider (the Duetto name was dropped), which replaced the original, this car having 14in wheels. Less than a year later, Alfa Romeo

also announced the Spider 1300 Junior, which had the 89bhp/1,290cc twin cam engine, very few of which were sold in the UK.

For 1970, Alfa, and Pininfarina, had second thoughts about the rear style, chopping short the sweeping lines in favour of a 'Kamm' tail which reduced the length, and the overhang, by six inches (and slightly cropped the luggage space). At the same time, the car was given a revised facia, still with the same range of instruments.

The definitive model, the 200 Spider Veloce, was launched in June 1971, and differed from the 1750 by having the final stretch to the famous twin-cam engine, to 1,962cc/132bhp. In its original form, so equipped, it was good for 120mph, with acceleration to match.

And that, except for minor style and updating changes, was that as far as the British and European versions were concerned. Right-hand-drive 2000 Spiders were built until 1977 (the last being sold off, here in 1978), after which the car was no longer available here. Left-hand-drive cars, of course, continued to be built, especially for North America, where their mechanical specification differed considerably in detail.

Cars called 1300 Roadster Junior and 1600 Roadster Junior were re-introduced in 1974 (really as knee-jerk reaction to the energy crisis), and although the 1300 was dropped at the end of 1977, the 1600 carried on, and was still listed in 1985.

The cars were long considered to be quietly pottering on towards retirement, so it was a real surprise to see them slightly restyled in the winter of 1983, complete with a new grille, and large front spoiler, and a moulded rear spoiler around the top and sides of the 'Kamm' tail.

Nevertheless for 1985, the 2000 Spider was still made, with peak power (for Europe) quoted at 128bhp, or (with fuel injection, for the USA) 117bhp.

As far as the UK is concerned, the 1750 and 2000 models were the most numerous.

The Spider today

Officially none have been sold here since 1978, but in recent years Bell & Colvill, of West Horsley, Surrey, have been importing 'federal' versions, and converting them to right-hand drive, for a great deal of money.

Supplies in the UK are relatively limited, and most of them are 1750s and 2000s. Since total global production in the 1970s was of the order of 3,000 Spiders a year, it is easy to see that the total number of cars in this country may be little more than a thousand or so.

A few years ago, good examples would have been hard to find for the 'tin worm' syndrome would be well advanced, but, as they have come back into fashion, some cars have been nicely restored.

Are you interested in joining the Alfisti? If so, this is what we think you should be looking for.

Heritage

1954: Alfa Romeo Giulietta, with new twin-cam engine, first shown.

1962: Alfa Giulia range of saloons, complete with enlarged 1,570cc engine, put on sale.

1963: Alfa Romeo Giulia Sprint GT, with Bertone-style body, and 106bhp, plus 5-speed box, revealed.

Spider family history

March 1966: Launch of 1600 Spider (subsequently called 'Duetto') at Geneva Motor show, with 109bhp, 1570cc engine. Styling and body shell construction by Pininfarina, in Turin.

September 1966: First UK imports of Duetto.

September 1967: 1600 Duetto replaced by visually identical 1750 Spider Veloce, with 118bhp and 1,779cc.

Autumn 1969: Tail-end style changed, with bulbous shape abandoned in favour of square cut-off, but unchanged 'chassis' and running gear.

(**1968-72:** 1300 Spider also produced, with 89bhp 1,290cc engine).

June 1971: 1750 Spider dropped, in favour of 2000 Spider Veloce, having 1,322bhp/1,962cc engine.

Spring 1978: UK imports of 2000 Spider Veloce officially discontinued. Production continued, however, for USA market.

Early 1980s: Limited UK imports restarted, via Bell & Colvill, West Horsley, Surrey.

Winter 1983: Modifications to front style (spoiler), rear end (spoiler) and to interior.

Summer 1986: Received aerodynamic change (announced March 1986).

The body

Unfortunately, Pininfarina styled cars better than built them, and the fact is that a Spider might have rusted badly. Restoration is possible, of course, but the price is very high. Especially in the case of the Spiders, beware that the body has not cosmetically been 'dressed-up' to hide the horrors.

Look around the edges of the wheel arches, the 'splash' areas ahead of, or behind, the wheel arches, and the sills, especially towards the front, and around the jacking points. Front wings may rust along the top (close to the bonnet opening), and along their lower edges, while rear wings may suffer due to water having drained down, inside, from the convertible cut-out area.

As with many open cars, the Spiders sometimes get caught in the rain with the hood down, which lets water get at the floorpan. Seat runners and their mountings may have suffered, as might the footwells and inner sills, not to mention the inside of the doors, so look around the door edges, and along their undersides.

Boot floors may have suffered – again because of water leakage, and collection after storms – and around the tail you should also check on welded seams, and sharp edges (like boot lids) for chipping and other damage.

Incidentally, parts for early long-tail Spiders (1600s and 1750s, in the context of this survey) are now obsolete. In this, and all other cases, make doubly sure that the car you are inspecting is complete, down to badges, chrome strips, headlamp plastic cowls and other details.

Look around the front end for signs of repaired accident damage. This is not shameful, in itself, but has the repair been properly done, do all panels fit together properly, and has the structural underside been distorted? While under the car, look at the cross-member under the radiator (it tends to collect standing water), and the state of the inner wheel arches, particularly where they weld up to the rest of the monocoque. The structural underside, at least, ought to be sound, but have a look at the rear suspension mountings, to be sure.

Power train

The engine is magnificent – if it has had regular care and attention. Properly serviced, and with correctly set-up valve gear, it can run and run. There may be some evidence of oil leaking out, perhaps down the side of the block, which is often due to failed rubber 'O' rings under camshaft bearings.

Be sure that there is no evidence of engine oil in the cooling water, or evidence of water loss, either. In fact, is the right sort of inhibitor in the water, too? These engines have aluminium blocks and heads, both of which are susceptible to frost damage, and to corrosion from cooling water.

Oil pressure? There should be about 4kg/cm^2 at moderate engine speeds and, of course, there ought not to be blue haze from the exhaust. Valve clearances might have gone astray over the years, perhaps with the last owner not troubling to have this rectified. The car might still go well, but have a very thrashy unit; attention to valve guides, and to re-shimming, might be needed – that's not an easy DIY job.

Perhaps every 50,000 miles a strip-out should be tackled, at which point the lower timing chain should be changed. The good news about wear, of course, is that this is a wet-liner engine, so piston and liner replacement (more straightforward than boring and sleeving) might be tackled. At this point, by the way, be sure the cylinder head gasket is in good condition, and that the engine mounts are still sound.

Clutches on these cars, even though they are quite light, have a hard life, so you ought to budget for a new one (heavy-duty examples are available), but the gearboxes are quite sturdy, except for a tendency to lose second gear synchromesh, and a frequent tendency to jump out of reverse gear when manoeuvring; this last may be due to bent selector forks. Is the rubber doughnut behind the box in good condition?

Back axles are usually sound, but may have become a bit loose and noisy. From mid-1973 there was a limited-slip differential in the 2000 Spider's axle; if so, is it still working properly?

Suspension, steering, brakes

All these, like the power train, are basically

Everything about the interior, from that crazy gearshift column to the deep instrument binnacles, indicates the sort of Italian overstatement that you either love or hate. (Courtesy Philip Young/ "Sporting Cars" magazine.)

the same as the Coupe components, so parts supply is assured. The handling on these cars should be crisp and predictable, but if not, look to the front end for worn joints and bushes, particularly in the steering, which is not a simple rack and pinion, but a more complex worm and sector unit.

Check for ball joint wear in the front suspension – particularly in the steering system – and if the front end is noisy (some would say 'squeaky') suspect worn bushes in the wishbones. Anti-roll bar brushes, too, may suffer, and the mountings have become corroded. Coil springs themselves have been known to sag.

At the rear, the various bushes in the axle location might be worn (which will allow axle steer, and clonks on torque reversal, to take place); this might show up in a lack of straight-line stability on undulating road surfaces. Check up on the axle bump stops, and on the condition of springs.

Dampers, front and rear, will almost certainly be tired, and Alfa specialists recommend fitting heavier duty, firmer, replacements. One front end oddity might be noise from the steering gear when winding it from lock to lock, at rest. This often means a loose nut on the drop arm. If you are lucky, tightening it up, and Loctiting to make sure, will solve the problem.

Brakes, all disc, have their problems, not only worn or rusty discs, as one might expect, but corroded cylinders (particularly master cylinders, under the bonnet), and even pedals rusting on to their pivot shafts (which is due to water leakage on to those pivots, and might also affect the operation of the clutch pedal as

well). Fluid leak causes will either be obvious, or will be due to a faulty servo.

On cars which have been carelessly stored, or neglected after salt-covered road journeys, there may be brake pipe corrosion, and the hand brake cable may be rusted solid.

While you are under the car, look at the exhaust system, which is in three parts. The rear box suffers badly. If you plan to buy a Spider, and keep it for some years, it may be worth investing in a properly fitted stainless steel (non-factory) system.

Trim and furnishing

The problem here is that so many Spiders might have suffered from rain damage, either because of hoods being furled, or being defective. The standard hood itself, could chafe badly between framework and body every time it was raised or lowered, and leaks could ensure.

'Your' car, indeed, might need a new hood, especially as the transparent panels might have gone opaque with age, and the heating systems seem to operate very eccentrically after a few years. Best, if possible, to have a road test to check all this out.

Earlier examples had rubber mats on the floor. If these are worn through, you might find replacements difficult. Expect, too, the car to be in a rather tatty condition (there are specialists to aid a rebuild . . .), and be sure that all the electrical fittings, and instruments, are present and correct.

Pre-1970 models had a very plain facia, with a painted panel, which might have been scratched; later panels were more opulently presented, but there was so much brightwork to go missing, be vandalised, or even be 'modified' by a previous owner. The moral is to look carefully . . .

On the road

More than anything, the Alfa Romeo Spider is a sports car, an Italian sports car at that, and has all the character to back up those definitions. A poor example will feel woolly, imprecise, and might have hesitant performance (all of which we've mentioned, previously), but a good one, with the chassis in good condition, will have crisp roadholding, good response, accurate steering, and that little 'something' which an MGB or a TR6 could not match. Sure, the driving position leaves something to be desired (it helps to have short legs and long arms . . .), and in winter it is not the most cosy of open two-seaters, but the true enthusiast puts up with that. Where a Spider is in its element is in a fast, cross-country, journey in high summer, when the traffic is light, and the hood can be furled.

The engine is tourquey, but still zaps up to 6000rpm when you feel like it. The five-speed gearbox is the sort that *all* sports cars have, and – when properly used – can help the engine produce those urgent, 'out-of-the-way, this is a real car coming past you' engine noises.

A 2000 Spider can certainly be cruised at 100mph where conditions are suitable, and you can push it through long sweeping bends with that straight-arm driving position beautifully posed ('Of *course* I could have been a racing driver, but there was the wife and kids to consider'), all with a reasonable standard of ride comfort.

Drive it slowly in towns, and the radio can certainly be heard above a mere tickle of tappet noise, the engine being so flexible that you don't actually need to change down two cogs merely to swoop past the local school bus. (But you might enjoy doing just that, for the joy of the noise it all makes!)

More than anything, the Spider is never dull. You might not like its styling, (but from the inside, looking out, who cares?), and might wish for a more ergonomic control and instrument display, but unless you left your heart in the West Midlands you would never get bored with the way it goes. Treat it strictly as a two-seater (there's really no nonsense about ' + 2' accommodation in that package), and as a leisure-time machine, rather than for day-to-day transport, and you may fall hopelessly in love with the Italian character of it all.

The delight of the 2000 Spider (for that is what is most numerous in this country), is not that it can nudge 120mph, but that it can surpass the legal limit in third gear. Drop it into fifth gear at 30mph, boot it, and it pulls uncomplainingly away, all the way to top speed. Buy it the correct (premium) grade of fuel, and it will reward you with about 25mpg – and up to 33mpg at steady speeds of 70mph

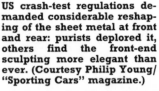

US crash-test regulations demanded considerable reshaping of the sheet metal at front and rear: purists deplored it, others find the front-end sculpting more elegant than ever. (Courtesy Philip Young/ "Sporting Cars" magazine.)

on motorways.

Way back in 1976, *Autocar's* road test suggested that: 'the 2000 Spider Veloce is something to treasure – that rare thing today, a car of character. And what character – it goes well, it steers perfectly, it stop well – it is probably the most satisfactory of its range . . .'

Do you want more, of a sports car, than that?

Best buys

There's no doubt, here. You get what you pay for, and you should always go for the most modern, and the best possible condition you can find.

Discard the 1300 and 1600 versions, quite simply because the 1750 and 2000 models are the faster, and more flexible, machines. Some enthusiasts prefer the 1750s for having slightly livelier engines, but there is little in it. If you can find one with the rare factory hardtop, that is to be recommended.

How much to pay? Surprisingly, these cars are still not going for silly prices. You should be able to strike a bargain for a 1750 for around £3,500 and a 2000 for £4,000, at which level you would expect the corrosion to have been tamed, and the cars to be complete in every detail. Take off £1,000 in each case, and you will get a car in which many horror stories may be hidden. Add £1,000 or more, and it should truly be immaculate.

Too much? How much do you have to pay for a *new* sports car today?

Where built?

Alfa Romeo provided underpans to Pininfarina in Turin, who produced the complete body shell, painting and trimming it, before sending it back to Arese, Milan, for completion. Alfa Romeo built their own engines and transmissions in Milan, too.

Even though the design is now 20 years old in the showrooms, no change has ever been made in these arrangements. Pininfarina's quality standards, they say, have improved markedly in recent years.

Parts supply

Mechanically, there should be no problem, especially if you don't have to be too pernickety about absolute period authenticity, as the power train is still in production.

Body panels, at a price, are still available for the short-tail version (which is still made), but long-tail rear panels are long gone, and some nose sections might be difficult as the detail of their construction has changed markedly over the years.

Alfa Romeo (GB) Ltd are no longer officially interested, so we recommend that you cultivate a specialist. Three noted ones are:

Benalfa Performance Cars,
Fore Street Garage, Trowbridge Road, Westbury
Tel: (0373) 864333

E.B. Spares,
2 Washington Road,
West Wilts Trading Estate,
Westbury
Tel: (0373) 823856

Richard Banks,
Commerce House,
Wickhambrook,
Nr. Newmarket,
Suffolk. (He sells them too).
Tel: (0440) 820291

Join the Club?

There are several Alfa Romeo specialist clubs in the UK, but none looks after the Spider to the exclusion of all else.

For that reason, it is best to join the Alfa Romeo Owners Club, and they may be contacted at:
Michael Lindsay, Alfa Romeo Owners Club, 97 High Street, Linton, Cambridgeshire. Tel: (0233) 894300 (Office hours, only).

The aims of this club are: 'to provide an atmosphere in which owners of post-war Alfa Romeos can join together to share interests.'

Services include advice on spares, technical information, and preservation of cars in the marque.

"Super Spider" appeared first as an article in "Sporting Cars" magazine.

In all its forms, the twin-cam engine is robust – and a delight to harken unto! (Courtesy Philip Young/"Sporting Cars" magazine.)

Alfa Romeo Spider production: 1966 to date

1600 Duetto: 6,325
1750 Spider: 8,723
1300 Spider: 7,237
2000 Spider: 50,000 approx (still in production)
1300/1600 Roadsters: n.a.

Armstrong Siddeley

Jeremy Coulter looks at a car that was "well-finished without ostentation" – the Sapphire.

One of the highlights of the 1952 Earls Court Motor Show was the unveiling of a new car from Armstrong Siddeley. Named Sapphire, the car's flowing, elegant body reflected the traditional styling and quality long associated with the rather staid Armstrong Siddeley marque and was assembled using the latest pressed steel construction techniques. However, the most noteworthy feature of the new model was the 3435cc six-cylinder engine which had hemispherical combustion chambers, a crossflow cylinder head, and inclined valves operated by an ingenious unequal-length pushrod system from a single side-mounted camshaft. The unit produced some 125bhp and endowed the Sapphire with quite lively performance and a top speed of over 90mph.

On road test, *The Autocar* found that the new car would cruise comfortably at 75 to

A pristine example of the Armstrong Siddeley Star Sapphire, probably the most desirable variant: 902 examples were built between 1958 and 1960.

80mph. Large power-assisted Girling hydraulic drums gave safe braking from these impressive speeds. The name 'Sapphire' had been taken from a turbojet engine produced by the aircraft division of Armstrong Siddeley whose products had also furnished illustrious names for two of the company's earlier cars, the Hurricane and the Lancaster.

The Sapphire's steel body was mounted on a sturdy pressed-steel chassis which was extremely rigid for its weight. Front suspension was by independent coil-sprung wishbones and the rear by half-elliptic leaf springs; front and rear anti-roll bars were fitted. This arrangement gave safe, predictable handling, combined with a comfortable ride. Two transmission options were offered

on the first Sapphire; an all-synchromesh manual gearbox and an electrically operated pre-selector unit. The latter had a small five-position steering column-mounted lever which could be pre-positioned before selection by pressing the gearchange 'clutch' pedal.

The Sapphire's outer elegance was complemented by interior quality and an abundance of top-quality leather and polished hardwood. *The Autocar* deemed this 'well-finished without ostentation ... a feature which contributes greatly to the car's very definite air of quality and well-being'. Asking price for a Sapphire at the time of test in 1953 was £1537 12s 6d with a radio as an optional extra for an additional £43 18s. In September 1953 the

Production: six-light – 6869; four-light – 377; 234 – 803; 236 – 609; Star Sapphire – 902; limousine – 382.
Specifications (1954 Armstrong Siddeley Sapphire 346, single-carb.)
Engine: cast iron block and cylinder head, 3435cc, 7:1 compression, 125bhp at 4700rpm, maximum torque 182lb ft at 2000rpm, four-bearing crankshaft, hemispherical combustion chambers, inclined valves, single side-mounted camshaft.
Transmission: four-speed manual, 10ins dry single-plate clutch. Four-speed preselector, $9\frac{1}{2}$ins dry single-plate centrifugally operated clutch. Three-ratio automatic, fluid coupling and four-speed planetary gearbox. Final drive, hypoid, 4.091:1.
Chassis: box-section steel.
Suspension: front, semi-trailing wishbones, coil springs, telescopic dampers, anti-roll bar; rear, half-elliptic leaf springs, telescopic dampers, anti-roll bar.
Brakes and steering: Girling, servo-assisted 12ins drums front and rear, Burman recirculating ball steering, three turns lock to lock.
Wheels and tyres: 6.70-16ins tyres on 5.50 x 16ins rims, five-stud steel disc wheels.
Performance: maximum speed 92mph, 0-60 15.5 seconds. Fuel consumption, 18mpg.

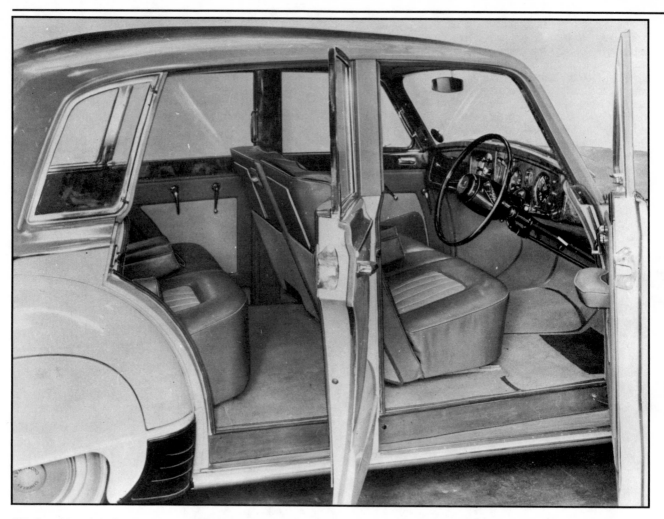

All Sapphire interiors were notable for their abundance of polished wood and top quality leather.

Sapphire range was supplemented by a more powerful 150bhp, 100mph version with twin carburettors, and four or six-light bodies became available. The company had delayed introducing the 150bhp cars as they felt that too much initial emphasis on performance might deter long-standing customers who liked the rather staid image of the marque. Refinements followed between 1954 and 1956 on the Mark II Sapphire with the introduction of optional fully automatic transmission and power-assisted steering. Larger brakes and a redesigned facia were also instituted as were optional electric windows and adjustable shock absorbers. The Mark II could be distinguished from the early car by its winking indicator, lack of boot lid central chrome strip and the rubber stoneguard on the leading edge of each rear wing. Limousine versions of the Sapphire became available in 1955.

1955 also saw the introduction of two smaller, lighter Sapphires, the four-cylinder 2.3-litre 234 and the six-cylinder 236 also of 2.3 litres. Both were intended to compete with the well-established P4 Rovers. However, it was the super-value-for-money 2.4 Jaguar introduced soon after which was to foil the small Sapphires, aided by rapid and serious decay suffered by the composite steel and hiduminium bodywork. Neither the 234 nor 236 made any real impact so both were dropped by

1958, leaving the company with only one model, the Mark II 346.

What was to be the last Armstrong Siddeley, announced in late 1958, was the four-litre Star Sapphire. Available also as a Limousine, the front disc-braked car resembled earlier models but had a lower bonnet line, a new grille and other subtle styling changes as well as a redesigned interior. A Borg-Warner automatic gearbox was standard and power came from a bored-out version of the six-cylinder engine to give 165bhp and a top speed of 105mph, making the Star Sapphire the quickest of the series.

In 1959, Armstrong Siddeley amalgamated with Bristol Aero Engines to form Bristol Siddeley, but after the merger, the Armstrong Cars limb of the combine fared less well than its Bristol counterpart. Faced with declining sales and an irresistible Jaguar onslaught, the company decided to wind up Armstrong Siddeley car production. The last Star Sapphire was completed on July 5th, 1960 and the final limousine on September 6th, bringing to an end 41 years of Armstrong Siddeley production.

Body and chassis

Rust is the main concern. As is often the case, elegant styling has created mud and water

traps in the body which exacerbate the problems suffered by even the best designed steel cars. The small 234 and 236 were constructed from a steel and hiduminium composite and the unforeseen electrolytic reaction between the two metals caused alarming decay; relatively few examples have survived.

The Sapphire's wings, door pillars and sills are bolted to the inner body shell, so renewal of a rotten section is not too difficult. But beware! New parts are very expensive. Supplies of original body panels are all but used up and the investment required for production tooling has prevented the Armstrong Siddeley Owners Club from attempting this type of manufacture. However, they can arrange for new panels to be made individually, but at a price. A front wing can run to many hundreds of pounds and rear wings to only slightly less; the lesson is clear – go for the best bodywork available.

The sills usually rust severely so examine these areas very carefully as they are structural members that support the body. Open the doors to expose the sill faces for a thorough inspection. New sills can be fitted by the DIY mechanic but it's a tedious job. Only one sill should be detached from the car at any one time, incidentally, otherwise the bodyshell will twist. Useful pointers to sill rot are unevenly fitting closed doors. The front doors in particular should open cleanly without catching on the screen pillars. The inner sill faces are partially open – allowing airflow but also permitting the ingress of water and road dirt which soon blocks up the drain holes. Water trapped in the sills tends to work its way out by rotting through the base.

After checking the sills, examine the door posts and check the state of the hinges. It's worth remembering that a broken or badly worn hinge could account for an ill-fitting door. The doors themselves often rot along the base but new original doors are still available. The doors on early cars open from the front pillar: only on later Star Sapphires did the doors hinge conveniently from the rear pillar.

Moving to the wings, the bottom edges are the areas most likely to decay as they receive the full blast of road dirt and water thrown up from the wheels. The wing tops also

gather water-retaining mud and tend to be eaten away; so do the formed sections around the head and sidelights. Rear wings are similarly vulnerable along the base and at the frontmost section which joins to the door pillar. The boot floor tends to disappear at the edges if the appropriate drainage channels aren't kept clear.

The time it takes to remove a rusty wing varies enormously from car to car and depends very much on the condition of the mounting bolts. The front wings are held by reasonably accessible free-bolts and they respond quite well to liberal applications of penetrating oil. The rear wings are held by captive nuts which tend to rust solid so loosening them can be a real problem. In extreme cases, the simplest way to remove a totally rotten wing is to cut it away with a suitable power saw and then remove the smaller pieces bit by bit.

The box-section chassis is fairly resistant to rust and has no fundamental weak points as long as the drain points are cleaned regularly. The secret of indefinite chassis life is to treat the underside annually with a high-pressure water or steam cleaner.

The capacious boot with spare wheel and tool kit.

More of the plush leather and wood interior.

This is the 1956 Armstrong Siddeley Sapphire 346 Countryman by H. Radford.

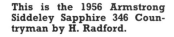

It's unlikely that you'll find an example as pristine as this; many will have rusty wings, door pillars and sills.

Suspension, steering, brakes

These three areas are marked by the soundness of the basic design. There are few weak points and any problems that are encountered are likely to be the result of long usage and general wear and tear. The king pins endure a heavy loading and are the components which most often show signs of wear. The Club is able to supply replacement king pins although they are rather expensive, so it's worth jacking up the front wheels and checking the amount of play. This check will also help expose steering wear which is likely to be at the idler arm rather than in the box. The power steering system, of Girling origin, is long lasting although the drive-belt tension and the fluid level in the Hobourn-Eaton pump fluid reservoir must be maintained correctly.

Drum brakes were fitted to early Sapphires but later cars had front discs. The brake servos can be a little troublesome; the problem is often a leaking vacuum reservoir as the tank is chassis-mounted and rather exposed to the elements. It is worth checking for servo action by depressing the brake pedal several times after running the engine briefly and then switching off. After two or three applications the pedal should go 'hard', keep your foot on the pedal and start the engine, whereupon the pedal should go 'soft' once more and move down perceptibly. Brake parts are readily available, so remedial work on a brake defect is no real problem.

When road testing a Sapphire, be on the look out for front-wheel imbalance transmitted to the steering wheel as vigorous shaking. Although this may be caused simply by imbalanced wheels, the true culprit may be decayed Metalastic engine mountings causing excessive engine vibration which in turn upsets the steering balance. So, carry out a check to the mounting in the engine bay after driving the car.

Engine, gearbox, transmission

Even in its most powerful form, the Sapphire engine produces only 165bhp so it's by no means highly stressed though it does have to propel a 32cwt car. The engine's 'square' dimensions and the massive big ends ensure a long life. As with most of the other mechanical components, any engine maladies are likely to be the result of wear and tear through old age rather than because of a design flaw. Sapphires have covered 250,000 miles without any major work on the engine – strong evidence of their durability.

The cast iron tappet barrels in the cylinder head can become noisy as they wear, and worn rattling timing chains can also boost engine decibels, so listen carefully and find out whether the odometer is on its second or even third circuit!

The inlet manifold is mounted on the offside of the cylinder head with a rubber gasket sandwiched in the joint. This gasket splits and perishes with age and often leads to a water leak (the crossflow head design necessitates water-heated induction). If the coolant level is low or if you can see rust traces on the block under the inlet manifold, the gasket may need renewing.

Engine spares are readily available but the work involved in a top end or full rebuild is time-consuming and likely to be rather expensive, so if possible go for an engine that has already received some love and attention or, if you're very lucky, one that has done a relatively low mileage. Not that you're likely to find one as the youngest example is now over 20 years old. An acceptable engine oil pressure reading when hot is around 35psi but note that the oil gauge calibration varies from car to car and can be confusing.

You are faced with a choice of three transmissions on the Sapphire. The automatic is likely to be the most common and fortunately it's very sound. Old age or impending failure is indicated by very jerky engagement, particularly of second gear, and generally juddery take up, the latter pointing to problems with the fluid coupling. Armstrong Siddeley were one of the last car manufacturers to employ a preselector gearbox. On later Sapphires it was superseded by a fully automatic unit which was simpler and therefore cheaper to manufacture as well as being the type preferred by customers. The preselector mechanism gives a rapid, quiet and smooth change, and because the gears are in constant mesh they suffer relatively little wear. Even clutch band wear is low as the pressure is spread evenly over a large surface area. Excessive wear will show itself as a rather distinctive whine when stationary, tailing off when the drive is taken up. The preselector 'clutch' pedal stops at a different point in each gear, so don't be alarmed if the system is unfamiliar to you. If all the preselector gears are lost, trouble is probably electrical – a blown fuse in the engine bay bulkhead-mounted fusebox or greasy contacts on the steering column-mounted selector lever. Alternatively, one of the actuating solenoids on the box could be jammed and this naturally calls for rather more advanced

remedies.

The four-speed Humber-derived manual gear-box can withstand a long, hard life and any ratio engagement difficulties can probably be traced to linkage wear. The gearlever is column-mounted and, in common with most systems of this type with a large number of pivots, wear is magnified, resulting in a very sloppy lever. Even when new, the lever is rather loose so expect some play but be wary of a lever that appears to be stirring thin air!

A conventional open propshaft with a centre bearing transmits the drive from the gearbox to the live rear axle. Both these components give reliable service if maintained and lubricated correctly.

Interior

A leather and wood cabin may be attractive but it's also expensive to refurbish. Recovering the Sapphire's ample bench seats (from the Mark II on, individual front seats were options) is unlikely to leave much change from £1000 if the job is done professionally and items such as door trim panels, carpets, headlining, etc., are similarly expensive to have made. The alternative is to obtain serviceable secondhand parts but these are fairly rare. Naturally, the interior responds to careful valetting and the seats to regular treatment with leather food.

Electric windows were a novelty for their day on some Sapphires. They are driven by an electric motor via a chain which must be lubricated from time to time if smooth operation is to be maintained.

Spares and the Club

Armstrong Siddeley merged with Bristol Aero Engines in 1959 to form Bristol Siddeley a year before the end of Armstrong Siddeley car production. Hawker Siddeley (the holding company) in turn sold their share in Bristol Siddeley to Rolls-Royce in 1968 and it was from Rolls-Royce that the Armstrong Siddeley Owners Club were able to purchase the entire stock of Armstrong Siddeley spares. Naturally this forms a fine basis for the Owners Club and membership is a must for any Armstrong Siddeley owner. The Club has some 800 members at present and owners regularly join. If you would like membership details, send a SAE to Alan Swainson, 193 Clockhouse Lane, Collier Row, Rowford, Essex R45 2TL, Tel: 0708 46570.

Prices for a Sapphire vary greatly depending on the age and condition. The later cars tend to fetch more than early examples and the Star Sapphire most of all. Rough examples of any age seem to sell for between £300 and £500 – but the expenditure of around £1000 should be enough to obtain a sound, but 'used' car. To buy a really nice Sapphire, you'll have to dig a little deeper in your pocket and find upwards of £2500 for an early car and £3500 for a later version. Owners of really outstanding cars can naturally ask considerably more but then few will want to part with their prized possession!

This buyer's guide first appeared in "Thoroughbred & Classic Cars" magazine.

Austin Seven

John Williams looks at the varieties of this perennial favourite

When Sir Herbert Austin envisaged the design of the legendary Austin Seven it was his intention to capture the enormous market for a small, cheap, but entirely practical car – a car which would bring motoring within the reach of ordinary people instead of a wealthy majority. He appreciated that Britain had just emerged from the First World War which had brought thousands of young men into close contact with motorised transport and brought about what amounted to a social revolution. He meant to give them their own means of transportation.

In 1922 when the car was introduced many, including most of the directors of the Austin Motor Company believed that the tiny Seven was a joke that could not succeed and would almost certainly ruin a company which was far from being financially secure. In fact, the Seven made the Austin Motor Company's fortune and remained in production until 1939 by which time around, 300,000 had been made. While the Austin Seven remained the butt of music hall jokes throughout its life, the jokes became affectionate and the car did play an important part in bringing motoring to the masses, not only during its production life but for the best part of fifteen years after production ceased.

The Austin Seven was a remarkable car. It was not the first small car and it was not the first cheap car, nor was it an advanced design when it appeared in 1922 but merely a scaled down medium sized car of the type that was commonplace in 1914. It is fair to say that the only advanced feature of the car was its four wheel brakes and those brakes were not even particularly effective by the standards of 1922! Much of the success of the Austin Seven was not merely that it was cheap but that it contrived to be built cheaply with good materials which helped make the car almost indestructible and it was also relatively easy to drive by the standards of the period.

Mention Austin Seven and most people would think of the Chummy, but there were and are many other forms of this successful car.

A typical interior layout of earlier Austin Sevens with the starter motor inside the car (moved into the engine compartment in 1932), the speedometer drive cable clearly visible, and the advance and retard control and the hand throttle at the centre of the steering wheel.

Brief Specifications (as introduced in 1922):

Engine – bore 2 1/8" stroke 3" capacity 696cc (increased to 747.5cc March 1923). Four cylinders, water cooled, side valves.

Transmission – three forward speeds and one reverse (four forward gears from September 1932).

Suspension – transverse semi-elliptic spring at front, quarter elliptic springs at rear.

Brakes – on all four wheels, the front brakes being controlled by the hand-brake lever (all brakes coupled from June 1930).

Electric lighting and starter motor on all production models.

Over the car's seventeen years long production life a confusing variety of Austin Sevens were produced not only to broaden the car's appeal but also to give it the outward appearance of being abreast of the times. Mechanical refinements were introduced as the model matured but it has to be admitted that many rival small cars at home and abroad were introduced during the Seven's lifespan and in terms of sophistication and refinement many of them were better cars. That aside, none of the rivals usurped the Austin Seven as *the* pre-war small car.

The Austin Seven range included tourers, saloons and sports versions and a great many versions of the same produced by independent body-builders ranging from department stores to tiny concerns in back street sheds.

Today the situation is further confused by the number of privately built specials and by the increasing numbers of replicas. In the limited space available here I can only offer a general guide to the Austin Seven and the photographs will assist in identifying the principle types.

A little History

The first Austin Sevens, produced in 1922, were open cars with an engine capacity of 696cc, increased in March 1923 to 747cc. These early Sevens were dubbed "Chummies" (a term in vogue at that time for small open cars) and they remained in production until 1930, by which time they were being built with aluminium bodies. Some steel bodied four seat tourers were produced in very small numbers up to 1934, but by then they had become larger cars with little pretence at chumminess. The first saloons were actually made for Austin by Gordon England Limited in 1926 but body distortion became a problem because the chassis extended only to the forward end of the quarter elliptic rear springs and in 1928 chassis extensions became available in the hope of overcoming this problem. Numerous modifications and improvements were made, each year and in 1931 it was deemed necessary to produce a car which would be more convincing as a four seater. In October of 1931 the De Luxe Saloon was introduced

In all engines the cylinder head, block and crankcase were separate components and early engines had magneto ignition as shown here.

This engine is fitted with coil ignition and note the height of the radiator which is necessary for the efficient performance of the thermo syphon cooling system.

Suggested further reading

"The Austin Seven" by R. J. Wyatt, published by David & Charles.

"The Austin Seven Companion" published by the 750 Motor Club Ltd.

"Austin Seven 1922-1982" published and distributed by Brooklands Books.

"Austin Seven" by Chris Harvey, published by the Oxford Illustrated Press, Haynes Publishing Group.

"Austin Seven Specials" by L. M. Williams, published by G. T. Foulis, Haynes Publishing Group.

with a chassis that was six inches longer, supporting a slightly larger body which offered more legroom for the passengers in the rear. That same year the Opal two seat tourer appeared, extending the Chummy-style lineage.

In August 1934 the Ruby saloon and Pearl cabriolet were introduced, together with a more up-to-date Opal. The Ruby was also available as a four seater open tourer.

Driving Impressions

Unlike so many motoring writers I had not driven an Austin Seven previously when Ken

Front suspension is by a transverse semi-elliptic spring with a single shock absorber mounted centrally behind the number plate. Note the surplus brake cable and the small brake drum.

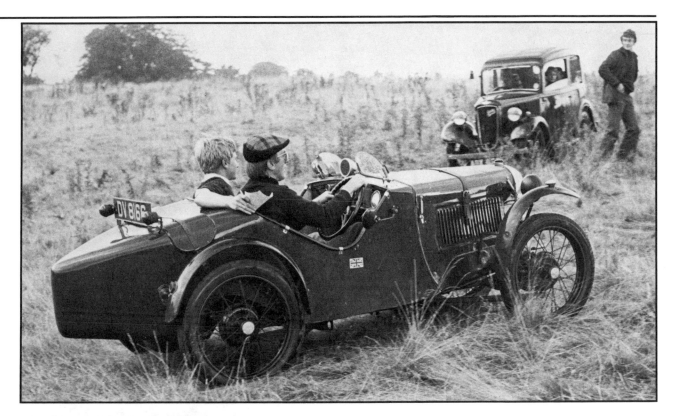

Cooke of the 750 Motor Club kindly (and bravely) invited me to drive his 1930 Chummy at a 750 Club Trials Meeting in Kent during 1981. What a strange impression it must have made in the minds of the many other owners who observed my sparrow-like progress across the very uneven field, and my unofficial attempt at one of the trials courses.

The abrupt "in or out" clutch of the Austin Seven is notorious and will take any newcomer by surprise. It has an effective travel of only a quarter of an inch. The engine's smoothness and flexibility are better than would be expected and the performance and pulling power are very good for an engine of such small size and power output – in 1938 the standard output was a mere 17bhp.

The Austin Seven's brakes were never a strong point and take a bit of getting used to in modern traffic densities – they encourage anticipation and defensive driving tactics. On pre-June 1930 examples the footbrake operates the rear brakes and the front brakes are applied by the handbrake – an arrangement which will take a little learning.

Pre-1934 Austin Sevens had a hand throttle and an advance and retard control for the ignition mounted at the steering wheel centre. The hand throttle is best left closed while driving and the ignition need only be fully retarded for starting and slow running. The lighting equipment is perhaps adequate for the available performance but inefficient by modern standards.

The steering is light and should be fairly accurate. The ride is quite comfortable but fast cornering is an acquired art and should not be attempted by the novice.

Describing the limitations of the Austin

There is a steady market for replica bodywork and this is a glass fibre replica of the Ulster sports model which dated from 1928 – we think the wings are wrong!

Here is a chassis with extensions fitted – previously the chassis ended at the forward end of the quarter elliptic rear springs.

A 1926 two seater coupe, a very rare example even in the replica form seen here.

Seven and what the driver has to contend with, always make the car sound difficult and demanding, but in practice it is an easy and entertaining little car to drive.

Prices and What to Look For

Of the various Austin Sevens which have been advertised for sale in the specialist magazines over the last few months three-quarters have been described in such a way as to suggest that little or no repair or restoration work would be needed. Most of the others were late Box saloons or Ruby saloons which were runners but required "some work" – probably quite a lot of work. Very few total rebuild projects are advertised in the magazines but such cars do change hands within the owners clubs, and owners will tell you how it can be easier to acquire one's second or third Austin Seven from complete strangers who will stop them at petrol stations and elsewhere to offer anything from a few odd spares to the complete car which has remained unused for

The Sports 65, later known as the Nippy, competing in a recent trial.

years at the bottom of the garden.

The market seems to divide into three fairly clear groups of cars according to the prices being asked. At the top end, between £3,000 and £5,000, will be found the immaculate show cars and the rarities (in their owners' eyes at least), and there is evidence to support the view that initial prices asked in this category are not usually realised but have to be reduced by perhaps 20% or more.

Over half of the cars advertised fall into the £1,500 to £3,500 group. These include the widest variety of models and are generally described as ''good'' to ''excellent restored'', and in fact most will have been extensively

restored at some time in their life. Many Austin Sevens lost their original saloon or tourer bodies in the post-war years and were given sports bodies, and some of these cars survived to be restored to their original form.

If your initial budget is limited you might consider buying a Seven for restoration. Few cars which are advertised for under £1,000 are runners, and the choice is limited as they are usually Ruby saloons or occasionally a late Box saloon.

Austin Sevens underwent an enormous number of modifications during their long production run, and there were several body styles too, some made in aluminium and some

Sporting achievements helped to develop the Austin Seven and its reputation. This is a sidevalve racer of the type which first appeared in 1935.

Fabric bodied saloons are also scarce – mainly because the bodies tended to disintegrate.

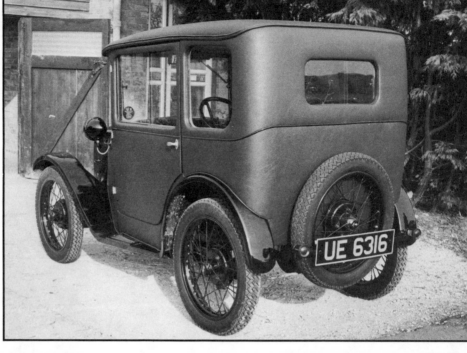

Top right. The Ruby appeared as a saloon, some of which had sliding roofs ...

Bottom right ... and as a four seater tourer (right) of which few have survived, and also as a cabriolet (left) known as the Pearl.

It is perhaps the rear view which reveals more clearly than any other the pram-like appearance of the early Austin Seven, in this case a pair of Chummies. The first saloons and the later long wheelbase "De Luxe" Saloon all had this style rear end.

in steel and many having wood in their construction. All models had a chassis but in the case of the Ruby's the chassis extended to the rear of the body, giving a degree of support which was not necessarily present in earlier models. Sills, wheel arches and the lower edges of the body (particularly adjacent to the mudguards and at the rear of the car) are all rot prone areas. The spare wheel

carrier should also be inspected as should the bottom of the scuttle on most models. The floors of all open models should be checked, especially as the rear and seat supports are prone to collapse on the 1931-35 models. These models also suffer rot at the base of the door pillars and the doors rot badly.

The chassis itself should be inspected as far as possible even though its preservation

This is a long wheelbase saloon, (introduced in October 1931) the immediate predecessor of the Ruby. Earlier saloons were shorter and narrower and the doors were cut away to accommodate part of the rear wheel arch.

The Opal two seater tourer introduced in 1931 retained the old style radiator and bodywork but remained in production alongside the Ruby models which appeared late in 1934.

may well have been guaranteed by the amount of oil ejected by the engine. Pre-1927 chassis are especially prone to cracks just forward of the front cross members, but later chassis should be examined too, particularly at the rear spring mounting points and the shock absorber flanges.

The writer would like to thank Ken Cooke and Barry Martin and any other members of the 750 Motor Club who assisted in the preparation of this article which first appeared in "Practical Classics" magazine.

Production of Swallow tourers started in Blackpool and saloon bodies soon followed, production of both continued after the company moved to Coventry in November 1928. Austin Swallows had no performance advantages over the 'standard' models.

Clubs

There are about thirty clubs catering for owners of the pre-war Austin Seven, some of which are listed in "Practical Classics" Register of Motor Vehicle Clubs. Additional information on the whereabouts of clubs can be obtained by sending a stamped and addressed envelope to the Secretary of the Austin Seven Clubs Association who is Robin Newman, Dixton Cottage, Monmouth, Gwent NP5 3SJ.

Vans were also made, this being a partly constructed reproduction of the early type.

Alongside this 1938 Special is the later type of van which remained in production until the frontal styling was brought into line with the Ruby in about 1937.

The Swallow Sidecar and Coachbuilding Company was one of the many independent concerns which built bodies for the Austin chassis. The two seater tourer was the first of the line in 1927.

Between 1928 and 1937 military versions of the Seven were produced for use as scout cars.

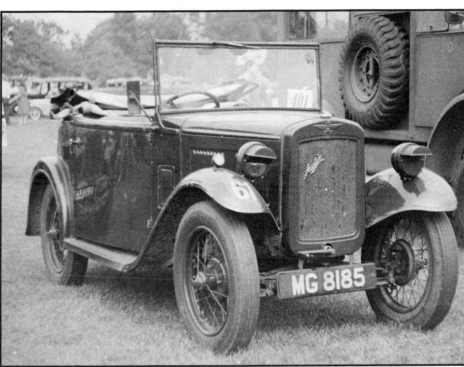

The Specialists

Austin Seven Services, Kirby Wiske, Thirsk, Yorks (0845) 587201. New & used parts.

The Seven Workshop, Denvers Yard, Barwick, Nr. Ware, Herts. (027-984) 2076. New spares.

John F. Heath, Kettle Green, Much Hadham, Herts. (027-984) 2735. Bodies, body parts, restorations.

Austineers, Denvers Yard, Barwick, Nr. Ware. Mechanical specialists, some used parts. (027 984) 3134.

Vintage Tyre Supplies Ltd, 12, Dalston Gardens, Honeypot Lane, Stanmore, Middx. (01-206-0722). Tyres for all years.

The Austin Seven was built under licence in France, Germany and America, the German version being called the Dixi and the American the Bantam. The Rosengart in this picture is an example of the French version whose production began in 1928.

Spares availability

If Austin Seven parts specialists are not numerous they compensate by giving very comprehensive services and nearly all parts are available, the interior fittings being the only difficult parts to find.

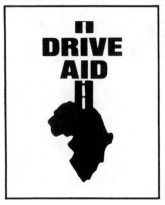

DRIVE AID

Buying a Bentley

The Mk VI and R-type Bentley standard steel saloons. Value for money or best avoided? John Williams investigates.

If you would like, and can afford, a really nice Mk VI Bentley, or its successor the R-type, you *can* go to a reputable specialist dealer and see a good selection for a little less than you might pay for a new Rover. The new Rover will have many advantages over the Bentley – better performance (by a large margin) and better amenities such as lighting, ventilation, screen-wipers etcetera, etcetera BUT, a modern Rover is just a good modern car, it will depreciate, it might actually be more expensive to run and it will not be a Bentley. it will not look like a Bentley, it will not feel like one, and you will always *know* that it is not a Bentley.

You *could* go to a less reputable dealer who may know, or may not know, that for the price of a good fifties Bentley or slightly less he is selling you a car that will shatter your dreams and do its very best to bankrupt you. However, if you shop carefully – take your time, and see – no, examine as many cars as you can – you could find a good car cheaper than you expected and one that will quickly prove that running costs are considerably less than you might fear.

The truth is that a Bentley of the early fifties represents no more of a challenge to the skills of the owner prepared to carry out his own restoration and maintenance than a Rover P4, and the beauty shared by Rover P4s and Bentleys is a big strong chassis.

When you go to drive a thirty-year-old Bentley, do not fall into the trap of assuming that Rolls-Royce could build a car that was thirty years ahead of its rivals, although it might be added that in the areas of comfort and braking performance they are not far behind modern standards. The atmosphere and feel of a good Bentley will encourage a tendency to drive "by the book" and enjoy doing so.

That feeling of pride in the car is nothing to do with snobbery and, incidentally, people who do buy an old Bentley to impress the neighbours generally neglect the cars terribly. Here it seems sensible to offer a few words of warning – do not be fooled by statements like, "It is a bit smoky but you can pop in some new rings if the smoke bothers you – they go on for ever," or, "Just needs the brakes adjusting" or perhaps, "Do the clutch and it will be a perfect motor" – if you fall for those lines you will soon discover that not only is the fault much more expensive to put right than you might expect but that it is also only

the tip of the proverbial iceberg. Rebuilding a rusty, worn out Bentley takes a lot of money, time and enthusiasm.

With some cars you can sometimes take a few short-cuts and save a bit of money but with any Rolls-Royce product take our advice, buy the right part (save for it if you have to), fit it properly and restrict the money saving measures to doing what you can yourself and going to specialists for their skills and knowledge for what you cannot attempt.

You may come across a reasonably priced car that has already had some work done on it and it may be a very sound buy, but do exercise caution. Let us assume the vendor tells you the engine has been "re-conned a couple of thousand miles back" – now if that is true the vendor should have some bills for parts bought and work done, they *should* relate to the car you are being offered and the parts suppliers and the overhaulers *should* be known Bentley and Rolls-Royce specialists

What to pay

It is advisable to spend as much as you can on the initial purchase, but only if this will result in savings during the restoration work which will follow. Mk VI Bentleys can still be found "just about running" for as little as £1500, but a respectable Mk VI is likely to cost at least £6,000, and the very good specimens will command prices around £10,000 to £11,000. The R-type Bentley will cost rather more, perhaps £1,000 more than a Mk VI in similar condition.

Little more than twelve years ago the Mk VI and R-type Bentleys offered the prospect of motoring in the grand manner for well under £1,000. They can still offer outstanding value if you buy warily. At 16'7½" the R-type is the longer car with the elegant sweeping tail.

The Mk VI has the smaller boot with a lid which opens downwards and a separate compartment below for the spare wheel.

Bottom left. The modest proportions of the Mk VI boot, but note the folding stops which allow the lid to be used as a platform for additional luggage. Get the owner to show you how the spare wheel compartment is opened; if the inner hinge mountings have been weakened due to rust this operation poses a serious thread to your toes!

The R-type bootlid is hinged at the top and there is a compartment for the spare wheel and some tools inside the boot.

Examine the lower rear floor of the spare wheel compartment (Mk VI) or of the spare wheel and boot compartments (R-type) as this can rot away completely, especially if rain gets into the boot.

The early style of upholstery shown here was replaced by pleated leather in 1949. Note the right-hand gear lever.

A lot of polished timber is used in the interiors of these cars, in the dashboard, around the windows, and in these folding tables. The woodwork tends to last quite well and it seems likely that the most serious problem affecting the interior will be deeply cracked or torn leather, especially in the front seats.

The restoration of an interior may well cost as much as the price of an otherwise promising car

The dashboard layout is simple and functional. The gear-lever quadrant for the automatic gearbox can be seen in this picture beyond the centre of the steering wheel which incorporates levers controlling the suspension firmness, the fuel mixture and the throttle.

Given a full-flow oil system and reasonable care these Bentleys should be capable of at least 100,000 miles between major engine work. Some cars were fitted with a fibre timing gear which tended to disintegrate – this was replaced by an aluminium gear and where this was done the letter 'A' was stamped on the timing case. However, it is not safe to assume that the presence of the letter means that there is definitely an aluminium gear.

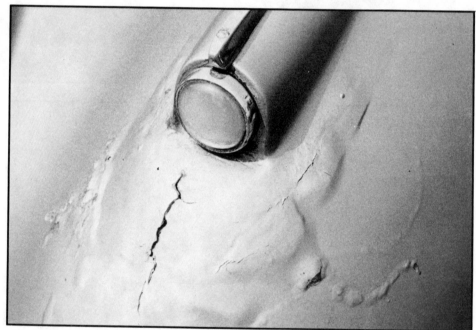

Look for signs of rust around the front sidelights; it is quite common here.

who will confirm all details for the price of a telephone call. A full engine rebuild costs about £5000 and it is no fun paying for it when you buy the car only to discover that you have to pay a second time to have the job done properly!

Some history

The Mk VI Bentley was introduced in 1946. It was the result of a major effort to produce a car which would be much more simple (and therefore less expensive) to maintain than its predecessors had been. Labour costs had risen sharply during the war years and Rolls-Royce designers felt the need to reduce the running costs of their products and, indeed, to rely less upon relatively expensive coachbuilt bodywork. Thus, the Mk VI Bentley was the first Rolls-Royce product to be clothed in a standard body from Pressed Steel, although it was also available in chassis form to independent coachbuilders and many splendid examples of their work still survive.

At its introduction the Mk VI had the six cylinder in-line engine of 4256cc. In 1949 the Rolls-Royce Silver Dawn was introduced for export only with the same engine, but by 1951 more power was wanted and both cars had their engines bored out to 4566cc. By 1953 the Silver Dawn and Mk VI Bentley had been restyled to accommodate a larger boot. The same engine remained in use but the restyled Bentley became known as the R-type. These cars were discontinued when the Rolls-Royce Silver Cloud and the Bentley S1 models were introduced in 1955.

What to look for

The Mk VI and R-type are undoubtedly superb motor cars. They are, after all, Bentleys, moreover, they were made by Rolls-Royce. But do not allow yourself to become overawed by these great names when you are inspecting a prospective purchase. Remember instead that it is a car, and that unless your assessment of it is hard-headed and thorough it may prove to be a most expensive liability.

Start by examining the outer bodywork. The areas to check are shown in our pictures. Look for evidence of previous repairs, satisfy yourself that they have been carried out correctly and that the end result looks right. It really is important to have access to the underside of the car. The chassis itself is of very generous dimensions but body mounting points should be examined thoroughly, especially the two on each side adjacent to the rear wheels and one on each side just behind the front wheels. While under the rear of the car try to assess the condition of the fuel tank, and don't overlook the exhaust system A twin system for one of the later cars will cost over £500. Bear in mind that the one-shot chassis lubrication system leaks oil when worn and if the system fails or is defective, some components, such as the clutch bearing, will be starved of oil and if no lubricant is reaching the bottom of the front suspension the silent bloc bushes at the top of the suspension itself should be checked – we have been quoted over £500 for an overhaul, and kingpins alone cost over £120 each. Whilst under the car check the condition of the rubbers on the rear gearbox mountings. The housing at the rear end of each steering torque arm is lined by a rubber cup and these are subject to wear. Start to examine the tyres whilst under the car. Dunlop RS tyres (6.70 x 16) are used and these are available from stock at Vintage Tyre Supplies at about £120 each including VAT and carriage.

Early engines had a couple of features which have proved to be weaknesses. They had a by-pass oil filter arrangement which was responsible for some oil starvation and accelerated wear, and also a fibre timing gear which tended to disintegrate. Full flow oil filters were fitted later and many early cars will have been converted by now, and aluminium timing gears often substituted for the fibre gears in earlier cars. Where the aluminium gear has been fitted the timing case will have been stamped with the letter 'A', although the presence of the stamp is not necessarily a reliable guide. Look for signs of overheating and a clogged radiator and note in this connection that a water pump repair kit will cost around £115.

Lower front wings and valances also rust and if it is as bad as this it must make you wonder what else has been neglected by the same owner.

The edges of wings are prone to rust, but the damage may not be this obvious ...

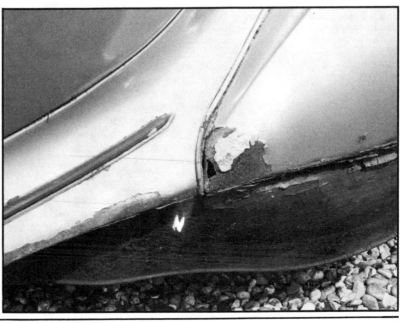

... and the rear ends of front wings and adjacent areas are also rust-prone.

these cars for restoration it is likely that the braking system will require attention sooner rather than later and we have been quoted £130 and more for a full set of eight brake shoes. An overhaul kit is available for the master cylinder but we were told that overhaul work on the brake servo "is not a do-it-yourself job". The mechanical servo is driven from the gearbox.

The interior is most attractive and, equally, most expensive if a full restoration is needed, £4,000 to £6,000 could be spent inside the car quite easily. Choose a car, if you can, in which what little renovation is needed can be done by yourself over a period with the aid of professional advice. Note that the folding tables in the backs of the front seats and the pleated upholstery were introduced in 1949.

The bottoms of doors, the centre posts and the sill structures should all be examined with care. Perhaps you have not seen a thoroughly rotten Mk VI or R-type but don't be misled into thinking that they are immune.

The Club

The Bentley drivers Club arranges social and sporting events, publishes a quarterly review, monthly notes and a bi-monthly advertiser, has advisers through whom members can obtain technical information, and is represented throughout the United Kingdom and in many countries abroad by its regional groups. Further information can be obtained from Mrs B.M. Fell, Bentley Drivers Club, W.O. Bentley Memorial Building, 16 Chearsley Road, Long Crendon, Aylesbury, Buckinghamshire, telephone: Long Crendon 208233.

The right-hand gate change manual gearboxes are exceptionally nice to use and not particularly troublesome but they are getting on in years now. It is important to avoid forcing it into first gear whilst the car is moving, for this could be an expensive mistake since the layshaft alone for these boxes could cost several hundred pounds. The manual gearboxes are said to be no longer available new but the Rolls-Royce Hydramatic 4 speed (automatic) box is available on an exchange basis (foul smelling oil is a sure sign of a worn out automatic gearbox). We have been quoted from £500 upwards for a replacement automatic box.

A front suspension overhaul may cost £500 or more and the lever arm shock absorbers at around £250 each on exchange are not to be overlooked during your inspection of the car. If you are buying one of

A do-it-yourself project?

There is no technical reason why one of these cars should not be restored by an amateur. Much the same skills and equipment would be required for any restoration project. However it is worth bearing in mind the size and weight of these cars in relation to the space available and to the capacities of your lifting and supporting equipment (the cost of suitable equipment would amount to a small part of the overall budget).

Perhaps the cost of such a project is the more worrying factor. I would argue that this need not be prohibitive if you shop carefully for your car with a view to saving or at least postponing some of the restoration expenses. The key question for most prospective owners is whether one of these cars and the restoration which will be needed will be affordable. As with any car this is a matter for the individual to decide by an honest appraisal of how much can be spent on the initial purchase and how much more can be allocated to the project each year, at least until the car is reasonably sound and usable, and thus how long the project will take.

I would like to thank the following companies for their willing assistance with the preparation of this article: Frank Dale and Stepsons, (01-385 9724). Balmoral Automobile Co Ltd (01-761 1155), Healey Bros. (Automobile Engineers) Ltd (0933 650247), Appleyard-Rippon Ltd (Leeds 32731), and Vintage Tyre Supplies (01-206 0722).

"Buying a Bentley" first appeared in "Practical Classics" Magazine.

The sliding sunroof is a desirable feature but should be examined with care. Drains lead from its outer front corners through the windscreen pillars to below the rear of the front wings – if these drains become blocked, serious rusting is likely to occur.

Production, specfications and performance

	M VI	R type
Period of manufacture	1946-52	1952-55
Number produced	5,201	2,320
Engine	Alloy head and linered block, 6 cyl in line.	
Bore (mm)	88.9	92
Stroke (mm)	114.3	114.3
Capacity (cc)	4256	4566
Comp. ratio	6.3:1	6.75:1
Valves	Overhead inlet, side exhaust.	
Carburettors	Twin SU	
Suspension – front	Independent, coil wishbone and anti-roll bar.	
rear	Semi-elliptic springs.	
	Lever arm shock absorbers all round with manual ride control.	
Brakes	Drums all round, servo assisted hydraulic front and mechanical rear.	
Kerb weight (cwt)	35³/₄	37
Length	16'0"	16'7¹/₂"
Width	5'9"	5'9"
Height	5'4¹/₂"	5'4¹/₂"
Tyre size	6.50 x 16 originally, now using 6.70 x 16	
0-50 mph (seconds)	11	10.1
Max speed (mph)	93	102
Overall fuel consumption (mpg)	17	16.5

DRIVE AID

Citroën Traction Avant

Jonathan Wood extols the virtues and vices of the revolutionary Traction Avant Citroën, a front-wheel-drive car in production from 1934 until 1957

Nineteen thirty four was a significant year for motorists on both sides of the English Channel. In Britain it witnessed the appearance of the Morris Eight which was destined to be the best selling home produced car of the pre-war era, 25,000 being sold in four years. By contrast, the great event in France was the announcement of the Traction Avant Citroën, the car that proved front wheel drive a mass-production reality. Unlike the Morris, the Citroën was so far advanced that it was manufactured up until 1957 by which time 758,917 had been built in four and six cylinder form.

But how much trouble is a Traction to own and maintain, and what points should you look for when contemplating the purchase of one of these truly revolutionary cars? To find out, I went to see John Gillard, who looks after the Traction Owners' Club spares and has recently established the club's garage just

round the corner from the *Thoroughbred* and *Classic Cars* offices in Waterloo. Before looking at the sort of shortcomings you're likely to experience when checking over a second-hand Traction, some details of the various models would be appropriate. Cars are available in left and right hand drive form, the latter examples emanating from Citroën's British assembly plant at Slough. These differ from their French counterparts in a number of details. The principle differences are a chrome plated radiator grille in place of a painted one, 12 volt electrics instead of 6 volt, leather upholstery as opposed to cloth on Gallic examples and the addition of semaphore indicators.

Now for some history. The Traction Avant was a modern car in every sense of the word

when it was launched in 1934, having a monocoque pressed steel body, torsion bar suspension, a wet liner overhead valve engine and hydraulic brakes. Unfortunately, the financial strain of taking such a monumental technological bound forward was too much for the already strained resources of the Citroën company. The result was that Michelin, the company's largest creditor, took over control in 1935.

The model first appeared in rather pedestrian 1300cc form, being rated as a 7CV, though it soon joined the 11CV 1911cc version. By early 1935 the designs settled down in forms that would be produced up until the outbreak of the Second World War. The 7CV was sold as the Twelve in England, while the 11 Legere was also known as the Sports Twelve and later the Light 15 across the Channel. Both these variants shared the same styling though the 11 Normale was an altogether bigger car, being both longer and wider, and was available in Britain as the Big 15. As the Traction was an outstanding example of progressive European engineering, it is no surprise to find that telescopic hydraulic shock absorbers took over from the original friction devices in 1935, while rack and pinion steering was adopted the following year. Introduced in the 1938 season were the distinctive and heavily spoked Michelin Pilote wheels which were specially designed for radial ply tyres. The six cylinder variation on the theme appeared in 1939, having a 2.9 litre engine which shared the same pistons, con rods and liners as the 11. It was, in short, a scaled up 11 Normale, though the front shock absorbers were vertically mounted rather than inclined as on the four cylinder cars, and the drive shafts incorporated a bulky rubber coupling.

Production was, of course, severely curtailed by the war and the pre-war models continued to be made up until 1946. From the following year the four cylinder car was only available in 1911cc form. Gone were the handsome Pilotes, being replaced by cheaper discs, though Slough used perforated examples. An instant way of telling the post-war four cylinders from the pre-war cars is that the later vehicles use conventional louvres on the bonnet in place of the small ventilating doors that dated back to 1934. The six used louvres from the start.

Rather like the Model T Ford, Tractions were only available in black for a time, though in 1954 grey and blue hues were introduced. However, 1953 saw the familiar silhouette slightly altered with the addition of a larger boot, the spare wheel now being contained within instead of being mounted on the boot lid. In 1954 came the first major alteration to the Traction's mechanical specification, the Six-H model having rear hydro-pneumatic suspension in place of the transverse torsion bars, foreshadowing the system to be used on the revolutionary DS 19 of 1956. The old model finally ceased production in 1957, the final example bearing the appropriate legend *fin,*

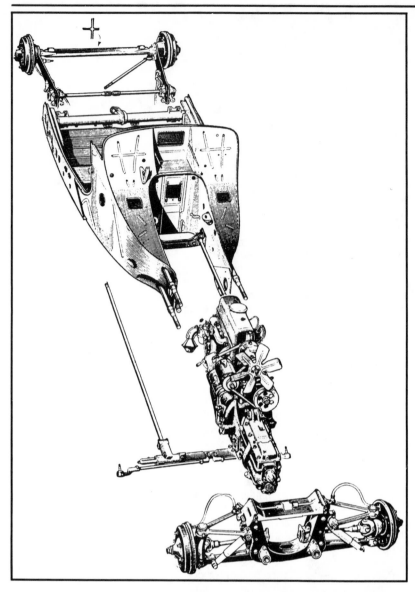

Citroën exposed: in engineering terms, the Traction Avant, with front wheel drive, unitary, chassisless construction and innovative suspension, was way ahead of any other mass-produced car of the time.

way they fit. If they're out of alignment be particularly suspicious, taking special note of the trailing edge of the rear doors. Weakening of the body structure can also put undue stress on the door hinges, so subject these to close scrutiny. While you're at it also check the condition of the doors themselves; there's very little to prevent rain getting straight past the windows and if the drain holes are blocked then the door bottoms can rust badly.

On the pre-1953 examples with the smaller boot have a careful scout around the interior, particularly in the vicinity of the lid's hinges which are attached to the boot floor. These boots aren't particularly waterproof and rusting tends to break out on the apron. The weight of the lid (remember it also holds the spare wheel) can result in the hinges breaking away from their mountings.

A sunshine roof was another distinctive feature of the Slough assembled cars and this is also another potential trouble spot. The lid was made of wood up until 1937 and thereafter metal. Drain tubes get blocked and rot away so carefully check this area.

The front of the car is fairly rust free in view of the proximity of the engine, though there is one point that really is worth checking. Look underneath the front engine/transmission mounting "horn", near the point where the steering column passes through the body member. This position will obviously vary on right and left hand drive examples. Also, all cars have a scuttle mounted ventilator flap. Inevitably the rubber seal gets damaged over the years (the Traction Owners Club can supply replacements) but the water gets in and rusts the floor directly beneath.

Engine, Gearbox Transmission

The Traction's engine is a robust and reliable unit. As already mentioned, it is fitted with wet liners and is quite capable of running for 100,000 miles without a major overhaul.

and left the Paris assembly line on July 25th of that year. Since 1934, 708,339 four cylinder cars had been built while Six production totalled 50,518.

So much for the model's history, but how does this pioneering front wheel drive design shape up as a practical proposition in the 80s? Let's start by considering the bodywork, always an important consideration on any classic car but a particularly vital one on the Traction with its monocoque hull.

Bodywork

The first port of call should be the sills. As we have seen, the Slough assembled cars were fitted with semaphore indicators and, unfortunately, water enters this slot and rusts out the sill directly below the door pillar. Also have a look at the rear end of the sills adjoining the back wheel as this is open to the elements and can also rust badly. Any corrosion at these joints may well indicate that the whole body structure has been badly affected, so turn your attention to the doors and particularly the

Although the engine was very advanced in most respects it is surprising to find that white metal main bearings and big ends were used right up until 1955: however, the 11D of 1956 used only white metal mains, the big ends being converted to shells; an unusual arrangement.

We now come to the model's Achilles Heel – its gearbox and transmission. First, the gearbox. This is a three speed affair and has a working life of 50 to 60,000 miles, with second/third gear synchro probably being the first component to give trouble. Contained within the casing which is mounted forward of the engine, is the crown wheel and pinion, the latter part of the union being liable to shed its teeth. A replacement crown wheel and pinion unit costs around £160. You can tell whether all is not well in that department because the car emits a howling noise rather like a low-flying aircraft! And never bump start a Traction, the crown wheel and pinion simply doesn't like it.

Now to the drive shafts which transmit the power from the gearbox to the front wheels. Unfortunately, they don't have a particularly long working life, about 15,000 miles is an average replacement period for the inner joints and 60,000 for those at the gearbox end. The wear occurs mostly in the bushing of the double Hooke joint which permit the driven power being transmitted through the steering arc. It is absolutely vital that these shafts are regularly greased. As the T.A.'s handbook states: "these joints cannot be over lubricated". Citroën recommend that the two grease nipples per shaft be attended to every 1,000 kilometres (that's about every 600 miles)

and you ignore these instructions at your peril. To check the state of the joints, grasp the shaft and twist it. If the joint isn't covered by a rubber gaiter (it should be) you will be able to see and hear movement in the joint, but if it is correctly contained then you should at least be able to hear any slack being taken up. Also, if the vehicle is a runner, drive it round in circles, alternatively to the left and right, to check that both sets of joints are in good condition. If they're not you should hear them knocking. As you can see from the photograph, the "wheel' end of the driveshaft contains a tapered stub axle, and it is important that the taper and the Woodruff key

A later six-cylinder version of the car.

it contains is in good condition as the nut on the end of it has to be tightened to a torque reading of 210lbs/ft.

Usually, wheels aren't much of a problem, but the Traction is an exception in this respect. During the 1938/39 season and also on the cars built in 1945/46 which were essentially pre-war models, Michelin Pilote wheels were fitted. Good as these wheels look they are vulnerable to rusting and unfortunately, the only way to tell whether they're in sound condition is to remove the tyre which is not always possible!

Steering, Suspension, Brakes

Practically all the cars we are concerned with are fitted with rack and pinion steering. The rack itself is adjustable and some wear can be taken up by shims. Other shortcomings are confined to wear on the inner ball joint of the pins that transmit movement to the track rods. Also look out for splits on the rack's rubber gaiters; unfortunately, fitting new ones is an awkward and time consuming job, but if it isn't done mud and grit can enter and MoT failure if likely.

The Traction's suspension is by torsion bars: longitudinal at the front, in conjunction with a semi wishbone layout, and transverse at

the rear where a dead axle is employed. The bars themselves should present no troubles at all. At the front, lubrication is again an important factor as the upper swivel link ball joints and the upper link arm pins and bearing also require greasing as often as the drive shafts! By contrast, the single bottom arm is rubber mounted and requires no attention.

Brakes are hydraulic all round and are remarkably trouble free. Fortunately, all the parts are still obtainable and were Lockheed from the very first. Post-war examples used steel hydraulic piping which should be examined for rusting and this particularly applies to the part of the pipe immediately adjacent to the bodywork.

Interior

As has already been noted, the French-built cars have cloth interiors while those built at Slough have leather, the latter option certainly being more desirable from a wear point of view. Incidentally, even the door panels were leather-covered on the pre-war Slough cars though leathercloth was used afterwards.

If the car is fitted with a sliding roof check the area immediately around the hatch for instances of leakage.

One of the Traction's big plusses is that the floor is completely flat as there is no obtrusive propellor shaft, the Normale being a particularly roomy offering.

Spares, Clubs and Prices

It is worth saying, avoid an example which is obviously suffering from bad rusting. Apart from the fact that it weakens the body structure, replacement parts are virtually impossible to obtain. By contrast, mechanical components are plentiful, so the moral is obvious.

As far as prices go, you can pick up a non-running Traction from about £300 to £500. Running examples are available from that top price, though nowadays you can get a good car for around the £2,000 to £3,000 mark; however, restored examples are now fetching about £5000.

The Traction Owner's Club caters for cars in this country and if you own one of these distinctive Citroëns then I would thoroughly recommend joining. The secretary is Steve Reed, 1, Terwick Cottage, Rogate, Petersfield, Hants. They have an excellent club magazine and a spares service. Parts are also available from Classic Restorations at Arch 124 Cornwall Road, London SE1 on Saturday mornings, which is presided over by John Gillard. My thanks to him for his help in the preparation of this feature.

This article first appeared in ''Thoroughbred & Classic Cars'' magazine.

DRIVE AID

Citroën SM

L.J.K. Setright profiles the Citroën with Maserati connections.

There must surely have been, in the early 1970s, more than 12,854 purists in all the world of motoring. There quite certainly were more customers than that who could have afforded the price of a Citroën SM – even though it rose, during that period, from 46,000 to 84,000 Francs. Yet that number is all that Citroën managed to sell, of a car that had been acclaimed, by the critics of the international motoring press, with a rare unanimity; that number is all they managed to sell, of a car that was tremendously strong, extraordinarily stylish, and uncommonly fast – a car blessed with aerodynamic properties that would be unbeaten for many years, and with steering and lights that have not been beaten yet.

One might think that purists would be attracted by such things. Alas, though many said they liked the car, few actually bought it – and the blame cannot be laid entirely at the doors of the Middle East, whence a mischievously political oil crisis cast its blight upon the world at the end of 1973. Sales in that year had only been half of what they had been in '72. The real fault was probably Citroën's own – not that of the designers and constructors – but of the sales and service departments.

The service network was incomprehensibly resentful. They, who could undertake work on the inaccessible complexities of the DS hydraulics without turning a hair or skinning a knuckle, raised no mean outcry over the comparatively simple task of caring for an engine with two more cylinders, three more camshafts and four more chokes than the familiar DS. Maybe they saw it as an opportunity to demand higher rates of payment; in the USA, what was needed was higher education. The typically brutal and deliberately uncomprehending xenophobe, for whose crass ignorance and insensitivity the domestic American car had been designed, having spent the 1950s trashing the SU carburettors of English cars and the 1960s abusing the transmissions of Italian cars, now took the opportunity to do to this French car such things as might have prompted a barbarian to pause and a vandal to discover finer feelings. Shocked and sickened, Citroën withdrew from the USA market in 1973, after selling about 2000 SMs there. Their feelings about the single examples sold in such places as Bolivia, Liberia and the Philippines must have been similar in kind if not in degree.

Considering the failure of the sales organisation to approach the targets forecast for the SM, one must hold them responsible too. It appears that they were out of their depth, dealing not only with cars but also with customers of a higher class than those with whom they had been familiar. Taking a Renault or a Ford in part exchange for a DS was a comfortable enough process, almost as comfortable as taking a fistful of grimy banknotes for a 2CV; but taking a Porsche or a Jaguar in part exchange for an SM, let alone recognizing the qualities in such cars with which the SM had to compete, were ideas above their station. Yet it was with the very intention of acquiring some glamour, some nobility of lineage and elevation of patronage, that Citroën had set Maserati to producing an engine for their social climber. Citroën had bought the Italian firm – quite cheaply – in 1968, during a wildly expansionist period in which M. Ravenel led them in numerous different directions simultaneously, doing various deals with Simca for factories, Panhard for everything, Berliet for a little while, and Fiat for crying out loud. Maserati fitted easily into his picture: with its reputation for bloodstock engines, it could provide the one thing that was missing from the Citroën armoury of talents.

The Citroën SM's value in Europe is boosted by those who appreciate the classical completeness of its engineering virtues but, paradoxically, is somewhat restrained by fear of its complexity. (Courtesy Thoroughbred & Classic Cars)

What was foreseen was a new, dramatic, high-performance, high-class Citroën to fill a gap which had grown distressingly obvious since the decline of the upper-crust French firms (Delage, Delahaye and so on) a decade earlier. In the new enthusiasm for refined and redoubtable cars which had blossomed in the 1960s, the scope for promoting Citroën was clear and tempting. The DS, or developments of it, could provide everything necessary in suspension, brakes, running gear, indeed in everything except an appropriate engine. Because the opportunity was immediate, and because the DS made everything else immediately available, the engine would be needed very quickly. Citroën told Maserati that it must be very light, very short, and develop at least 150bhp – and that they would have to create it within six months. Maserati told Citroën that a trivial little job like that would only take them about three weeks! Doubtless a sign of hurt pride (they may have been saved by the take-over, but they can hardly have been pleased), this was not to be taken too seriously – but in astonishing fact they took less than seven weeks.

They did not have to start from scratch. They had recently created a new engine for themselves, the 4186cm³ V8 of the Maserati Indy. Ing Alfieri sliced two cylinders off it, reduced the bore and stroke of the remainder slightly, and thus produced a 90° V6 of 2670cm³, just small enough to get below the 16CV fiscal rating beyond which French cars were punitively taxed and seldom bought. With a choice of camshafts he was able to offer Citroën three alternative power curves, one of which reached 200bhp. There was work to be done on rearranging the ancillaries and providing for a drive to the Citroën hydraulic clutch and five-speed all-indirect gearbox with spiral-bevel final drive, but when it was done he had created an engine weighing only 309lb and only a foot long.

It was impressive in its detail. The light-alloy castings were sandwiched together very firmly, the lower supports for the main bearings being integrated with a nether half-crankcase, beneath which the sump was a simple and separate casting. The main block of upper crankcase and cylinder blocks was immensely rigid, despite its open-deck construction, and above its banks a pair of remarkably shallow cylinder-head castings nevertheless accommodated hemispherical combustion chambers, in which opposed valves were inclined at an included angle of 76° for operation by paired overhead camshafts.

The drive to these camshafts was an ingenious replacement for that in the original V8. The new three-throw crankshaft (which allowed inertial forces to be balanced out as though the engine were three 90° V-twins, though it made unequal firing intervals necessary) drove a chain from its rear to a jackshaft lying in the V of the cylinders. From that jackshaft went two more chains, one to each head and staggered so that the heads themselves were identical and interchangeable; and by being set in the planes of the main bearings, these drives added nothing to the length of the engine.

It was ostensibly a beautiful arrangement, giving a very short and extremely stiff crankshaft, clear straight porting served by three twin-barrel downdraught Weber carburettors, and minimal torsional flutter in the camshafts. As installed in the car, however, the alternator, hydraulic pump and air-conditioning pump were all carried in a sub-frame well ahead of the engine, to which they were connected by a long and slender torsionally flexible shaft driven from the nose of the jackshaft. Whether that induced torsional flutter of the primary chain, or damped it at the expense of accelerated wear, is not clear; but that chain gave problems, and too often they were very costly ones.

That was the only operational flaw in the entire driveline, which was otherwise remarkable only for the precision of the gearshift and the appropriateness of the gear ratios; this gearbox was later to be used by Lotus in their Esprit. For the Americans, such as they were, Citroën sought Borg-Warner collaboration in confecting an automatic transmission – but that came later with an increase in displacement to augment the torque as

Although perhaps over-styled (because that style is now looking dated), the extraordinary interior layout adds to the message that this is the car for you; not you for it: an SM is taken entirely on its own terms! (Courtesy Thoroughbred & Classic Cars)

those shiftless customers begged. When the engine was enlarged in 1973 (by reversion to the original Indy bore, giving 2965cm³), European customers continued to enjoy the Bosch fuel-injection system (like that of the DS23i) to which they had been treated since 1972, and which had increased the power somewhat. The fact that the top speed rose without the acceleration being any better was due to the subtle increase in gearing brought about by fitting 205mm Michelins instead of the original 195 size.

Top speed and acceleration were both excellent without being incredible. About 136mph was the limit for the former, while the time for a standing-start kilometre was usually an irritating fraction of a second over 30. Both figures must be seen in the perspective of the big and heavy car that the SM was.

Its growth out of the DS was more than metaphorical. The running prototypes were actually DS saloons with the V6 inserted at one end and the wheel arches enlarged at the other. How else do you suppose so complex a car could have been created – from the go-ahead to the debut at the Geneva Salon Automobile in March 1970 – in just eighteen months?

As we have seen, the wonderful old DS provided much that was more than satisfactory. It provided a self-levelling self-damping and inimitably progressive-rate suspension system that was already so much superior to anything else in the world that nobody else in the world yet understood it; and there was already proven (but shelved) an active-ride version of it that would eliminate roll, and for which the extra-powerful hydraulics pump of the SM must have been eventually intended. Further, the DS provided a braking system of outstanding power, with inboard discs at the front reducing the unsprung mass (further enhancing ride and roadholding) and instant automatic load-dependent modulation of pressure to the rear drums so that they should never lock prematurely.

Further still, the DS provided the basis of a most remarkable steering system. It was further developed for the SM by the interpolation of a speed-related negative servo which progressively reduced power assistance from its maximum at standstill to zero at 124mph. Thus, the steering was light when manoeuvring slowly, full of feel when driving fast, and as precise as exceptionally high gearing could make it, with only two turns of the handwheel from one extremity of lock to the other.

Making it all possible was perfect steering geometry, such as no other car but the later (just a few months later, and still going strong) GS ever had. With a four-bar linkage (essentially that of the DS) giving strict parallelogram geometry at the front, and with zero camber, caster and kingpin inclination, the SM front wheels went through camber changes equal to body roll but did not suffer camber changes induced by steering, as in other cars, nor gyroscopic interference.

Strictly trailing rear wheels devoid of toe-in variation complemented this arrangement, accounting for marvellously consistent handling while leaving Michelin with their purpose-built XWX (a derivative of the XVR, and the best 70-series VR tyre then made) to arrange equally impressive roadholding. Only at the limits of adhesion, and especially when reaching them in the course of an S-bend, did the SM begin to reveal the seamy side of front-wheel drive.

Mere speed (sheer speed, rather) made no difference to it at all. Today's aerodynamicists might cavil at the lack of downforce, and suggest an abasement of the nose, but Citroën's styling chief, Robert Opron (subsequently purloined by Renault) and his assistant, Giret, extrapolated DS styling to combine low drag with directional stability by keeping close to zero-lift – something that the self-levelling suspension maintained by preventing pitch variations. It was a car still visibly descended from the wonderful design created by Opron's predecessor, Flaminio Bertoni, for the DS of 1955.

Partly because of that, it was a lot of car – especially in relation to the not extravagantly large interior. In fact the rear seats were derisory; most of the body was full of car, with the boot half-full of spare tyre and the bonnet absolutely crammed with engineering. It was a long body, too, following Citroën's established ideals by being very wide at the front and very narrow at the back; and it was its great length in proportion to its cross-sectional area which played a big part in minimising the drag coefficient.

Citroën took no chances whatever in its construction. The bodyshell was very strongly integrated with the floorpan to create an immensely strong chassis-hull, with little but the doors, lids and front wings removable. It was also heavy – but, after all, it was not a sports car, even though it did win its first rally. It was not a town carriage either, even though specialist coachbuilders laboured mightily to make swankmobiles for President, Premier, and visiting heads of state. Nor was it a mean-minded economy car meant for the parsimonious mobilisation of economists and calculators, although the advent of injection helped its thirst as much as its emissions.

Most of all, it was emphatically not a car that should have been doomed never to exceed half its potential speed; but this was what was imposed when the fuel crisis came to

cloud all other issues at the end of 1973. With sales already dropping dangerously low, the SM was doomed – a car with no future and very little present. Poor Citroën, sorely overtaxed by the investment in the GS of late 1970 and the CX of 1973, had seen the departure of Michelin who had been major shareholders since the death of André Citroën forty years earlier. Their new overlords certainly wasted no sympathy on the SM: once they had decided that its production should stop, they would not even allow engines to be installed in already completed body shells. Ligier could have the few engines he had been promised; as for Maserati, they were welcome to put the V6 into their nice little Merak for as long as their new and equally hard-headed owner Alejandro de Tomaso might let them; and as for those SM bodies, they were to be scrapped. But we should not be too hard on Peugeot: revivals are all very well, but keeping the dead alive can be more cruel than euthanasia.

This article first appeared in "The Car". It has been revised for this book.

However, if you're looking for an SM to buy, don't ever be dazzled by what you see, because a bad one would give you so very many problems. Search high and low, if necessary, to find someone who knows a great deal about the cars and, even if it costs you dearly, get him to inspect the car for you. It would be certain to work out both cheaper and more satisfying. (Courtesy Thoroughbred & Classic Cars)

Top of the Pops

It was crude but cheap and in one form or another ran for over 30 years. Jonathan Wood looks at the ubiquitous sidevalve Ford

The sidevalve engine is quite simple to work on and this one, with adjustable tappets, is the best of all.

Transverse leaf-spring suspension, a channel section chassis, sidevalve engine and mechanical brakes sound more akin to pre-First World War days than the post-1945 era. Yet, the Prefect/Anglia/Popular range of 'sit up and beg' Fords were produced until 1959, and over half a million were made.

But first some history. Ford's new Dagenham factory began production in 1931 and really got into its stride with the best selling Eight h.p. Y of the following year. This was sold until 1939, after a 1937 restyle, when it was replaced by the Anglia (Series EO4A), a basically similar confection but with a more imposing bonnet. This two-door model was

Autocar

similar in styling to the newly introduced four-door six light Prefect (E93A) of 1938 and the two cars remained in virtually unchanged form until the end of 1948.

It was an example of the well-established Ford formula of a crude but strong design which offered reliability and good value for money. Both models were basically similar in concept but the four-door Prefect demanded a longer wheelbase (7ft 10in, as opposed to 7ft 6in). The chassis was uncompromisingly simple. It was built up around a channel-section frame with transverse leaf suspension and radius rods and torque tube transmission, all found on the immortal Model T. Brakes were initially cable but a Girling rod system was soon adopted. The engines, largely inherited from the Eight, were of similar external dimensions, with the 933cc unit being fitted to the Anglia while the Prefect's capacity was 1172cc, achieved by increasing the bore from 56.6mm to 63.5mm. RAC ratings were eight and ten horsepower respectively. But

the very utilitarian nature of the vehicles was underlined by six-volt electrics and the retention of the infamous vacuum windscreen wiper, operated by suction from the inlet manifold that immediately ceased to function when climbing a hill or overtaking! I speak from experience, having owned a 1948 Prefect for a time. In addition to the saloons, a touring version of the Prefect was offered, about 1600 being produced in all.

Body and chassis production was the responsibility of Briggs Motor Bodies, whose plant was adjacent to Ford's Dagenham factory. Output was, of course, interrupted by the outbreak of the Second World War and production didn't re-start unttil 1946. Both the Anglia and Prefect continued to be made in their basic pre-war form until 1948 when they were mildly altered for the 1949 season. The Anglia lost its running boards, its radiator grille was altered and the model redesignated E494A. The Prefect's appearance was also changed with headlamps grafted into the front

The upright shape of the Ford 'Pop' was a familiar sight on postwar British roads. Today its simplicity – some would say crudity – is all part of the charm. And so is the price, because these are among the cheapest classic cars to buy.

wings (E493A). Both models remained in production until 1953 when they were replaced by the Popular (103E). This was basically the Anglia body fitted with the 1172cc Prefect engine, already fitted to some export Anglias.

Popular production continued at Dagenham until 1955 but in August of that year output restarted at Ford's Doncaster factory. (It is a matter of historical interest that this was the very plant where bodies for the ill-fated Jowett Javelin had been produced by Briggs. Ford, bent on autonomy in the body building field, had taken over Briggs in 1953). The Popular ceased production in 1959 – not bad for a chassis layout that dated back to 1908 and an engine design to 1932, though it should be added that at £390 in 1955 it was the cheapest car on the British market.

But what are the problems associated with buying one of these tough sidevalvers? To find out I talked to two leading members of the Ford Sidevalve Owners Club, Ivan Precieux, who is responsible for books and regalia, and Bruce Palmer who looks after the club's register of Populars. Both own 103Es.

remarkably immune to rust except where the front and rear cross members join the side frames. Have a look at all the corners on the members' flanged sides for signs of corrosion, too.

The body is also fairly trouble free. The doors, for instance, very rarely rust, but you are likely to experience problems with the wings. Rust festers around the bottom edges of the front wings and rain also gets in through the scuttle-mounted ventilators and corrodes the box section directly beneath. Take particular note of the wing area immediately adjacent to the running boards, if they're fitted. The boards themselves should be examined at their extremities; fourtunately

Body and Chassis

As we've seen, all these Fords have a channel-section chassis frame. Fortunately, it's

Production

Anglia: 50,684.
Prefect: 379,229
Popular: 155,350
Total: 585,263

replacements are available. Also have a look at the sills immediately above the boards. The rear wings tend to corrode faster than the front ones, particularly at their running board end. And like the fronts they also deteriorate along the flange that joins them to the bodywork, something that might not seem readily apparent at a cursory inspection. It is not possible to obtain metal replacements but a definite advantage is that they're bolted, rather than welded, in position which makes removal and rectification easier. As a matter of interest, the paint used on the wings was baked on, this enamelling ensuring a hard and lasting finish.

Although a sunroof was available before the war, the post-1945 cars had a fabric roof. The material is secured by a metal channel which is covered by a rubber moulding. This channel is another potential rust area and any trouble here can result in water getting in and damaging the head lining. Fortunately, it's possible to obtain replacement mouldings from the Ford Sidevalve OC.

The most vulnerable area of the Anglia and Popular (the Prefect has a different body layout) is the valance beneath the boot lid which rusts very badly. As there are no replacement parts available, pay particular attention to this area. Having sought out the rust, move on to the boot lid as that is also another vulnerable area. Open the boot and examine the floor immediately adjacent to the lid. You might be in for a shock, the corrosion being aided and abetted by water entering around the petrol tank filler. The boot hinges are rather brittle, incidentally, so breakages may be encountered.

Engine and Transmisson

The sidevalve engine is crude in the extreme – but reliable, though it does have limited life, which usually terminates at around 30,000 miles whereupon it starts to fume horrendously; in really bad cases the entire vehicle can

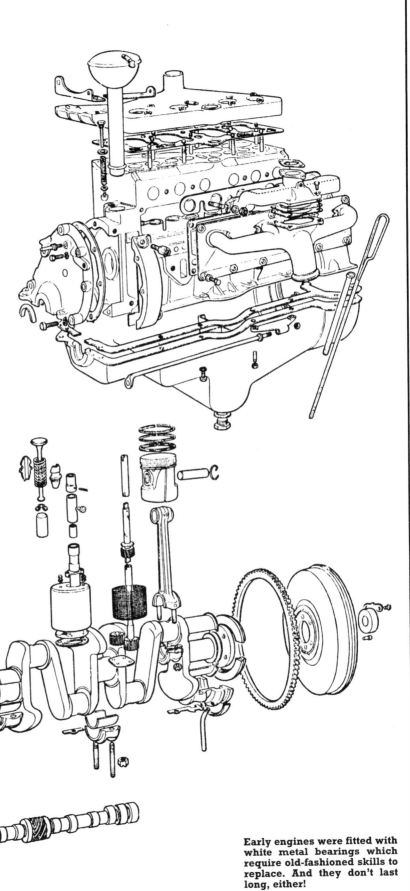

Early engines were fitted with white metal bearings which require old-fashioned skills to replace. And they don't last long, either!

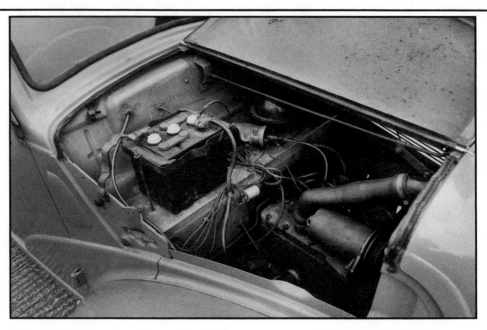

Why such a long bonnet for such a small engine? But what a charming way to inspect the engine! Just the car for a Sunday morning spin?

Specifications (1954 Popular)

Engine: cast iron block and head; side valves; bore/stroke 63.5/92.5 mm; 1172cc; three main bearings; max power 30.1bhp at 4000rpm.
Transmission: single-plate clutch; three-speed manual gearbox; spiral bevel rear axle.
Chassis: channel section with bolt-on body.
Suspension: front and rear transverse leaf with radius arms aided by Armstrong shock absorbers.
Steering, brakes: worm and nut: Girling mechanical drum brakes all round.
Wheels, tyres: pressed steel with 500 x 16 tyres (Popular: 4.50 x 17).
Performance: max speed 60.3mph; 0-50 24.1 secs; 30-50 mph in top 15.3 secs; fuel consumption; approx 35mpg.

be consumed in a cloud which belches forth from the oil filler. So these engines are bad liars about their age. Normal oil consumption is around 200 miles to the pint. One major spares shortcoming is that replacement valves are now almost impossible to obtain. The Ford Sidevalve club is now looking into the possibility of getting new stock manufactured, but it's also a point worth remembering. It's also worth noting that these engine don't have adjustable tappets so the valve stem has to be ground to achieve the correct clearance.

Fortunately, it is still possible to obtain completely reconditioned engines. Amongst companies that offer them are the Newford Parts Centre and Shepperds Grove Service Station. Traditional white metal bearings are employed but it is possible to fit the more conventional shells.

One of the engine's main idiosyncrasies is that it's prone to fuel vaporisation in hot weather, perhaps because the mechanical fuel pump is uncomfortably close to the exhaust manifold. It's not uncommon for a sidevalver to come to a grinding halt on a summer day; all you can do then is to wait for it to cool down. Re-building the petrol pump may cure the trouble and AC still recondition these units. As a last resort some owners have fitted a six-volt SU electric pump in place of the mechanical one. That said, it's worth making the point that these cars are, in the main, poor starters and a preparatory turn-over on the starting handle or operation of the priming lever on the side of the pump is a worthwhile routine prior to ignition (it takes 32 strokes of the lever to prime the system, incidentally).

The gearbox is a three-speeder and it's not uncommon for second gear synchromesh to wear badly. The result is that the lever jumps out of mesh and the gear will probably chatter badly as well. The drive is taken to the rear axle via a propeller shaft contained within a torque tube, and transmission chatter may be the result of wear in the universal joint

which is found directly behind the gearbox. In addition, the rear axle hasn't the best of reputations for reliability; the crown wheel and pinion and/or half shaft are all prone to failure, usually with the minimum of warning – as I once discovered myself. A rumbling noise will probably indicate wear in the wheel bearings as it's easy to overlook their lubrication via the appropriate grease nipple.

Steering, Suspension, Brakes

The steering on these Fords can be somewhat alarming if you've never previously experienced it! ''If it wanders it must be normal'' say Bruce and Ivan. It's possible that there'll be some play in the steering column itself but this can be corrected by adjustment at the top and bottom of the shaft. Otherwise the box doesn't seem to wear out. But the means of conveying the car's change of direction does induce wear as drag links, pins and track rod ends all suffer to a greater or lesser extent. Fortunately, the Sidevalve OC has had the drag links re-manufactured and they can also supply replacement kingpins and these are also available through specialist and trade sources. The difficulty at present is with track rod ends but it seems likely that the club will take it on themselves to have new ones made.

Suspension, such as it is, is simple and relatively trouble free. One fairly common shortcoming is wear in the A bush which secures the front radius arms to the chassis. A good indication of this having occurred is when the car judders badly when starting from standstill. It's far more likely that wear in this bush is the cause rather than in the clutch itself.

At the back of the car the single transverse leaf spring is secured to the axle by bolts and Silentbloc bushes. The rubber in the bush can break down leaving just the shackle pins which isn't particularly desirable:

a vital check point. Mention should be made of the Panhard Rod conversions, available front and rear, that were offered as a contemporary accessory through Ford dealers. If they're fitted, then they are well worth retaining.

Provided that the Girling rod brakes are properly set up they shouldn't give any trouble, and I'm assured that they have much to commend them. However, if they do give concern, the chances are that this is caused by wear in the clevis pins that are to be found throughout the system. Play in the brake compensator can also cause steering problems.

Interior

Although somewhat spartan in layout these Fords have well finished interiors. Although the upholstery was usually PVC, leather could also be specified. The window surrounds are made of Bakerlite and these are slightly prone to cracking though it is possible to obtain glass-fibre replacements. The floor in these cars presents few problems as it is made of marine plywood, but you might find the trim in the front foot well has warped, usually caused by water. You may also experience trouble with the window winder of the driver's side, making it impossible to raise the glass. The actuating gear wheel tends to strip its teeth but, fortunately, the ever vigilant Ford club has got the matter in hand and have just had a batch of gearwheels and their attendant spigots manufactured.

Spares and How Much

Metal body panels are, not surprisingly, no longer available but glass fibre wings, sills, boot lids and the like are available from Geoff Jago of Custon Automotive, Quarry Lane, Chichester, West Sussex. Glass fibre body parts are also available from DCM Mouldings of Haver Road, Exeter, Devon. These include wings and even a complete two-door body! Rubber mouldings for these models are available from Edgware Motor Accessories of 120 High Street, Edgware, Middlesex.

The mechanical spares situation is in a particularly healthy state and two sources of parts are the Newford Parts Centre of Abbey Mill, Abbey Village, Chorley, Lancs and Shepperds Grove Service Station of Stanton, Suffolk. And, as we've seen, the Ford Sidevalve Owners Club is initiating the re-manufacture of difficult-to-get parts. So membership of the organisation is an absolute 'must'. The club address is: 30, Earls Close, Bishopstoke, Eastleigh, Hants, SO5 6H7 and the secretary is Mick Crouch.

What would you expect to pay for one of these trusty Fords? Prices start at around £500 for an Anglia or Popular in good running order and out-standing examples have reached the £1,000 mark. However, Prefects tend to command slightly higher prices, concours vehicles fetching as much as £1200.

"Top of the Pops" first appeared as an article in "Thoroughbred and Classic Cars" Magazine.

Humber Hawk, Super Snipe & Imperial

Peter Williams analyses the 'Series' Humbers often called the 'English Buick' in America

If ever a car deserved better it was the big 'Series' Humbers introduced as the Hawk by Rootes in May 1957. Complemented by the Super Snipe in October 1958, and then later, in October 1964, the Imperial (a plush derivative of the Snipe), the Series cars followed the trend of 'Americanization' with wrap-around screens and plenty of chrome. This was a somewhat incongruous theme for cars which boasted burr walnut veneers and Connolly hides, both hallmarks of the marque. They were styled by the American Raymond Loewy organisation which had a substantial influence on the Rootes Group before and after the Second World War.

The Series Humbers were a departure for the Rootes Group and followed the trends of

the time. When it was first introduced in 1957, the Hawk was the first all-monocoque unitary construction Humber. It featured Humber's four-cylinder 2267cc 78bhp overhead-valve engine, based on the earlier side-valve unit the company had used since the war, and stayed in this form throughout the car's lifetime.

In October 1958 the Super Snipe was introduced and used the same bodyshell as the Hawk, but with necessary engineering changes to accommodate its all-new six-cylinder 2651cc overhead-valve 118bhp engine. Many Rootes *aficionados* would describe this engine as one of the smoothest and most beautifully-built sixes of all time. It was designed for the company by Armstrong-Siddeley.

The Series cars utilised straightforward engineering and were available in manual, manual with overdrive and automatic versions, with wishbone suspension at the front and a live axle at the rear. In sharing the same bodyshell, they measured 185 inches in length and used a common wheelbase of 110 inches. Inside they are roomy, though occupants sit high with a clear view out of the glassy cabin. They weighed between 3000lb and 4000lb depending on the model.

Rootes was obviously copying Detroit trends, but was some three years behind. The Hawk was supposed to resemble the Chevrolet and Buick models of the period. Apart from the wrap-around front and rear winds-

The Humber Hawk: Rootes Group Americana on display from 1957 when it was first introduced. (All pictures in this article courtesy of Thoroughbred & Classic Cars).

creens, the large horizontal chromed grille and single hooded headlamps were American traits. To set it apart from the Hawk, the Snipe was fitted with a rather gaudy grille which spoilt the 'cleanness' of the horizontally-slatted one on the Hawk.

Although the windscreen style did inevitably produce a 'dog-leg' in the door aperture, this was not the knee trap it proved to be with some makes, due to the enormous front doors which provided easy access, albeit at the expense of the rear passengers' entry, which was only adequate.

There were saloon, estate and limousine (featuring a wind-down glass partition) versions of the Hawk and Super Snipe.

The first change to the Hawk occurred in October 1959 when it adopted different gear ratios, while the 2.7-litre engine in the Snipe was uprated to 2965cc and 129bhp. Front disc brakes became standard on the Snipe at the same time.

A year later the Hawk (Series 2) followed with disc brakes, larger rear drums, redesigned rear suspension and an improved gearbox. The Snipe (Series 3) received the suspension modifications plus fresh air outlets at each end of the facia and new heater controls. The heater was now standard on the Hawk. Broadly speaking, the Hawk was one year behind the Snipe in the modifications made to the range, although both received larger fuel tanks, an improved steering system and overdrive (optional) on top (Series 4 Snipe) and third gear (Series 3 Hawk) in 1962. The Super Snipe had its power output increased slightly, to 132.5 bhp and the gearing was raised together with the rear axle ratio, which changed from 4.55:1 to 4.22:1

The Humber Super Snipe had first been introduced in 1958, still using the Hawk body shell but now with a 6-cylinder engine. This is a later version with a 3-litre engine.

Pre-dating the 3-litre, the rare Humber Super Estate car offered enormous accommodation and must have been among the most luxurious estate cars built.

Exterior styling was subject to minor changes at regular intervals mainly to waist mouldings and grille. The Series 2 Snipe saw the first noticeable change with reshaped front wings and twin 5¾ inch headlamps. The grille now consisted of all-horizontal bars, giving an impression of increased width. The Series 4 Hawk (Series 5 Snipe) featured a new, reshaped roof with squared-off six-light profile, flatter screens, narrower (and flimsier) bumpers and a restyled fascia to give the range another three years' life. Also introduced in 1964 was an executive version, the Imperial. This was a Snipe with more equipment, such as map reading lamps to both rear seats, rear heating, demisting from a separate heater in the boot, adjustable rear squabs (from control on fascia), radio with front and rear speakers, automatic transmission as standard, additional courtesy lamps. Reuter seats and choice of hide or West of England cloth upholstery.

During the production of Series models, several coachbuilders produced variations, notably Radford, Mulliner, and Thrupp & Maberley who put the finishing touches to the Imperial. Production of the Series cars ended in 1967 at around 50,000 units.

Bodyshell

The body and underframe are of all-welded monocoque construction using multiple panels in stress areas to achieve remarkable strength and rigidity. The full length 'chassis' is supplemented by the box-section sills which are made up from four separate panels, as are the door pillars and inner wing panels. The roof frame, again of multiple panels, provided a very safe passenger area.

As with all welded body vehicles, seams and edges are prone to rust, particularly wing edges and sill sections. Though these are not irrepairable, they may prove somewhat more expensive than many makes due to the multi-panel construction. Door bottoms should also be checked, Chassis corrosion is usually confined to the outriggers and an area of overlap just below the rear seats where the front and rear members meet. The rear inner wings also demand inspection, especially directly behind the wheel where a crossmember is welded in.

Do not discount a vehicle if it is rusty in these areas but bear in mind the cost. If there are any signs of corrosion or repair in the front door pillars around the 'dog-leg', the car is best left where it is, as this panel is so intricate that it is extremely difficult to repair satisfactorily. Brightwork is almost unobtainable and requires specialist production if badly corroded.

Engine and Gearbox

Most mechanical parts are still available for the Series cars. The four cylinder 2267cc

With burr walnut, leather and thick pile carpet, the cars were redolent of genteel British luxury from an earlier age on the inside, which jarred, aesthetically speaking, with the relatively brash 'American' styling on the outside: at least, that was how it seemed at the time, although shifts in taste have reduced the visual conflict.

engine fitted to all Hawks was a direct descendant of the pre-war side-valve unit and still retained several common components. The bhp/cc ratio would be considered laughable by modern standards but the amazing torque available made it a very 'easy' car to drive. It is common for vehicles to go 'round the clock' without overhaul.

The cylinder head was of conventional design with vertical valves operated by hollow push-rods from a camshaft on the right of the engine. It features combustion chambers in the head and flat top pistons. There was so much 'spare' metal in the head that cracking and distortion were unheard of in normal use. There's provision on the pistons for an additional scraper ring below the gudgeon pin, which was normally fitted at the first 12,000 mile service.

If the unit had a weakness, it lay in the connecting rods. The long 110mm stroke which helped produce the desirable torque also produced an undesirable strain on the bottom end. Any attempt to take advantage of modern high-octane fuels by increasing the static ignition timing of two degrees after TDC could very easily result in a 'leg out of bed'. Drive was through a Borg and Beck single-plate clutch which was well up to the job. Operation was by long pendant pedals and Lockheed hydraulics on Series 1 and 1A, with Girling on later models. A carbon thrust-bearing was in common with that fitted to all Rootes cars.

The new six-cylinder 2.6-litre engine fitted to Series 1 Snipes had many features which made it one of the most advanced of its time. The crossflow cylinder head with inclined valves on either side and central spark plugs was somewhat revolutionary in a production vehicle. Although soon enlarged to 3.0-litres, it continued until the end of the models' lifespan. At first glance it gave the impression of being a twin-cam unit but this was due to the two rocker shafts, one along each side of the head. Push-rod-operated valves from a single camshaft were inclined and offset in the bowl like combustion chambers with the spark plug entering in the centre. A very 'tidy' unit, it produced the smooth power expected of a large six-cylinder quietly and, even by modern standards, efficiently. If it had a weakness it would be with the crankshaft but failure of this item was rare and usually followed abuse. The rocker shafts were prone to wear but only after considerable mileage.

All models should maintain 40-50lb oil pressure at 1500rpm and any noise from the crank should be treated with suspicion. Tappet noise on the six-cylinder may indicate worn rockers and, while most Hawks tend to smoke a bit, the Snipe should not. Water pumps are prone to failure but are not expensive.

Pay particular attention to the transmission on the Hawk. Noise when idling which occurs with the clutch in shows wear on front bearings while on the move, if it happens in top, there are worn rear bearings. The gear change may not be too positive, which was a feature of the model.

Operated by a column change which had rather too much linkage for its own good the gearbox was the source of most trouble in the Hawk range. Series 1 and 1A models shed teeth from first and reverse gears at the slightest provocation while later, modified units, possibly helped by the uncertain selection provided by the linkage, would slip smoke a bit, the Snipe should not. Water pumps are prone to failure but are not expensive.

Pay particular attention to the transmission on the Hawk. Noise when idling which occurs with the clutch in shows wear on front bearings while on the move, if it happens in top, there are worn rear bearings. The gear change may not be too positive, which was a feature of the model.

Operated by a column change which had rather too much linkage for its own good the gearbox was the source of most trouble in the Hawk range. Series 1 and 1A models shed teeth from first and reverse gears at the slightest provocation while later, modified units, possibly helped by the uncertain selection provided by the linkage, would slip out of gear like a bar of soap from a wet hand. The ratios were somewhat widely spaced on the 1 and 1A, the very low first being ideal when moving heavy loads, but almost embarrassing in normal use, most drivers preferring to start in second. In the modified later models, ratios were much closer and a definite improvement. The optional Laycock overdrive operated on top only on Series 1 and 1A, and on third and top in later models.

The rear axle was somewhat prone to pinion bearing failure and the subsequent floating of the shaft allowed lubricant to escape through the front oil seal resulting in wear on the gears and an accompanying whine. This was modified in the Series 2, identifiable by fine splines on the shafts, but this did not really solve the problem.

Fitted with a three-speed, column change gearbox as standard, the Snipe did not suffer the linkage problems of the Hawk. A new unit, the box provided a first gear low enough for any purpose but without being extreme. Second was very useful, pulling from a virtual standstill up to 50mph or so, while top could be engaged at speeds as low as 10mph. Overdrive was available as an extra and operated on top only. Automatic transmission was also available, early models being fitted with type DG boxes, later being replaced by Borg Warner type 35.

The Snipe transmission should be like silk with no noise and an easy, positive change. Type DG autos were very smooth. These units are very expensive to repair and if suspect expect a bill for at least £500! Type 35 autos, although not as smooth, have the advantage of being economically repairable. The Hawk retained the transmission from the earlier 'Mark' cars with minimal modifications. It was available with a four-speed column change, with overdrive and automatic as extras. Axle ratios of 4.22:1 and 4.55:1 were similar on both cars with a very rare option of 4.778 available on the Snipe for heavy towing. The differential was much heavier than that on the Hawk and was trouble-free in normal use.

Suspension and Steering

All models share a front suspension comprising unequal length wishbones with coil springs and telescopic shock absorbers mounted on an enormous cross member, fitted to the chassis on rubber mounts. The wishbones pivot on threaded fulcrum pins which require regular greasing to prevent wear. Pay close attention to the pins as to replace all of them is costly. Stub axles were carried on 'old fashioned' king pins with two more grease points. There's provision for adjusting the camber angle by shims at the upper wishbone mounting, though the castor angle built into the king pin carrier is not adjustable. Leaf springs feature at the rear with telescopic shock absorbers and an optional anti-roll bar. There are no particular weaknesses if these are kept well greased but drivers should be wary of considerable understeer if cornering at more than sedate speeds.

Recirculating ball steering had a chassis-mounted idler on the nearside while manual steering models had a Silentbloc bush on the nearside of the drag link which was prone to wear. Power steering was available and most desirable, as town driving of manual models develops muscles like Garth. Dunlop 6-70x15 (6-40 on Hawk) RS5 nylon tyres were fitted on five-stud wheels. They give adequate traction and very long life. If radials are used there's increased understeer and a 'wallowing' feel.

Brakes

Brakes are an all drum system by Lockheed on Series 1 and 1A Hawks. Girling on Series 1 Snipe. Series 2 versions of both models were changed to a Girling disc/drum set-up with remote servo-assistance. Adjustment is through the wheel and drum on the Lockheed system and through the backplate on Girling drums.

Early systems were adequate but faded with prolonged use. The later disc/drum set-up was exceptionally good requiring only light pedal pressure. A long handbrake lever is mounted through the floor on the right of the driver's seat. Cable-operated with a compensator in the centre of the axle it is said to be capable of holding the car on the side of a cliff!

Interior

The interior was well appointed in all models, the Hawk having vinyl upholstery with hide on the Snipes which also had upholstered door cappings, picnic tables for the rear seats and cigar lighters in each rear door together with ashtrays. Rear seat courtesy lamps were also fitted to Snipes. The standard bench front seat could be replaced with 'Reuter' recliners which had arm rests. Rubber mats were used on estate versions for obvious reasons but these cars retained the copious amounts of underfelt and soundproofing.

Facia layout was impressive, providing all necessary equipment set in a walnut panel. The large speedo was complemented by a multi-dial ammeter, oil and temperature

... and wrap-around rear screen, of which the makers were inordinately proud.

areas to look out for when purchasing a 'Series' car.

Most mechanical parts for the cars are available though in some cases they will be re-conditioned or good used spares. Exhausts, brake pads and shoes, water pumps and track-rod ends are all generally available from Humber specialists.

Spares from outside the club are available from R J Grimes of Hadleigh Garage, Marlpit Lane, Coulsdon, Surrey. This company has been a Humber and Rootes specialist since the Thirties. PVHCC members have a 15 per cent discount and the contact is Brian Lewis on 668 1455/8.

Gwent Humber Spares on 0633 854026 is also another company which specialises in Humber and other older car spares. A number of these specialists break unrestorable cars which enables a good stock of bits and pieces to be built up. Apparently, few panels are available except pattern sills and the club is actively considering manufacturing new panels.

Club and Buying

If you're thinking of buying a 'Series' Humber, or already own one, it's essential to be a member of the Post Vintage Humber Car Club. The formation of the club was announced in T&CC's May 1974 issue so it is now twelve years old. In that time the club has grown, at present boasting around 1000 members with an active calendar and area meetings.

Registers take care of specific models and the one for the 'Series' cars is David Clark. He presently has 650 cars on the Register and can be contacted at 18a Kentwood Close, Tilehurst, Reading, Berks RG3 6DH.

If you see yourself driving a large late Fifties/Sixties saloon the Humber way, then you'll find prices start at around £100 for a car which will probably need a part or complete restoration, with a decent runner costing £600 plus and one in first class condition fetching more than £1500. Series 1 Snipes should be avoided because they use the 2.6-litre engine as opposed to the 3.0-litre of the Series 2 onward. Later cars fitted with disc brakes at the front are preferable, too.
PVHCC, 81 Gordon Road,
Herne Bay, Kent.

This article first appeared in "Thoroughbred and Classic Cars" magazine.

Buying an XK for Restoration

It's still just possible to get into the Jaguar big-time league for under £2,000. XK owner Paul Skilleter tells you what you should expect for the money – and how to cope afterwards!

The XK Jaguar is a big, beefy car in the true British sports car tradition; most weigh around 30 cwt (almost as much as an XJ6), do 120mph, and give inferiority complexes to all other sports car owners except those with Ferraris. To most of us they are very beautiful cars, and they are very expensive – or are they?

Well, like almost every other 'classic', XKs have had their ups and downs pricewise over recent years, but even so a quick look at our Price Guide will tell you that anything from £10,000 – £15,000 has to be forked out for a good one, and true concours examples can (if a buyer is to be found) enter the giddy realms of twenty grand plus. So where does that leave the hopeful XK enthusiast who reckons he could just about raise £2000 if he sold his Midget and raided the home

improvement money? Possibly in a better position than he might realise.

Large, semi-exotic classic cars aren't selling very well at the moment, particularly those which can't be driven away by the proud new owner to display in front of his friends. So unless the seller has priced his XK rebuild prospect stupidly cheaply, he isn't likely to have much of a queue at the door when the advert appears, at least, not a 'buying' one. One reason for this lies with some of the XK's disadvantages, like the bodyshell's propensity to rust which makes restoration difficult and expensive – make no mistake, rebuilding an XK is 'A' level stuff and makes a similar exercise on a Sprite or TR seem like a weekend's routine maintenance. Don't kid yourself, therefore, that buying a rusty XK means that the hardest bit is over, even though the bottom-rung approach is feasible, as we shall see.

Sorting Out the Types

The original XK 120 was based fair and square on the big Mk VII chassis frame, engine and suspension, which explains its excellent ride for a sports car, and rigidity which was much better than most sports cars of the period and which contributes towards the car's good handling characterics. The craze for torsion bars was in full swing at the time (1948) and Jaguar's chief engineer, William Heynes, designed an excellent wishbone system for the Mk VII and the XK which lasted in its essentials right up until the E-type left

Motor Wheel Services, 65, Jeddo Road, Shepherds Bush, London W12. Tel: 01-749 1391/743 3532. (New and rebuilt wire wheels).

Bill Lawrence, Unit 7, Sway Park Industrial Estate, Sway, Lymington, Hants. SO4 0BA. Tel: 0590 683288. (Manufacturer of body panels, etc).

F.B. Components, 35-41 Edgeway Road, Marston, Oxford. Tel: Oxford (0865) 724646, Telex 83767. (Brake and suspension components a speciality. Worldwide service).

Ce Be Ee Components, Unit 11, Holly Park Mills, Calverley, Pudsey, West Yorkshire. Tel: 0532 573700. (Brakes, suspension, steering, some chrome parts).

Phillips Garage, 206 Bradford Street, Deritend, Birmingham. Tel: 021-772 2000. (Engine rebuilds and spares).

Pieter Zwakman, C. de Vriesweg 17, Industrial Estate, 1744 CL, Dirkshorn N.H., Holland. Tel: 31-2245-848. (The best-known XK specialist on the continent).

All the three types of XK are shown here – XK 120 open two-seater in the foreground, XK 140 on right, and XK 150 fixed-head in the background.

Wire-wheeled cars are considered more valuable but will add to your restoration expenses, as new hubs (if needed) are costly to buy, and the wire wheels themselves may well need overhauling.

First of the breed was the open two-seater or 'roadster'; when fitted with pressed steel wheels, all XKs had the spats covering the rear wheels.

production in 1975. Rear suspension was by leaf spring and the engine was, of course, the famous six-cylinder XK power unit of 3442cc. In due course three body styles arrived, roadster, fixed-head and drop-head, and the XK 120 was succeeded by the XK 140 and XK 150 as shown in the accompanying tables.

There is really no 'best' XK which you should aim to get, as each of the types has its own adherents who prefer it to the other variants. The first XK to be restored by enthusiasts was the XK 120 roadster, because

it was both the first of the line and, to many, the prettiest and most sporting XK. It is still about the most popular model, which means that it's also the most expensive to acquire even as a wreck or near-wreck. On the other hand, having once purchased it you'll find more reproduction parts available than for any of the other models, and it may be worth more when you've restored it.

The XK 140 brought the heavy, Mk VII-type bumpers, a thicker, cast grille and generally more chrome and weight. Whether

or not you like these extra adornments is up to you, but certainly in the 140's favour is its more responsive (rack and pinion) steering, telescopic rear dampers, and a more forward engine position which allowed 'plus two' seating for the fixed-head and drop-head models (though not for the roadster, which remained a two-seater with XK 120-type detachable windscreen, hood and sidescreens). Traditionally, the XK 140 has always been the cheapest XK to buy and whilst amongst the really top cars prices have evened out amongst XKs, a tatty fixed-head 140 especially is still cheap.

Either you like the more bulbous coachwork of the XK 150 or you don't; however, no-one can deny the attraction of the 150's disc brakes, which means you can use all the performance without worrying about the earlier XK driver's nightmare, brake fade. Beggars can't necessarily be choosers, but if possible avoid the pre-May 1959 XK 150 with round-pad brakes, as these require dismantling of the wheel cylinders to change the pads. Interior appointments and controls are more modern in the 150, which again has become a matter of taste. The roadster was given a proper windscreen and wind-up windows, by the way.

The biggest advantage of the XK 150 is that there seem to be more of them about, and fixed-heads in particular are still to be found in rough order, because many of the more sought-after open cars have already been restored. All XKs are now old enough for rust to be a serious problem so it doesn't follow that just because it's younger, an XK 150 will be less rusty than a 120.

How to Pick a Bargain

When you're buying for restoration you're generally in a safer position than if you are shopping about for a so-called 'good running

The XK 140 brought wth it more cockpit space; this is the fixed-head coupe which in unrestored condition is one of the cheapest XKs to buy.

The drophead body style was introduced with the later XK 120s and was continued with the 140 and 150 ranges. This American export car has been fitted with chrome wire wheels which again can add to your restoration bill if you elect to fit them instead of the standard painted type.

Chassis Number sequences

Model	Type	Period built	First Chassis No. Rhd	Lhd
XK 120	OTS	July 49-Sept 54	660001	670001
	FHC	Mar 51-Sept 54	669001	679001
	DHC	Apr 53-Sept 54	667001	677001
XK 140	OTS	Oct 54-Feb 57	800001	810001
	FHC	Oct 54-Feb 57	804001	814001
	DHC	Oct 54-Feb 57	807001	817001
XK 150	OTS	Mar 58-Oct 60	820001	830001
	FHC	May 57-Oct 61	824001	834001
	DHC	May 57-Oct 60	827001	837001

Engine Number sequences

XK 120:	From W.1001 to W.9999, then from F.1001
XK 140:	From G.1001
XK 150:	From V.1001 (standard 3.4)
	From VA.1001 (standard 3.8)
	From VS.1001 (3.4S)
	From VAS.1001 (3.8S)

On all models Engine Number suffix /7, /8 or /9 indicates CR.

The XK 150 drophead coupe was the last (and heaviest) of the XKs.

The door shut pillar on this XK 150 has been "botched up" by plating the wheelarch area – all the internal supports which it should contain have rusted away. Pay close attention to this and where the hinges enter on the front pillar – XK doors are heavy and these structures will have to be made sound.

car', because nobody's going to bother to fill and spray over rust to sell you a rebuild prospect. However, you still want to take a careful look at the bodywork if for no other reason than being able to point out the serious faults may persuade the vendor to lower the price.

All XKs are built on the same general principles and the main places for rot (apart from self-evident rust in outer panels) are the box-section sills (attack from behind with a screw-driver, but they're almost certain to be gone unless they've been replaced at some stage), door pillars and shut faces, all round and underneath the boot and spare wheel well, bottoms of the front bulkhead, the rear tonneau panel above and all round the wheel arch, the floors, and the battery boxes and valances up inside the front wings. That's another advantage of buying a heap – you can be more vicious with the old screwdriver in uncovering rot and filler.

That immense chassis frame is not particularly rot-prone, but check especially the much thinner members which arch over the rear axle – these rust on their top faces and are difficult to repair if you're not taking the body off (which is normally essential, though). Very rarely will you find an accident damaged or bent frame, however.

When it comes to engine and gearbox, then possibly *authenticity* is more important than condition. That is, they should be of the correct type for the model of XK you're buying. The table accompanying should help your investigations. A number of bottom-market XKs have acquired Mk 2 saloon engines, later cylinder heads and so on and

tracking down correct, original units could be a problem, especially with the XK 120s. The same goes for an XK 120 or 140 that's had a disc-brake conversion; if you want originality, finding the authentic drum brakes complete might be awkward now.

One would assume that the interior of an

Club details

The XK Register, co-founded incidentally by the writer, is a branch of the Jaguar Driver's Club and has recently been re-organised. Membership costs no more than the JDC annual subscription of £15 plus £5.00 joining fee and a useful 'XK Bulletin' is contained within the professionally produced monthly "Jaguar Driver" magazine; plus you have the opportunity to pick the brains of the experts. Membership application forms are obtained from the JDC at Jaguar House, 18 Stuart Street, Luton, Beds. The Jaguar Enthusiasts' Club is a later arrival but is rapidly growing in popularity, and specialises in helping members with parts and technical advice. Contact Graham Searle, 37 Charthouse Road, Ashvale, Surrey. GO22 5LS.

Specification identification

'S' prefix to XK 120 Chassis No. denotes Special Equipment model.
'A' prefix to XK 140 Chassis No. denotes Special Equipment model with standard cylinder-head.
'S' prefix to XK 140 Chassis No. denotes Special Equipment model with C-type head (also denoted by suffix 'S' on Engine No.).
'DN' suffix on XK 140 and XK150 Chassis No. denotes that overdrive is fitted.
'BW' suffix on XK 140 and XK 150 Chassis No. denotes that automatic transmission is fitted.
'E' after the prefix 'JL' on XK 140 gearbox indicates that overdrive is fitted, as does 'S' after prefix on XK 150 gearbox; 'CR' suffix on 'JL' gearbox indicates close-ratio gears.

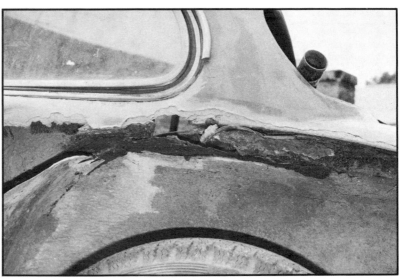

The top of the inner rear wings rust and so does what is termed the tonneau panel (which surrounds the boot aperture) and the upper part of the XK's body where it meets the outer wing beading. This is an XK 150 fixed-head but the same damage occurs in the other models.

Location of numbers

Chassis, body, engine and gearbox numbers are found collectively on a plated fixed to the bulkhead in the engine bay. If the plate is genuine and the car retains its original components the numbers should correspond with those stamped on the individual components as follows:
Chassis: stamped on top of chassis-frame opposite flywheel housing and sometimes on front cross-member under radiator.
Engine: stamped on left-hand side of block above oil filter assembly and at front of cylinder-head casting.
Gearbox: stamped on boss at left-hand rear of unit.
Body: stamped on plate attached to left-hand side of bulkhead in engine bay.

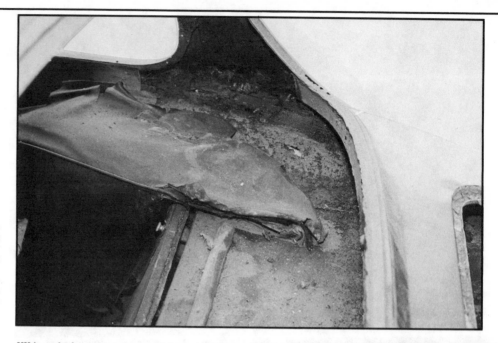

This area on a fixed-head is usually covered by trim, but on this car it's decayed away to give a good view of rust above the rear wheel arch. This area is particularly vulnerable on drop-head (not roadster) XKs, because of the wood surround here on which the hood material anchors.

Values

An indication of values is given in the text. 'Special Equipment' denotes wire wheels, a more powerful engine for the XK 120 (only), and spot/fog lamps on XK 140s and 150s; these add to the value of a car. A further option on XK 120s and 140s was the C-type head giving a 210bhp rating as opposed to 160/190bhp of standard and S.E. heads; on the 140 only, cam covers with 'C-type' badges were used with this head, though bear in mind that cam covers are easily swopped, and C-type heads on XK 140s should carry 'S' prefix on the engine number stamped at the front of the cyl. head. The existence of a straight-port ('S') head on an XK 150 can be similarly verified from the engine nos. listed. Overdrive and automatic transmissions were further options on XK 140s and 150s; value is enhanced by the former, but probably not affected either way by the latter. Genuine XK 150'S' models are worth 10-20% more than standard cars, at least. Only a very few XK 140 and XK 150 roadsters stayed in this country and attract a rarity value in addition.

XK bought for restoration would need just that – restoring. But take a look round to see whether all the instruments, fixtures and fittings are in place, even if the dash and upholstery needs re-doing. If many of these bits and pieces are missing, time and expense will be needed to replace them. The same applies to the outer brightware like bumpers and grilles; ignore the Mazak stuff because that'll need renewing anyway.

The 'ideal' XK for restoration would be a rusty but unbodged car that is totally complete, hasn't been dismantled (so you can see that everything's there), and has been dry-stored. However, this sort of project is likely to cost a good deal more than £1,000, maybe double that figure – and a lot more besides if it's a roadster. Examine carefully a car that has sat outside on damp grass for ten years or so – however 'complete' it looks, the bodyshell will almost certainly be totally rotten.

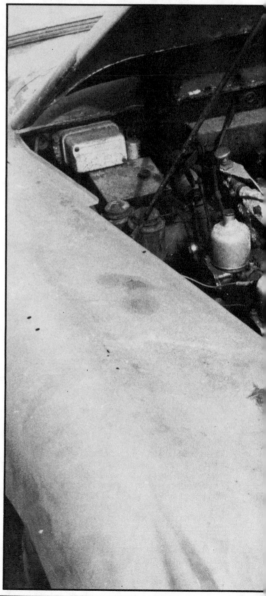

But at this stage we come up against an anomaly: with an XK, the totally rotten example mentioned may also be just the thing to buy. This is because it will come cheaply (around £1,000 unless it's a roadster), and you know exactly where you stand regarding bodywork – it will all need throwing away. This is a perfectly feasible way of looking at things because you can buy an entire new XK bodyshell (except possibly for the roof of a fixed-head) in either component form or in built-up front and rear sections. Having bought your total wreck, you then buy these major assemblies as you can afford them, doing the same with the chrome parts and the upholstery kits which are similarly available from the XK specialists. The 'total wreck' philosophy thus means the lowest initial purchase price, the most accurate assessment of what needs doing to the car (everything), and the advantage of working with mostly new body panels instead of patching-up rusty bits and pieces. Assuming, that is, that you want to end up with a really good car, and are not just aiming to produce a running XK in the cheapest way you can.

On the other hand, don't underestimate the difficulties of rebuilding an XK's bodywork; even complete new front and rear sections take a lot of fitting and aligning on the chassis frame, and while these units are probably the best answer for the home restorer, I've heard at least one professional XK rebuilder of repute state that he'd gone back to repairing rather than replacing internal steel structures on XKs.

Mechanically, the reasonably adept home mechanic should be able to cope with re-bushing and fitting new ball joints to the front suspension (apart from ball joints instead of trunnions, it's all a bit like an oversize Morris Minor), and with overhauling the engine. Here again you can order complete kits of parts to suit your particular power unit. Corroded cylinder heads can usually be

Wire wheels add to the value of an XK, but bear in mind that those splined hubs are expensive to replace if the splines are worn, as they probably are. All XKs had 16 inch wheels – smaller wheels are not original. Brake parts (this is an XK 150 with discs) are generally available but all new parts for an overhaul will cost several hundred pounds.

One would normally assume that all mechanical components will need reconditioning, unless the vendor has very clear evidence to the contrary. All you can do otherwise is to check numbers stamped on head and block against the car's chassis plate mounted on bulkhead (although even these get swopped around!) This is an XK 150 bay.

Watch out for missing items on the outside of the car too; even if you can locate them, parts like bumpers and lights will be expensive to buy separately later on.

Trim kits are readily available to refurbish interiors like this on all XK models (this is an XK 150 with its 'modern' dash), but those missing door handles could take ages to track down – so check for missing parts.

repaired, or, if very bad. better examples can be found after a bit of searching. In short, suspension, brake and mechanical parts are in good supply, although certain components for gearboxes and early drum brakes are difficult.

Cost, therefore, is the biggest item to consider when rebuilding an XK; to properly rebuild a 3.4 or 3.8 engine will take from £500 – £900 for parts, front wings are £500 each, rear wings £200, and complete rear ends including sills but excluding outer wings about £1,800; although a number of XK panel specialists can also quote for such things, watch the delivery dates quoted! Professional restoration? Forget it – a complete rebuild to the correct standards will not cost less than £10,000 – £15,000; if it does, it hasn't been done properly.

One important point to consider is the very basic one that not many XKs are offered for sale as total wrecks in the first place – you really have to get out and look for them,

maybe joining the XK Register of the Jaguar Driver's Club, placing the odd 'wanted' advert, and generally prowling around looking for 'leads'. You are more likely to be offered a part-rebuilt car, often with the engine and chassis done but with the bodywork very incomplete, by some over-enthusiastic soul who's realised that the task is beyond him. It then becomes a case of assessing the value (and quality) of the work already done, what remains to be carried out, and thus the worth of the car as it stands, bearing in mind that arriving at a nice gleaming chassis with an engine in it is the easiest part of the whole exercise. Assuming that the standard of workmanship has been good, then such a part-finished car probably has a value in excess of £3,000, up to as much as £5,000 depending on how much of the body has been restored. This can still be a means of obtaining an XK cheaply, again because the car in question isn't on the road.

Rarest of the XK 150s in this country is the open two-seater, though it is relatively common in the USA. It has no occasional rear seats, unlike the other two types. As with the fhc and dhc XK 150s, it was available in 'S' form, which meant the straight port cylinder head and triple carburettors – on either a 3.8 or 3.4 block. 'S' versions command rather higher prices restored or unrestored.

The XK is not a beginner's car, but thanks to the availability of parts it *is* a practical proposition for the experienced home restorer, and great things can be done over a period of time – I know of one enthusiast who actually fabricated his own XK 150 front wings himself, using home-made formers! To what standards you work is your own business, but as a true 'concours' car largely depends on detail finishing, by buying an XK for restoration and doing it all yourself, you could end up with a £15,000 car for an expenditure of half that amount.

This article first appeared in "Practical Classics" magazine. Much of the data comes from "The Jaguar XKs – A Collector's Guide" by Paul Skilleter, published by M.R.P.

Right-hand-drive/left-hand-drive breakdown of XK production

Model	Roadster	FHC	DHC
XK 120	175/6437	194/2484	294/1471
XK 140	73/3281	843/1965	479/2310
XK 150	92/2173	1368/3094	662/2009

Note: XK 140 production totals include 396 fixed-heads and 385 drop-heads with automatic transmission. A breakdown of XK 150 production by engine and optional overdrive or automatic transmission is as follows:

		3.4	3.8	3.4S	3.8S
Roadster	Auto	71	1	–	–
	O/drive	489	30	888	36
FHC	Auto	674	197	–	–
	O/drive	1651	334	199	150
DHC	Auto	440	209	–	–
	O/drive	789	264	104	89

Buying an E-Type for Restoration

The impossible dream? Former E-type owner Paul Skilleter, and former E-type restorer Michael Brisby, say that a six-cylinder E-type for restoration could be a good bet – if you know what you are in for ...

The E-type Jaguar was a legend in its own time – between 1961 and 1975 when E-types offered a combination of refined but potent performance, looks, quality and value for money that was unrivalled. Even today it is still *the* dream car for many people.

It is over twenty years since the announcement of the E-type, but it is unlikely that anyone driving one for the first time will be disappointed – provided that the car is in good condition it is remarkably easy to drive on the open road or in city traffic. By sports car standards it is quiet, comfortable and practical, and yet if required, there is still more real performance than most people will ever want to use. In short, the E-type is one of the most practical supercars ever made, and also one of the cheapest to run.

Unlike many other great cars the Jaguar E-type has never been reduced to the level of being something you could not give away with a year's tax and a full tank of petrol! While prices definitely did suffer a serious set-back about two years ago, they have steadied and it would not be surprising if they now began to climb again a little each year, because demand exceeds supply. Good unrestored cars have become few and far between, and as the cost of a full professional restoration is frightening, the price trend for a good or restored example can only be upwards.

Unfortunately, the E-type has not been granted immunity from rust, or deterioration of its suspension, braking and mechanical components, and all too often buyers underestimate what they are taking on when they land themselves with a superficially reasonable E-type.

An E-type which is not right in all the important departments can be described as a dangerous animal waiting to kill, and there are no shortcuts to getting a good E-type – you either search very carefully and pay a lot for a genuinely good one which must then be carefully preserved, or you spend a lot of time, money and effort putting a bad one to rights step by step, from end to · end. Experience shows that a mediocre E-type which "needs tidying" almost always needs a total rebuild just as much as a rough one "suitable for restoration" – which costs much less to buy in the first place.

If you are buying an E-type the condition of the bodyshell is more important than any other aspect of the car. Unfortunately, other than in exceptional cases, the only way to be absolutely sure that the precious shell is sound is to see it stripped bare of paint and trim – a

What to Pay

A non-runner in almost any condition from a pile of bits to a recent MoT failure can be described as 'for restoration', so the price paid for an off-the-road E-type is wide. However, the price should hinge on monocoque (centre section) condition, and completeness (many of the smaller chrome fittings are hard to find now). Dismantled cars with possibly the wrong engine, 'scrap' monocoque and front sub-frame, and perhaps incomplete can be bought for between £800 and £2000. Complete cars, with correct engine, (albeit needing an overhaul), reasonable front sub-frame, and a restorable monocoque go for between £2000 and £3000, depending on condition and whether open or closed (the former fetching approximately 20 – 40% more than a fixed-head).

Insurance

You would be foolish to try and insure your E-type with a High Street broker – join one of the car clubs, or go to a specialist classic car insurance broker, who know that E-types are now treasured 'weekend' transport and have a far better claims record than, say, new Fords do. If you are over 25 and have a good record, then an E-type will actually be cheaper to insure than the said Ford through one of these special schemes. But watch out if you are under 25 and/or have a bad record.

fresh coat of paint and a partial re-trim can be a cover-up of all sorts of major faults. Fortunately, however, there are other checks you can make inside half an hour that will tell you what sort of car you are faced with, without the need for such drastic measures.

But before you get too depressed about the whole idea of owning an E-type, the following points should cheer you up – few E-types have been bad enough to have been scrapped over the past five years or so, and a determined person with skill and sufficient funds can rebuild a car from little more than fragments. The scarcity of parts that arose as factory spares ran out, has been very largely met by the specialist firms who are generally more interested in acting as suppliers to home restorers than in doing full restorations on their premises.

Not that rebuilding an E-type is something we would recommend as a first restoration project, although several people have done it. It is a major undertaking, but the trade and knowledgeable Jaguar enthusiasts know that it is possible, which is one of the factors that have kept the price of complete wrecks, especially Roadsters, very buoyant.

Driving the Car

With a car which can deteriorate so badly if neglected, it pays to look over the danger points of an E-type carefully before getting behind the wheel, always assuming that the car you are contemplating buying can actually be driven! *Then* you can see what you can

An E-type is a complex car to restore, having a central monocoque from which projects a tubular frame carrying the engine and torsion-bar front suspension. With bonnet removed accessibility is excellent, though.

The front sub-frame must be carefully checked for cracks, pin-hole rusting and kinks; although of welded construction, frame unbolts into sections which can be replaced, or you can now buy complete new frames from such as Martin Robey Engineering.

Rust often forms behind the bumpers, as demonstrated on this Series 2 bonnet. This particular example wasn't too bad and this section of wing was repairable; a new wing costs about £100.

Typical parts/service costs

Front floor section	£22.00
Inner sill	£18.00
Boot floor	£45.00
Door skin	£27.00
Rear wings wheelarch repair	£10
Bonnet complete	£830.00
Monocoque rebuild based on existing front bulkhead and tunnel	£2,800
Engine rebuild	£1,200

Note: all prices approximate and not inclusive of VAT.

learn from a drive.

Jaguar engines should start promptly and within two or three minutes it should run evenly and without very much clatter – though some detectable tappet noise is a good thing. Oil pressure should be 40 lbs per square inch hot, and if it is less than thirty pounds per square inch something is wrong – either minor like the sender unit, or oil pressure relief valve, or major like bearing trouble.

The gearbox should not be too noisy and the clutch should begin to take up quite early in a long travel. First gear is high and some care wth the clutch is required to get away smoothly. Both the early gearbox and the later all-synchromesh unit are strong but the early cars have usually very little synchromesh left and welcome a fairly slow, gentle, change. First gear, especially on the 3.8 cars, is far from quiet, but beware of grinding or grating noises from this ratio or reverse – parts to repair are both expensive and scarce.

This is the stage when many would-be E-type restorers give up! A stripped E-type shell is a daunting prospect as, with all the paint off, the true extent of the rot is revealed. Rear wheel arches, sills and front bulkhead are all affected on this car.

Clonks as the drive is taken up can come from any number of sources including worn hub splines, universal joints and differential and sub-frame mounting bushes which have deteriorated. Before the car has built up any appreciable speed try the brakes gently. The early 'bellows' servo has been known, on isolated occasions, to go off duty just when it is needed and is therefore viewed with suspicion, but most owners have driven thousands of miles and never been given cause for panic or complaint.

The steering of an E-type should be reasonably light, and being rack and pinion you can expect accurate response accompanied by some kick back at the wheel rim over broken surfaces.

Those of us who have served our apprenticeship with ageing E-types would urge newcomers not to try using a fraction of the car's potential performance until the car has been given a very thorough going over, and we would not place any particular reliance on an MoT – so please take it very gently at first!

The E-type's excellent ride and effortless performance can land a newcomer in trouble – it is easy to arrive in situations going a great deal faster than you expected. However, while the E-type's grip is easily bettered by many modern family saloons, its safe handling qualities make it fair to say that the car is both easier to drive – and to drive briskly without much effort – than most people would expect. Just watch that long and partly invisible snout when manoeuvering in tight corners, though!

Restoration – how Difficult?

Finding an E-type for sale at a price which takes into account the need for a rebuild is not all that easy; today you stand very little chance of finding anything below £1,000, and may well have to find nearer twice that for an open car, but scouring classified advertisements in magazines and even newspapers and being prepared for a long search would be a wise approach. A very worthwhile move would be to join one or both of the Jaguar clubs and studying the pages of their magazines.

Before even considering buying a Jaguar E-type for restoration, it is a very good idea to think for a long time about what you are letting yourself in for. Some novice restorers have tackled an E-type and carried out a very good job, but many others have found that they got into trouble and either had to sell the car for what they could get or call in professional assistance.

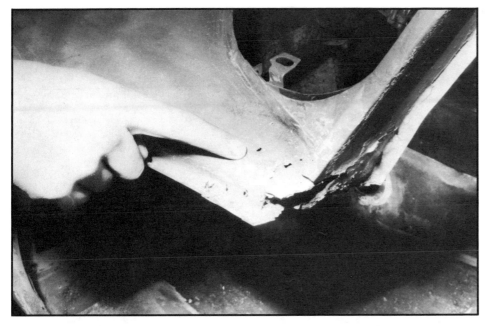

Rot is not confined to the lower areas of an E-type – water can lie at the base of the screen pillars and rust through where the bulkhead meets them.

Norman Motors, 100 Mill Lane, London NW6. (01 431 0940). Wide range of parts.

Suffolk & Turley, Kelsey Close, Attleborough Fields Ind. Estate, Garrat Street, Nuneaton, Warks. (0203 381429). Trim and interior restoration, trim kits.

Jag Unlimited Ltd., 36, Druid Street, London SE1. (01 237 5529). New and s/hand parts.

Barry Hankinson, 15 Copse Cross Street, Ross-on-Wye, HR9 5PB. (0989 65789). Trim kits, materials, chrome and trim parts, seals. etc.

Rebuilding the bodyshell is indeed a major undertaking requiring considerable skill (your welding will have to be particularly good), and constant reference to how the car was made and to the correct shapes and profiles is necessary. The trim, although comparatively straightforward, is still a major hurdle for amateurs and no matter how well you carry out the metalwork, the trim and especially the final paintwork will make or break the end result.

The mechanical side of the car cannot be ignored simply because of the cost (you could easily spend £1,500 on the engine and gearbox), but it is still structural condition of the shell and front sub-frame, and the need to get the brakes and steering working properly, which *must* be the principal concerns. Remember – even an E-type with a badly running, worn-out engine can go quite fast enough to be lethal if the other basic essentials of the car are not up to the mark.

Rear wheel arches and quarter panels can sometimes be repaired locally using repair sections; otherwise, replacing a full rear wing on a fixed-head especially is a very big job.

The rear suspension assembly is quite easily detached from the car as a unit, but with its four springs and dampers, four universal joints, numerous bushes, bearings, inboard discs and handbrake assembly and limited-slip differential, it is expensive to overhaul. Wheels and hubsplines should not be forgotten either. Radius arm mounting can also be seen, and check condition of bump stop mounting and box sections which take the sub-frame mountings on the body.

Martin E. Robey Engineering, Camp Hill Industrial Estate, Nuneaton, Warks. (0203 386903). Monocoque rebuild systems, extensive range of body, mechanical and trim parts.

Ce Be Ee Automobile Components, Unit 11, Holly Park Mills, Calverlet, Leeds, West Yorks. (0532 573700).

Clubs

There are two clubs catering for E-type owners in Great Britain, the Jaguar Driver's Club, 18 Stuart St, Luton, Beds. with its long-established E-type Register, and the relatively new Jaguar Enthusiasts' Club, G. Searle, FREEPOST, Aldershot, Hants GU12 5BR. Both offer a monthly magazine and technical advice, while the latter club has a club Spares Shop and remanufactures parts in addition. Both clubs hold the usual rallies while the JDC offers a variety of racing events, too.

To sum up, the rules of the game are: make sure you know exactly what you are buying by examining every part of the car's structure carefully and persuading the vendor to adjust the price according to what's rotten and what is missing. Then cost out the work needed by obtaining quotes for parts and (if you cannot do it yourself) the all-important monocoque rebuild (allow an amount for 'extras' for hidden defects discovered during this work). If you can still afford it, then go ahead!

A rebuilt or good original E-type is (and I speak here as a past-owner of a 1962 3.8 litre fixed-head which I used every day) an extremely reliable and practical sports car even in the eighties – though remember that in today's terms (if the original purchase price of around £2,000 is adjusted for inflation) it is a £16,000 motor car and has maintenance and parts prices in line with such. So while an E-type *is* cheap to run compared with an Aston Martin, Ferrari or Maserati, do not expect to be able to rebuilt or maintain it on an MGB-type budget.

It is hardly possible to restore an E-type Jaguar to 'new' standards and hope to get your money back in the short term, so if you are determined to tackle the job, it makes much more sense to think about what you *really* get for your money and effort – and that is, one of the great high performance cars of all time.

This article first appeared in ''Practical Classics'' magazine.

Inside the boot, and the spare wheel well on this car is in a very sorry state; it is unlikely to be any better under the petrol tank which is on the left out of the picture. A new floor is obtainable for less than £50 but don't forget that you've got to have a sound structure to attach it to.

Compared to the expense and time needed to rebuild a poor body, the engine and transmission of an E-type are less daunting. However, in the likely event of your restoration prospect needing an overhaul of these components, you'll have to budget for anything between £500 and £900 for parts alone to do the job properly.

In recent years the parts supply for E-types has improved enormously and most 'difficult' trim parts, internally and externally, can now be purchased new. A re-trim kit including leather seat covers costs, for instance, about £700 with VAT. This picture shows a 3.8 roadster interior with its characteristic aluminium dash and console – later cars had vinyl covering.

Production figures

Model	RHD	LHD	Total
3.8 Open two-seater	942	6885	7827
3.8 Fixed-head coupe	1798	5871	7669
4.2 Open two-seater	1182	8366	9548
4.2 Fixed-head coupe	1957	5813	7770
4.2 2-plus-2	1378	4220	5598
4.2 S2 Open two-seater	775	7852	8627
4.2 S2 Fixed-head coupe	1070	3785	4855
4.2 S2 2-plus-2	1040	4286	5326
Total 3.8 Cars:	15,496		
Total 4.2 Cars:	22,916		
Total 4.2 S2 Cars:	18,808		

6-cylinder E-Type Specifications

	3.8	4.2	2-plus-2	4.2S2*
Capacity	3781cc	4235cc	4235cc	4235cc
Wheelbase	8'0''	8'00''	8'9''	8'/8'9''
Length	14'7$\frac{1}{2}$''	14'7$\frac{1}{2}$''	15'4$\frac{1}{2}$''	14'7$\frac{1}{2}$/15'4$\frac{1}{2}$''
Max. speed	146mph	147mph	140mph	137/143mph
0 – 60mph	7.5 secs	7.3 secs	7.8 secs	7.5/8 secs
Av. consumption	18.5mpg	18.5mpg	17mpg	18/16.5mpg
*2nd figure, 2-plus-2				

DRIVE AID

Buying a Second-hand S-Type Jaguar

Cheaper than a Mk II Jaguar to buy, cheaper than an XJ6 to run. Paul Skilleter brings you the facts and helps you choose the right one.

S-Type Facts

Introduced October 1963 with 3.4 or 3.8 litre engines, based on Mk II saloon but with revised front and rear end treatment, and independent rear suspension. Available with manual, o/drive or automatic gearbox. Would have appeared with the '420' front if the factory had had time! Top speed of 3.8 manual overdrive model approx. 120mph, with 0 – 60 mph in around 10½ seconds. Fuel consumption for both types ranges from 14 – 19 mpg for manual cars, automatics about 2mpg less. Discontinued September 1968.

Have you noticed that for the price of a rather tatty XJ6 you can buy a very decent S-type? If you've been looking around for an XJ and got fed up with viewing dogs, you could do worse than consider Jaguar's older barouche – slightly cheaper to run, slightly easier to maintain, and with all the depreciation finished. It's also pretty well as comfortable, virtually as fast, and getting more exclusive. Beginning to make sense?

Not that we're running down XJs – one that's in perfect order will out-handle and out-quiet almost any other saloon on the road, including S-types of course. But S-type fans claim more character and walnut for their steed, and say that money properly spent on them will be more than recoverable on resale, which is more than you can say for most XJs at the moment. However, it's essential to choose

Top of the range – a 3.8 S-type with chrome wire wheels; overdrive gearbox adds further to value, and in any case the S-type represents better value for money than the Mk II.

a good one, or at least to buy at the right price – and it's worth remembering that compared to the average familar car, *any* Jaguar is expensive to run and so there's a lot more to it than scratching together the initial purchase price.

Our picture guide shows you the main things to watch for, but remember that, in common with most cars of this age, it's body corrosion you have to look out for. Not only can it cause the car to fail the MoT test, but also there are hardly any new steel outer panels to be found apart from sills, although several specialists offer repair sections for wheel arches and the like.

Try and take a test drive – that shows up a lot of faults, from poor or uneven braking to bad suspension (e.g. clonking over bumps, though this can sometimes be caused by a decayed gearbox rear 'steady' mounting, or engine mountings). Bear in mind that these cars always rolled a lot, and feel rather unsporting at first. New springs and dampers, plus a properly set-up front suspension, does wonders for the feel of the car, but that exercise alone could cost you a couple of hundred pounds!

If an automatic, the box should change up and down without slurring or undue hesitation – see how it behaves on full throttle acceleration. If non-synchro manual, beware of very noisy first and reverse gears because new parts simply are not obtainable. The later all-synchro box (adopted from March 1965) is much nicer to use and spares are easier to find. Try the overdrive if fitted – though these are normally rather idiosyncratic and usually benefit from minor sorting.

Production changes

Brake disc shields added and larger Lockheed servo fitted October 1964. All synchro gearbox introduced as optional extra Dec 1964, at chassis numbers: 1B.2192 RHD/1B.25302 LHD (3.4); 1B.52078 RHD/1B.76410 LHD (3.8). This box standardised Sept 1965. Improved torque converter and auto box June 1965 at 7B.3557 (3.4), 7B.5557 (3.8). S-type range cheapened in Sept 1967 with Ambla instead of leather seat facings, tufted instead of pile carpeting, and fog lamps deleted.

New wire wheels with forged hubs and straight spokes fitted, and grease nipples on rear half shafts. Jan 1968. Modified handbrake lever (part no. C.27021) to reduce effort fitted July 1968.

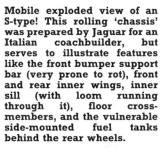

Mobile exploded view of an S-type! This rolling 'chassis' was prepared by Jaguar for an Italian coachbuilder, but serves to illustrate features like the front bumper support bar (very prone to rot), front and rear inner wings, inner sill (with loom running through it), floor cross-members, and the vulnerable side-mounted fuel tanks behind the rear wheels.

The more common steel-wheeled S-type – but still fast and luxurious.

This is what people buy Jaguars for – a sumptuous leather and walnut interior which complements the car's superb ride and silence. But most S-types aren't as good as this immaculately preserved left-hooker being sold by Graig Hinton, so bear in mind that a re-trim runs into hundreds of pounds. Faded or creased leather can sometimes be revived with hide food and special dyes (Woolies market a good one), but actual cracks and tears mean new leather. Beware too of clumsy re-varnishing of woodwork – it really needs to be removed to make a good job of it, something which the amateur can do very effectively if the time is taken. A really good interior rates very high marks indeed.

Parts suppliers

Some items for engine, transmission and suspension can still be obtained from your local Jaguar agent. However, this includes few body panels, and for these and elusive mechanical items, you could try contacting the following specialists:

David Manners, Jaguar Daimler Spares, 991 Wolverhampton Road, Olbury, West Midlands B69 4RS. Tel: 021 544 4040. General spares and exhaust systems.

Martin E. Robey, Engineering, Camp Hill Ind. Estate, Nuneaton, Warks. Tel: 0203 386903. Body parts.

Classic Spares, 501-503 Southbury Road, Enfield, Middlesex. Tel: 01 805 5534. New and used parts.

Norman Motors, 100 Mill Lane, London NN6. Tel: 01 431 0940. General spares.

Identification

Commencing chassis numbers were:

3.4 S-type	RHD:	1B.1001
	LHD:	1B.25001
3.8 S-type	RHD:	1B.50001
	LHD:	1B.75001
Engine No. prefix: 7B		

Numbers made

3.4 S-type	RHD:	8665
	LHD:	1371
3.8 S-type	RHD:	9717
	LHD:	5418

Start at the front: examine underneath the radiator grille and the valance behind the bumper, then look closely for rust bubbles or filler around head and side lights, caused by a build-up of mud inside the wing. Because of the compound curves, this is a very dificult area to repair properly. Headlight rim is missing on this very bad example.

Continue round the side of the car and look for a disintegrating wing lip, plus (in very poor cars) a line of rust marking the spot where closing plate inside the wheelarch meets the outer skin of the wing. Wing repair kits are, however, available from most Jaguar specialists, as fronts are the same as Mk II.

What to Pay

As with most production cars of this age, price varies widely according to condition. Running examples with MoT can still be bought for around £700 but are doubtful prospects for restoration and may cost a lot just to keep going. You are in with a chance for between £1000 and £1400, but bank on paying £1800 – £2500 for a really excellent example. Almost rust-free examples with a genuine low mileage (i.e. 30,000 – 50,000) can fetch well over £2500 but this is fairly rare. The price of petrol has kept prices fairly static, although inevitably, as the cars are bought increasingly for 'collectability' rather than for every-day use, petrol consumption becomes less important and values can only rise in the end.

'Plus points' which, besides condition, add to a car's value are; manual gearbox with overdrive (especially if the all-synchro box); wire wheels, (especially if chromed and in good condition); 3.8 engine, but only marginally; leather interior as opposed to the later 'Ambla' upholstery. Power steering was an optional extra, but remains a personal like or dislike and doesn't appear to affect value now.

This article first appeared in "Practical Classics" magazine.

The bottom of the front wing forms an ideal mud-trap and can result in sorry sights like this; it can be patched with new metal ...

... or just plugged with filler as has happened on the other side. The closing plate directly behind the road wheel can also separate from the outer wing (especially if the car's been thumped) or become holed, which opens up the main sill to water and mud, and results in the obvious.

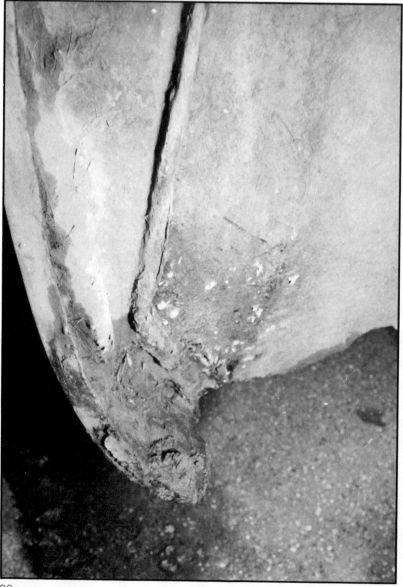

Towards the rear, examine sill/rear wing join for decay, and for rot caused by mud lodging inside rear wing lip. Inner wing leading to sill can often hole too.

Top centre. Look inside the front of the wheel arch too – note build-up of mud around side light (if only people would remember to wash underneath the car too!) and badly corroded 'crow's foot' and bumper mounting beam; if left, the bumper can drop off altogether ...

The vacuum tank for the brake servo is mounted on the other (off-)side. Road dirt can get trapped between the 'protective' shield and the servo tank itself. You can get new crow's feet and cross-members from Abercorn Motor Panels, Olaf P Lund and a number of other sources.

Having dealt with the front of the car, look carefully along the sides, especially under the sills and around the jacking points, which often suffer as badly as this. It's important too that you should reach right under and feel the condition of the reverse side of the sill, pressing outwards with your fingers. While outer sills and jacking points can be renewed, serious corrosion of the inner sill and floor areas is much more difficult to rectify. Inside the car, lift the carpets and check the inner sill where it meets the floor in each footwell. Dampness of carpets gives advance warning of holes too.

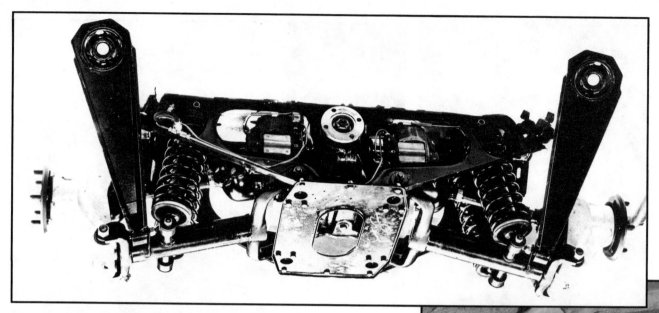

The S-type's rear suspension was basically a narrower version of the Mk 10 saloon's, and is very similar to the XJ6's having twin coil spring/damper units acting on tubular lower wishbones, radius arms, and a solidly mounted diff. unit – all contained within a detachable sub-frame. Most common faults are oil leaks from the diff. (which effect the inboard brakes), UJ wear, and bearing failures in the cast aluminium hub carriers after high mileages or lack of maintenance. Replacing diff. seals and inoperative rear wheel brake cylinders really means dropping the entire suspension unit, so beware of oil, rusted discs, and bad clunking noises. Outboard parts like bearings and UJs are much easier to service.

Front suspension is also mounted on a detachable sub-frame, whose rubber mounts can decompose resulting in a drooping front – though this is commonly caused by tired front coil springs as well, because around 57% of the car's entire weight is over the front wheels ... Tyres actually foul wheel arches if this is really bad. Top and bottom ball joints wear quickly if not kept greased – bottom ones can be shimmed incidentally – and can contribute to stiff steering. Replacements are same as XJ6. Bad clonks can denote perished anti-roll bar rubbers, ball joint wear, or worn out rubber wishbone mounts onto sub-frame – in more or less ascending order of seriousness.

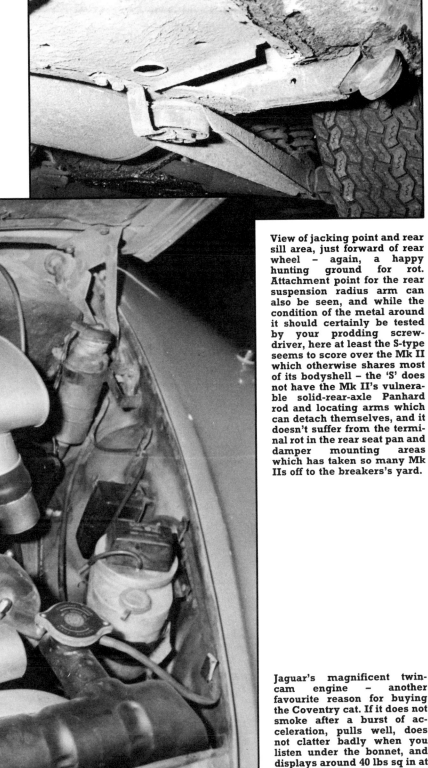

View of jacking point and rear sill area, just forward of rear wheel – again, a happy hunting ground for rot. Attachment point for the rear suspension radius arm can also be seen, and while the condition of the metal around it should certainly be tested by your prodding screwdriver, here at least the S-type seems to score over the Mk II which otherwise shares most of its bodyshell – the 'S' does not have the Mk II's vulnerable solid-rear-axle Panhard rod and locating arms which can detach themselves, and it doesn't suffer from the terminal rot in the rear seat pan and damper mounting areas which has taken so many Mk IIs off to the breakers's yard.

Jaguar's magnificent twincam engine – another favourite reason for buying the Coventry cat. If it does not smoke after a burst of acceleration, pulls well, does not clatter badly when you listen under the bonnet, and displays around 40 lbs sq in at 2,500rpm, you should be OK for a further 30,000 miles. Worn engines often exhibit excessive piston-slap and a noisy bottom timing chain – a noisy top one (you can usually tell the difference) isn't so serious.

Jaguar XJS

Is an older XJS a realistic option for the private buyer?
Jeremy Coulter investigates

When it was introduced in 1975, the Jaguar XJS did not receive altogether rave reviews, but these days, in terms of exceptional performance and value for money, older examples of this flagship of the Browns Lane fleet are almost impossible to ignore when scanning the 'for sale' columns. If you're looking for a car to use for quality motoring on high days and holidays, one that you can pamper, and one that, in good condition, will doubtless be collectable in years to come, the XJS might just be the car for you, even though it's not all that old in Classic terms. Mechanical complexity and a great thirst for fuel need not be a recipe for financial disaster, but obviously they can be, so unless you are habitually rash with your money, this is not a purchase to rush into! The line of reasoning that leads you to consider buying an XJS might also lead you to look at some Italian exotics that seem to change hands very cheaply – Lamborghini Espadas, Maserati Meraks and cars of that ilk. They certainly have the edge in terms of exclusivity but the Jaguar has an almost unassailable advantage when it comes to the availability of spare parts and expertise.

The XJS was of course the actual, if not *the* spiritual successor to the E-Type. It was based on the early short-type XJ saloon floorplan shortened by almost seven inches. The saloon's all-independent suspension was retained although moved forward at the rear with double wishbones fore and aft. Coil spring rates and damper settings were adjusted to accommodate the slightly different weight distribution and lower overall weight – 3892lb compared with the 4117lb of the XJ saloon.

Heart of the XJS was the 5.3-litre Jaguar V12 engine, a simplified(!) and refined version of the Harry Mundy/Walter Hassan quadruple-cam V12 that had been developed for the racing XJ13. The existence of the 'secret' new V12 had been public knowledge for several years before it was eventually announced in the new generation Series 3 E-Type in March 1971. The engine subsequently found its way into the XJ12 saloon, thereafter gaining Bosch-Lucas fuel injection, and it was in this latest 285bhp form that the unit was fitted to the XJS. The block and cylinder heads are of light-alloy and there is a single cam per bank, with drive coming via a long single duplex chain. The more recent versions of the XJS benefit from having more fuel-efficient HE (high efficiency) versions of the V12, but since

these fall into the 'new car' bracket they need not concern us here.

As far as the transmission is concerned, for the first two years of production, the XJS was fitted with the ageing Borg-Warner type-12 automatic box but after 1978, like Rolls-Royce, the company adopted General Motors' Type-400 speed unit which was better matched to the V12's huge torque and performance characteristics. As an alternative to the auto 'box, purchasers of XJSs could initially opt for a four-speed manual gearbox but this option was deleted when production of the 'box ended in 1979.

The basic specification of the XJS is high, with central locking, air conditioning, electric windows etc etc, all as standard, which is fine when everything is working, but exceptionally annoying when they're not. The trim, too, is fairly plush with leather facings to the seat and plenty of soundproofing that makes for an exceptionally quiet ride, all the way to the car's 150mph top speed. To find out quite what is in store for the potential XJS buyer we spoke to various Jaguar specialists including Ron Beatty of Forward Engineering and Chris

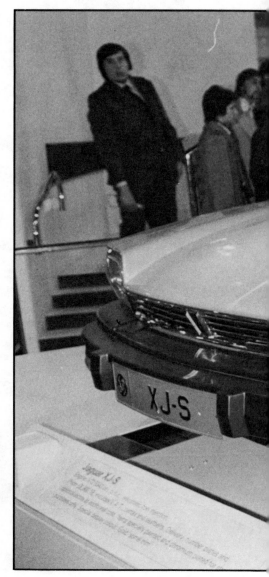

The original Motor Show XJS had some extra chrome plating when compared with those sold through dealers.

If only Jaguar's initial re-entry into saloon car racing had been with the XJS instead of the impossibly heavy XJ, they would surely have avoided the run of mechanical failures that plagued their efforts. The Group A XJS showed how it should be done!

Hopper of Jaguar Services, Peckham. This is a consensus of what they said.

Bodyshell

Unless an XJS has been horribly neglected, and bearing in mind that the oldest example is still not yet nine years old, it's unlikely that any car you look at will be completely rotted out. Rust is must more likely to have confined itself to seams and areas where water tends to lie. The latter includes bonnet and boot drain channels, door bottoms and the sill tops behind the rubber sealing strip that runs along its length. Whereas XJ saloons tend to rot out around the headlamp rims and along the wing bases, the XJS is rather more resilient in this respect, due to better design of the box sections and there apparently being fewer mud-collecting niches.

The problem of rust in body seams can be a difficult problem to defeat without major attention involving the removal of wings and other panels. However, judicious use of modern rust removers and treatments can certainly minimise the effects of this type of rot and as long as the car isn't left to stand out in the rain all the time, it should not fall to bits in front your eyes.

Should you wish to embark on a major bodily overhaul, the good news is that all the panels for the XJS are available at the moment. However, the prices quoted by Unipart might make you think twice as examples include a front wing at £212 and a new bonnet at £275. If you're viewing an XJS as a long term interest, it might not go amiss to lay up a couple of panels in the loft to tide you over the lean years that are bound to follow once the model has been superseded, although in Jaguar tradition that won't be for quite a while yet!

Among the important factors to bear in mind when buying an XJS is that, whereas with an 'ordinary' car, should you not be able to find an excellent example, it's usually advisable to opt for one with a sound body and suspect engine than vice versa, with the XJS the relative importance of finding one with a good engine is much greater. It is almost always possible to repair bodywork but fitting a new engine or repairing a damaged unit might be *impossibly* expensive.

Engine & Gearbox

The reaction of most people to their first sight of an XJS engine bay is a sharp intake of breath and a look of disbelief. This is entirely to be expected as the tangle of pipes and tubes above the engine is a real plumber's nightmare! The pipes relate variously to the air conditioning system – which is standard on this car – the fuel injection and cooling systems, plus sundry breather pipes. Despite its complexity, the truth of the matter is that the V12 is a reliable engine and most problems that afflict it are linked to faults in the ancillary components that surround it.

Twelve cylinders are sufficient to distri-

Rusty pock-mark at the top of the B-post.

Corrosion on the alloy wheels but nothing that a good polishing won't cure.

Clubs

The extensive and enthusiastic Jaguar Drivers Club and Jaguar Enthusiasts Club both have within them a register for XJS, including the S, and membership of these organizations is another good investment for the XJS owner. The JDC can be reached by writing to Jaguar House, 18 Stuart Street, Luton, Beds LU1 25L, and the JEC by contacting Graham Searle, 37, Charthouse Road, Ashvale, Surrey GU12 5L.

As a replacement for the
E-type, the XJS was a non-
starter, although from this
angle, their shapes are
surprisingly similar. Not too
many potential owners can
have seen things this way,
though!

bute the engine's work load fairly lightly so the V12 can be expected to cover at least 100,000 miles before major attention becomes necessary and distances considerably in excess of this are quite common. The secret is to keep the engine well watered and oiled, because if it runs low on either fluid, damage will quickly ensue. Water can escape from a bewildering number of places but a perished hose is the most likely cause, so it's worth checking that the previous owner has replaced these where necessary.

A check on seepage from the water pump and on the condition of the pump bearing is advisable too. As far as oil leaks are concerned, these are to be avoided at all costs as a repair can mean lifting out the entire engine which is a very time-consuming and expensive job. For example, a new rear main bearing oil seal costs approximately £1.00 but fitting it involves a complete engine-out job which, if undertaken professionally, might cost around £700. So be prepared to lift the car up and crawl underneath with a torch to check for tell-tale leaks.

An XJS that smokes is to be avoided; when checking this aspect, be sure to let the engine warm through first. Preferably check for blue smoke during and after a test run. Inspect the emissions from the exhausts at idle, then ask the vendor (or your moral supporter) to rev the engine and then see what comes out! Jaguar oil pressure gauges are notoriously inaccurate and although a good V12 will actually run at around 65psi, the gauge might read rather less. Short of substituting an accurate gauge to test the pressure during your inspection, a low reading on the standard gauge of 20/30psi should be enough to give you confidence that the bearings are sound.

It can be a problem judging whether all the XJS's 12 cylinders are working. The best method is to use a compression tester on each cylinder although this is a time-consuming business as the spark plug holes are by no means easy to reach and, after all, there are 12 of them. A simple check that each of the fuel injectors is working well is to feel for the pulsing of each feed pipe with the engine running – erratic pulsing or no pulsing at all means that all is not well. The injection system is controlled by a master electronic 'brain' which receives information relating to fuel flow, air flow, temperature, throttle opening etc, from a collection of sensors distributed around the engine. Although the 'brain' itself is generally reliable, faults in the electrical linkage to the sensors, or faults in the sensors themselves can cause bad running.

Drive for the camshafts comes from a long single duplex chain but the amount of wear that it suffers is surprisingly small. The chain tensioner is Molyslip impregnated, which minimises frictional wear of the rollers, so a chain life of 50,000 miles can be expected. The sounds of the rattling chain at the front of the engine, particularly at idle, is worrying but should not necessarily put you off buying an attractively priced and otherwise sound car.

However, renewing the chain calls for

fairly major work at the front of the engine which will take many diy hours or, if tackled professionally, will run up a tidy bill, even though once again the cost of parts is relatively small.

It simply isn't possible to check every aspect of the XJS engine, nor to diagnose quickly the cause of a malady that you identify. In the end the most reliable indicator of an engine's state is its service record. Jaguar's recommended service interval is 3000 miles, but evidence that the car has visited a Jaguar specialist every 6000 miles or so for checkover and adjustment should be sufficient to keep everything running sweetly. If you do take a chance on an engine that isn't running quite right, with an eye to carrying out some work yourself, at least make sure that the cooling system contains the correct Unipart corrosion inhibiting anti-freeze. The significance of this cannot be over-emphasised because the engine is all-alloy and corrosion within the block and head can often effectively weld the two units to each other on the studs, to the extent that dismantling is impossible. Many Jaguar V12s have been scrapped as a result.

Only a small number of early XJSs were delivered with manual gearboxes so it's more than likely that an XJS you are looking at will have either the Borg Warner or GM automatic 'box. The most important check to make with an automatic example is that fluid in the box is still red. This is a simple matter of pulling out the 'box dipstick and looking at the end. If the fluid is brown coloured, it probably means that the bands in the 'box are burned, which is not good. A more practical test of the 'box is on the move. Each gear should engage without too much drama or jerkiness but if you're checking the manual override, remember that first won't come in until the car is moving very slowly. Don't forget to check the box in reverse too and listen out for drive slippage when accelerating in second or top. The XJS is a very quiet car so back up the messages your ears give you with readings from the rev counter. The rare manual box is a tough ZF unit, also found on the V12 E-Type. It has a heavyish change quality but is well up to the job although it's worth listening out for whine on second gear in particular. The clutch, too, is heavy on manual XJSs and maladjustment here might account for any baulking of the gearchange.

With regard to the remainder of the transmission system, excessive wear on the propshaft centre bearing often reveals itself as an alarming rumble against the propshaft tunnel especially during cornering. The Powr-Lok limited slip differential is an important factor in the XJS's ability to transmit all its power to even slippery road surfaces. It's worth looking for oil leaks from around this component but apart from listening out for suspicious whining, there's little else that can be done to ensure that all is well.

Steering, Suspension, Brakes

The lightness of the XJS's steering might not be to everyone's taste but it certainly gives relaxing motoring. Screeching of the power steering pump drive belt from cold is generally cured by tensioning the belt correctly although reaching the adjuster bolts calls for considerable manual dexterity! The steering components are well-proved items common to the rest of the XJ range and, if the steering feels sound in operation, it remains only to check for fluid leaks from the pump, the rack itself and the pipe unions. As with so many other XJ items, repairing a faulty rack need not cost a great deal in hardware terms, it's simply the time and effort required to reach the parts needing attention.

At 3710lb the XJS is a heavy car and this naturally takes its toll on the suspension joints and wheel bearing. Regular maintenance is the key to prolonging the life of the suspension and steering swivel joints which can otherwise be knocked out quite quickly. Jacking up the front of the car and testing for unwanted movement at the wheels in both planes is worthwhile. Identifying worn subframe mounting bushes can be a little more tricky, but you should suspect their

Rot in the water trap in the boot channelling.

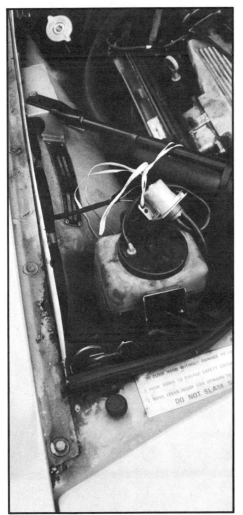

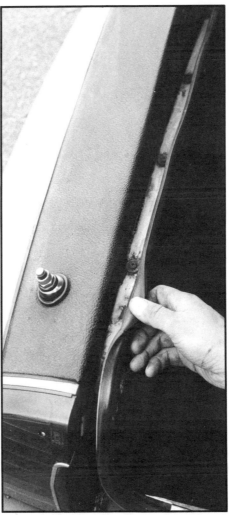

Plumber's nightmare – the engine bay.

Left. Typical decay in the bonnet drain channels (and typical 'bodging' of the electricals, which suggest that maintenance has been less than 'no expense spared'!)

Same again at the rear of the car hidden by the rubber seal.

condition if you notice any cracking noises and bangs on bumpy road surfaces. The XJS is softly sprung by 'sporting' standards so don't necessarily mistake the natural compliance of the suspension for a symptom of worn dampers. However, if the car bounces more than twice once you have pressed down a corner and let go, it may be that a new set of dampers is required.

The XJS has inboard rear disc brakes which fortunately aren't too difficult to reach to renew the pads. Renewing the front disc pads is a relatively straightforward operation which is just as well because their life is short. Indeed, you might realistically budget for a new set at every service as otherwise disc damage might result. The handbrake operates on separate calipers and a deficiency in this area is a common cause of MoT failure. The action of the handbrake level itself often causes confusion, because it's of the 'floppy' type which parks out of the way on the floor even when it's engaged, so don't immediately conclude that it's broken if it won't stay in the raised position!

An older XJS: the most afford-able high-luxury around and with the running and mainte-nance costs to match those of the newest versions – but without the reliability.

Other points to watch

Because the XJS has a relatively high level of trim and equipment, it's all too easy to forget to check significant items. Central locking, for example, is by no means essential but it is very useful, so take time to see whether the system works. The electric windows should work because a non-operational window causes real inconvenience. Repair parts are, however, readily available and problems can often be traced simply to faulty, or detached electrical connections within the door. Air conditioning is also standard on the XJS and the cabin can become very uncomfortable if the system isn't working. A system's old age is likely to be reflected in the temperature controls becoming inaccurate or the system performing inconsistently. Complete failure can be due to the loss of fluid from the compressor in which case a 'pump-up' by a Jaguar dealer might effect a repair. Should the system require major work however, it is bad news indeed, because it involves a great amount of stripping down to reach the 'works'.

In common with all the XJ range, the XJS conditioning system is installed at a point fairly early in the production process after which numerous other components are added around and on top of it, without much thought for future replacement.

As far as trim is concerned, the leather seat facings are attractive when new but can crack and decay badly with age and wear. Various leather treatments are useful in restoring the situation while the vinyl coverings of the rest of the trim is hardy. Jaguar switches have an annoying habit of falling to bits, which can make the facia look very tatty but repairing or replacing them is not difficult.

Spares and Prices

Because the XJS is still a 'current' car the spares situation is very good by normal Classic car standards. Jaguar dealers and branches of Unipart can supply just about every component, from a wing or a complete new engine to a bulb for any one of the 18 warning lights that adorn the facia and spares

are also carried by various Jaguar specialists, many of whom advertise their wares in the pages of *Thoroughbred and Classic Cars.* Some examples of prices quoted by Unipart in 1984 were: Front wing: £212; Door: £240; Bonnet: £275; Boot: £175; Complete exhaust system: £245; Engine, stripped: £1750; Cylinder head: £600; Fuel sensor: £28.60; Rear light lens: £24.65; Handbrake cable: £13.75; Brake disc: £52.50.

A new XJS will cost you a cool £25,000 today which compares with a total price of £11,243 when it was introduced back in 1975/6. The youth of the model means that 'normal' second-hand price trends tend to prevail and the oldest example is usually the cheapest. Asking prices tend to start at around £3000 for 1976 cars. A car a year younger will normally cost approximately £1000 more and this £1000 per year increment tends to persist right up to the last non-*HE* cars, of 1980/81 which change hands for around the £10,000 mark. A car with a full service history is obviously going to command a rather higher price than one that has suffered from neglect or diy meddling. 14,800 pre-HE XJSs were built, so there are plenty around at any one time *and* it's usually a buyer's market with all the implications that has for the buyer's bargaining position.

Regardless of the basic excellence of the product. Jaguar Cars reached a low in terms of quality control in the late seventies and a reflection of this is that there are very definitely 'good' XJSs and 'bad' XJSs. A bad car can be a nightmare to cope with as component after component fails or temporarily refuses to function. In that respect therefore many XJSs are 'cheap for a reason'. On the other hand a good car is a real delight and is quite simply 'a lot of car for the money'. It might not have particularly sporting handling but it is capable of being driven extraordinarily quickly in great comfort. Fuel consumption will always be a problem, however, and a featherweight right foot would be needed to see a figure above 15mpg while an average of nearer 12 or 13mpg should more realistically be budgeted for. Also included in the budget should be enough to cover the cost of regular servicing. A service visit to a Jaguar specialist might set you back around £300 which sounds a great deal but this pales into insignificance when compared with the costs of the alternatives, such as the fitting of a new engine.

This article first appeared in "Thoroughbred & Classic Cars" magazine.

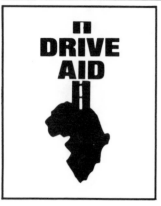

Healey Hunting

Lindsay Porter searches for a Jensen-Healey but first takes a hard look at the pros, cons and antecedents of this enigmatic British sports car.

In the seventeen or eighteen years I have been driving, I've owned countless numbers of different motor cars. I suppose it has something to do with the way a car sort of sidles up to you with a defenceless look on its grille, just when you're least able to resist it. Or maybe I'm just impulsive. Anyway, just for once I decided to sit down and rationally select my next car.

After spending all of the hottest summer on record without a rag-top sports car on the road, I decided that I just *had* to have another. It had to be quick, just a touch different – and cheap! The combination sounds impossible and, for a time, as I pored over pages of advertisements for the expensive exotica and the cheap'n seedy, I began to wonder. Then I rediscovered the Jensen-Healey!

The search began as a paper-chase and I read up dimensions, performance figures and checked out the cost price of the cars. So far seemed just too good to be true and the contemporary road test reports were no less flattering. On the other hand, those I spoke to were downright scathing about the car, saying that it drained its fuel tank if parked on a slope and blew its engine to pieces if over- or under-filled with oil. I needed some hard information on the car's faults so I called Ian Orford, Managing Director of Jensen Parts Service, and was invited to visit the spares and restoration company that was salvaged when Jensen Motors went under the hammer a few years ago. Ian, and his Service Manager, John Baker, exude enormous enthusiasm for everything Jensen, including the unfashionable Healey, and were able to give me a great deal of information on the car.

Parentage

The Jensen-Healey was conceived as the Anglo-American answer to the demise of the Austin-Healey 3000. Donald Healey was even

Many people find the Jensen-Healey's looks bland – and some even confuse it with the Triumph Spitfire when viewed from the rear! This car was offerd with the neat works hardtop that came with leathergrain finish and heated rear windscreen which plugged into appropriately positioned connections.

more horrified than most enthusiasts when the MGC was wheeled out as a replacement for the 'Big' Healey; he stood to lose a great deal of commission from BMC's non-use of the brand name! Jensen Motors were also hit heavily by the move: the Austin-Healey's bodywork had been assembled at their West Bromwich factory and the loss of this work threw their very existence into doubt. On the other side of the Atlantic, a little known millionaire, English car fanatic and key importer/distributor of British cars by the name of Kjell Qvale (pronounced Shell Kervarley) shook his head in disbelief at BMC's suicidal marketing policy and decided to do something about it. 'Doing something' meant buying out Jensen Motors from its worried owners, appointing himself as President and Donald Healey as Chairman (with

Geoffrey Healey also appointed to the board) and going hell-for leather towards the design and production of the Jensen-Healey, the car that should have replaced the Healey 3000.

It took from early 1970 only until 1972 before the first Jensen-Healey came off the line. Many people quote this incredibly short 2½ year gestation period as the reason for the car's early unreliability and there is doubtless some truth in that (although, in fact, the Healeys had already been working on the concept of the car for some time). John Baker at Jensen Spares assured me that most early cars would have had most of their teething troubles sorted out by now, but some of the owners and ex-owners I spoke to gave me the strong impression that 1972-73 Jensen-Healeys can give notably more problems than later cars, even eleven or twelve years on.

How Many

In all, a total of 10,453 Jensen-Healeys were built, of which, over 75% went to the USA. Only 1,914 stayed in the UK giving a year-on-year breakdown as follows:

1972: 343
1973: 899
1974: 484
1975: 180
1976: 8

In addition, 202 Jensen GTs (not properly Jensen-*Healey* GTs as they are commonly known) were released in the UK with almost Interceptor-like trim, a fixed-head and Healey mechanics.

Rot spots

The car was designed around a safe, strong and highly conventional monocoque chassis with bolt-on wings, and it seems to be in this area that the Jensen-Healey's lack of development and big-manufacturer expertise shows up most of all. The car goes together remarkably well, as befits anything that left a factory renowned for quality coachwork would, but the rust-inducing shape of the panel work makes the car way out of line with most rust-inhibited motor products of the mid to late seventies. Rust really is the Jensen-Healey's Achilles heel with front and rear wings, sills and, at a more advanced stage, outer floor panels suffering badly. Unlike, say, that massively strong MGB which can rot quite badly and still retain much of its structural rigidity, the Jensen-Healey starts to feel quite flexible on the open road when it corrodes badly which is no good for handling and no good at all for peace of mind.

Corrosion must be the area to check most thoroughly before buying a Jensen-Healey and, unless buying a restored or pampered car, any condition two car or worse will be bought with the expectation of rust. Any of these cars which have started to sag in the middle will be terribly expensive to restore properly: check the door gaps to see if they have closed in at the top. On the other hand, of course, there is the reassuring knowledge that every single body panel is available, usually ex-stock from Jensen Parts and Service (although steel bonnets are getting scarce; J.P. + S. are having steel framed GRP bonnets made up) and the even more reassuring thought that the parts are far less expensive than anything with a Jensen name tag would suggest.

Engineering

Actually, having said that the condition of the Jensen-Healey's bodywork marks the watershed of whether a car is worth buying or not, it must be remembered that the engine can cost an arm and a leg to rebuild, at least in comparison with the initial cost of most Jensen-Healeys. The story behind the choice of engine for the Healey is an interesting one and gives an insight into the problem of running a small-scale car manufacturing business. In 1968, two years before the Qvale deal, Geoff Healey's brother, Brian, had approached Vauxhall with a view to using their slant-four single-overhead-camshaft 2.3 litre engine in the still embryonic new Healey. Many engines had been considered but

The sill and the front wing area above them, as well as the front wing to engine bay flitch plate joint areas, are seriously prone to corrosion. The trouble is, there is nearly always ten times more hidden than visible rust in cases like this.

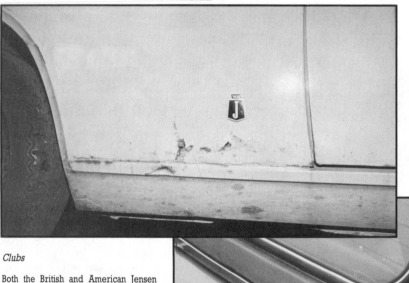

Clubs

Both the British and American Jensen Owner's Clubs accept Healey owners, while in the States Jensen-Healey owners proliferate and even dominate their Club's scene. The American club magazine is highly professional and greatly superior to the British offering.

Association of Jensen Owners, Membership Secretary – Pat Hill, 6814 Wayside Court, Tampa Florida 33614, USA.

Jensen Owners Club, Membership Secretary – R.P. Langford, 28, Cartford Drive, Norwich, Norfolk NR3 4DN.

Tops of the rear wings, where they meet the rear panel, are typical J-H rot spots. If the beading which sits between the two is missing and the panels flushed over with filler, expect the worst.

rejected because of a variety of problems; the use of a BMC engine was politically impossible; Lotus, Ford and BMW were all approached, found agreeable in principle, but each had supply problems; Mazda and Chrysler (France) engines were considered and rejected and so, by Hobson's choice, the Vauxhall unit was selected.

During the post-Qvale, pre-production phase of the car's development, work began on the Vauxhall 'Four' to see how it responded to American emission control requirements. The team were disappointed that the engine's performance dropped well below the 130bhp minimum which they had deemed necessary, and that the Vauxhall's price for putting back the missing 'go' was understandably steep. There seemed nowhere to go until negotiations were re-opened with Colin Chapman, who agreed to expand his Norfolk-based engine plant to cope with the 200 units per week which Jensen were then aiming for but were never remotely able to reach. (The highest figure was for 1974 when an average of 87.5 units per week were built).

By some coincidence, the Lotus engine had several confusing similarities with the Vauxhall engine and, indeed, the Vauxhall block was used as a test bed for the development of the exceptionally efficient 16-valve Lotus head. However, after running the engine on Vauxhall foundations, Lotus later went ahead and built their own all-alloy, open-decked block and it is this unit, used also in the Lotus Elite, that found its way into the Jensen-Healey. This engine – which ran so 'clean' that no emission control equipment was necessary even at the height of US regulations – is at the heart of the car's character. It runs with a throaty burble and responds to a dab on the throttle with an exciting pulse of power

that is equalled by very few other road-going engines of this capacity. Efficiency, of course, also means economy, and the Jensen-Healey returns a surprisingly good 25mpg average, even allowing for the irresistible temptation to enjoy the car's performance that the Lotus engine allows you.

As a production engine, all parts are available, but Lotus don't make oversized pistons available, so 'rebore' time means that a new piston and liner set becomes necessary. A full engine rebuild would set you back a hefty, four-figure sum, but at least the engine is as tough as old boots and goes on and on if looked after properly. But what was that about oil levels? "Oh, yes", said John Baker, "if you over-fill the engine it can pull the excess oil into the air box and cause misfiring, and if you under-fill it – well, you shouldn't under-fill an

engine anyway, should you? We make a point of filling the sump to just about an eighth of an inch below the 'Full' mark, said John, ''to ensure we won't have any trouble.''

Having looked at the body parts I was bound to need but which were relatively cheap, and the engine parts which I probably wouldn't want but which were relatively expensive, it was a relief to look over the rest of the car's running gear. Here, Jensen concentrated on simplicity and reliability and maintained the erstwhile strong Vauxhall connection. The Jensen-Healey's complete front suspension, comprising fabricated dou-

J-H wheels are rather difficult to keep clean and so become prone to pitting. A new batch has been specially made up and Jensen Parts and Service retail them at around £40 each, whilst existing wheels can be polished for around £25, provided that no metal needs to be removed.

From beneath the car (and ignore the two ramps, one on either side on which the wheels are resting), the highly complex, highly expensive, exhaust system can be seen as well as the standard Firenza axle with superior location points. The exhaust is so heavy that the rear exhaust bracket mounting area is prone to suffering stress fractures.

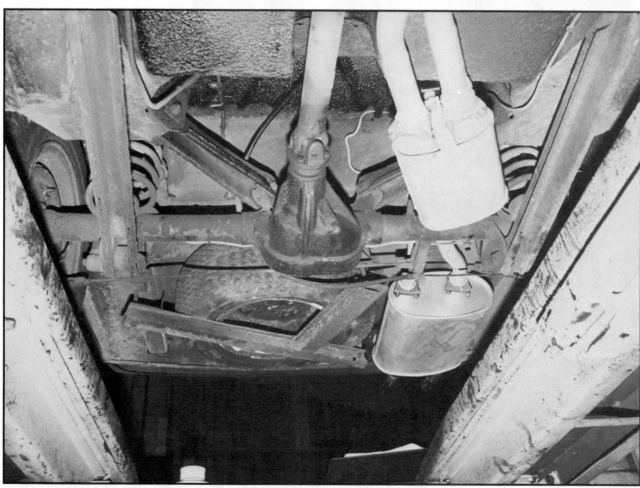

ble wishbones with coil springs and piston-type shock absorbers, came straight from the Vauxhall Firenza, while the standard Vauxhall steering rack, dual circuit brakes (disc front and drum rear) and front subframe carrying engine and steering), are all used. At the rear, the Firenza axle was fitted, though with superior location (see photograph). Shock absorber settings and spring ratings were, of course, adjusted for the lighter weight of the car.

Although a Vauxhall gearbox was originally to have been used, in the event the Sunbeam Rapier H120 box was selected because of its closer, sportier ratios. On the road, this box is a delight to use and its choice was an inspired one on the part of the Healey design team. The Rapier overdrive unit can easily be fitted to the car (although the prop. shaft would need some specialist shortening attention) and why Jensen never fitted it is a mystery. Instead, from 1974, they fitted the German Getrag 5-speed box with racing pattern gear change and a shift that, in my view when test-driving prospective purchases, is inferior to that of the good old Aunty Rootes/Chrysler box. However, styling changes in 1974 made the car a more attractive looking package with more aggressive bumpers, a body side-stripe that the car's styling had always screamed out for, and the option of a most attractive hard top with heated rear screen.

Buyer's market

Armed with all this information, I set out on my own search for the 'right' Jensen-Healey. I had already driven a rather worn 1974 example at Jensen and found it delightfully responsive, with lots of leg room even for a six-footer like me and with super handling and perfectly balanced powerful brakes. The only problem experienced in the handling department was a noticeable front wheel patter which occurred when cornering fairly hard on an uneven surface. I put that down to worn dampers on a car which was badly worn in other areas. I decided against the too bland styling of the pre-74 cars and in favour of the improved interior trim of cars produced after that date. In principle, I rather liked the idea of a 5-speed box, too.

The first car I looked at resided at a local garage and was for sale at 'around £2,200'. They had obviously bought the car in at the 'right' price, slapped filler over all the rust – then, as a sort of poetic justice, been unable to sell the car. (This, as I quickly learned, is a recurring feature among Jensen-Healeys offered for sale). As a result the car was everything that it shouldn't have been and because of the presence of filler, an unknown quantity to boot. The next was the right age, the right price (£1,250 or near offer) and in some ways the right condition. It had completed 60,000 miles and had been known to the owner since it was one year old, I was told. It was pretty rotten in its sills and wings

How Much

Virtually every spare part is at present available for the Healey (although the latest type front bumpers and bonnets are expected to run out soon), except for one or two items of dashboard trim. Some prices (without VAT) are:

Clutch, complete (Chrysler)	£66.93
Exhaust, complete	£265.98
Gearbox, recon: 4 speed	£450.00
Gearbox, recon: 5 speed	£532.00
Piston and liner	£115.00
Brake pads, set	£10.00
Brake shoes, Mk II	£20.76
Brake disc	£23.47
Front wing, Mk II	£131.00
Rear wing	£101.00
Outer sill	£33.86

Prices for Jensen-Healeys range from the very occasional £400 parts car to the even more occasional £4,000 concours example. Most prices range from between £1500 to £2000 and around £2500 + for a well above average specimen.

Jensen Parts & Service's vast array of spares makes a reassuring prospect for any potential owner. At least as reassuring is the friendliness of the staff and their evident delight in keeping as many Jensens on the road as possible.

A well used interior like this will require attention.

The Jensen-Healey's boot lid is a large, flat area. Catch the light on it to check for any of the dents and dings to which it is prone.

but the doors were sound, it hadn't sagged and the interior and mechanics seemed excellent. Disturbingly, it also pattered on cornering but it was fitted with the optional hardtop. I would have bought it there and then, but I decided that the total rebuild that would have been necessary would have put the full cost at around £3000, so I kept on looking.

The third car which I took a serious interest in was a 1975 Healey with Getrag box and heavy bumpers but without the interior carpets (rubber mats were fitted) with which the latest few cars were equipped. Although this was the latest car I saw, it was also the worst! It had been bought from a dealer a couple of months previously and was fully equipped with rust, filler, overspray and a horribly growling engine that gave the lie to its 45,000 miles on the clock. The 5-speed box is in the familiar H-pattern for the top four gears with first to the left and down. The change lacked precision, probably a fault of wear and a hard life, but the gate pattern was less than straightforward, not just because of the unconventional change but because it was so easy to change up out of third and go straight back into second which was almost where fourth should have been. These 5-speed cars were only sold in this country from some time in 1974 and so they are numerically the least common, but even so I decided that I was neither fanatical nor wealthy enough to tackle this little 'beauty', whose asking price was £2,500 so, as many reporters have done before me, I made my excuses and left.

I was offered a couple of very early cars (one *sans* engine) neither of which interested me and another filler-laden lump, vintage '74. I decided to ring the owner of the inexpensive and rusty 60,000 miles car in order to take another look only to find that it was sold. *C'est la vie!*

I knew that the ownership of a Jensen-Healey would no doubt be exciting and rewarding, but I began to realise that it would demand the sort of commitment of time and money that I could not afford to give.

In 1972, *Autocar* had summed the car up by saying, "It is everything a Healey and a British sports car should be, simple in concept, basic in construction, sporting in performance and nimble through the curves. It felt like a future classic, the kind of car that one day will become a collector's item". Those words have not yet quite come about; the day of the 'collectable' Jensen-Healey is only just starting to dawn. However, it's got so much verve, so much character, that *Autocar's* prophecy must surely come true, and now certainly seems to be the time to buy if you're interested, while prices are at a low ebb. I was still thinking of buying a Jensen-Healey when, just as I least expected it, a pretty little 1982 TR7 came up and started nuzzling my leg. I must admit that she was a bit ordinary after flirting with the last of the Healeys, but, dammit, a man has to settle down sometime!

"Healey Hunting" first appeared in "Thoroughbred & Classic Cars" magazine.

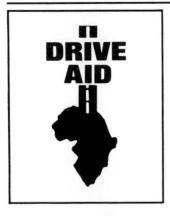

Jowett Javelin

by Jonathan Wood

The Jowett Javelin was first fully described in the motoring press in May 1947, and went into production later in the year. A 4-door, 5-seater saloon, it employed an A frame box-section chassis, joined at the rear by a sheet steel assembly. Suspension was by wishbone-and-torsion bar at the front and transverse torsion bar and radius arms to a live rear axle. Brakes were Girling Hydromechanical (hydraulic front and mechanical rear) and a quadrant-and-pinion steering box was fitted. The engine was an overhead valve, flat four of 1486cc (72 x 90mm) developing 50bhp. Leather or leather-cloth upholstery was available. The car costs £818.

For 1950, Standard and De Luxe versions appeared, the latter with a wooden facia with round-faced, recessed instruments, armrests for each passenger and a heater as standard; re-designed bumpers were fitted. Cars for 1951 featured separate sidelights instead of their being contained in the headlamps, while

No doubt coincidentally, the Javelin had, in outline, a similar mechanical specification to Alec Issigonis' original but partly thwarted plans for the Morris Minor, even though on the outside the Jowett was an everyday family car. (Courtesy National Motor Museum, Beaulieu.

at the rear, De Luxe examples were given a bumper mounted number-plate box. Major mechanical changes consisted of: conventional tappets replacing the Zero-Lash hydraulic ones; full hydraulic brakes and the fitting of an Idle built gearbox (from car no. EO/PC/11270) in the spring of 1951. Further changes at the beginning of 1951 included oil pressure increased from 60psi to 70psi and the oil filter being changed from a Vokes to a full flow Tecalemit. The radiator grille was also re-designed. Javelins for the 1952 season were fitted with Metalastik independent front suspension bushing. The De Luxe wooden facia was re-designed with flush-fitting instru-

ments with chrome bezels. The more reliable Series III engine was fitted in cars in 1953, which was the final year of production.

Body and Chassis

The Javelin's box-section chassis stops well short of the rear of the car and this is the first point of investigation. Underneath the car any suspect areas should be tested by prodding with a screwdriver. The forward end of the rear wheel arch is a particularly vulnerable section for two reasons. Apart from being blasted by grit and mud thrown up from the road, the location is also under stress as the

rear transverse torsion bars are mounted there. The chassis should be checked at the same time; rust may have attacked the front and rear outriggers. The latter also serves as a jacking point and is found immediately beneath the central door pillar which, in extreme cases, can also suffer. The front chassis cross-member should also be examined for splits along the seam (it was a favourite spot for a careless mechanic to place a trolley jack and the box section does not take the strain).

The bodywork doesn't seem to suffer too much at the front, but at the rear the floor of the boot should be checked as it is particularly susceptible to rusting. And on the De Luxe cars the steel surround containing the spare wheel is also likely to disintegrate. It is, undoubtedly, the rear of the Javelin that demands the most careful inspection.

A final word of warning: particular care should be taken when examining a Javelin registered in late 1952 or 1953. The sales dive of the previous year and resultant stockpiling of bodies outside the Idle factory meant that many of the shells were already starting to rust when they were assembled.

A few words are probably worthwhile on the Jowett numbering system. A typical Javelin number might be D9/PA/10631. The first letter indicates the decade, A is 1, B 2 and so on. The second digit indicates the years of the decade. The third letter P indicates a 'pleasure model',

car is a 1949 pleasure A model (early type) Javelin. As it happened, the model year was changed every year from 1949 to 1953. Therefore, a later model 1953 car would be E3/PE/28562.

Suspension, Steering and Brakes

Suspension faults are usually confined to the Javelin's front end. The main difficulty is that the upper wishbones pivot on single bolts and if they loosen the resultant movement can crack the chassis. To avoid this the Jowett Car Club recommend that a high-tensile Allan-headed unbreako bolt is fitted in place of the original. The upper wishbone brackets also act as oil reservoirs, which supply lubricant through a tube to the swivel pin yoke. This method of lubrication was discontinued after car number D9/PB/5979 and a grease-nipple substituted at the upper end of each upper link. The reservoirs require topping up with 40 grade oil every 500 miles and excessive wear of the swivel pin yoke indicates negligence in this regard. The system was replaced in 1952 when Metalastik joints were introduced. The rear torsion bar layout is comparatively trouble-free apart from rust of the torsion bar mountings already mentioned.

Steering gear require lubrication every 2,500 miles though the joints need greasing at 500-mile intervals, so excessive wear due to lack of maintenance is not uncommon.

The Javelin's less than ideal column gearchange must have made life difficult for this stage of the 1956 T.E.A.C. Cat's Eyes Rally. This is a 1953 car. (Courtesy National Motor Museum, Beaulieu).

as opposed to C for 'commercial'. The fourth letter shows the basic model type, which changed as modifications were introduced. The final figure is the engine and chassis number. The example given shows that the

There aren't any special problems associated with the brakes, and obviously the full hydraulic layout fitted from 1951 models onwards was a great improvement to the Hydro-mechanical system employed earlier.

Engine, Gearbox and Transmission

Although Jowett did have their fair share of mechanical misfortunes with the unusual flat four engine fitted in the Javelin, most examples have by now been rectified. The Series III engine of 1953 was the most reliable unit of all, but the much improved oval webbed crankshaft, designed for the company by Dr. Ker Wilson of De Havilland, was not fitted to reconditioned engines until about 1955, 2 years after car production had ceased. Nowadays, the main disadvantage with this engine is the aluminium block. Over a long period, the water within the block and weather conditions cause severe corrosion to the underside and repairs are tricky and expensive. If possible, the bottom of the block should be examined for signs of damage or bodged repairs. Also the cast-iron cylinder heads tend to crack between the valve seats and a damaged gasket probably means that the engine's wet liners weren't 0.008 – 0.010 proud of the block when the engine was reassembled after a de-coke. A torque wrench is a vital tool when working on this engine because of the amount of aluminium it contains. The distributor is rather exposed to the elements and misfiring can be prevented by wrapping it in a polythene bag. If the sparking plugs have to be removed, the plug wells should be free from stones and grit otherwise they will drop into the combustion chambers. An acceptable oil pressure reading for this engine is 50psi at 40mph.

The Javelin was fitted with two different gearboxes during its production life. Up until the spring of 1951 a Meadows-built unit was employed. This tends to be fairly reliable, though it can jump out of third gear. Thereafter a Jowett-built box was fitted and this, amongst other shortcomings, can strip the teeth of its second gear. Although in contemporary terms this gearbox was less reliable than the Meadows one, many examples have continued to operate reliably for years. The steering column gear change is a well engineered component and shouldn't develop any slack.

Power was transmitted to the rear axle via a two piece propeller shaft supported centrally by a bearing, which in turn was contained by a cross-member and held in place by fabric or rubber strips. The condition of this supporting material is vital and should be examined for chafing or wear, which could cause bad vibrations. The rear axle is not prone to trouble.

Spares

Like most saloons of its age, it is virtually impossible to obtain replacement body panels for the Javelin. However, so far as mechanical spares are concerned the Jowett Car Club has recently taken over a large stock, while another source is Dennis Sparrow and Associates of London who also undertake work on these rather unconventional cars.

This guide to the Jowett Javelin first appeared in "The Enthusiasts Guide to British Postwar Classic Cars".

Javelin Spares and Service

Dennis Sparrow and Associates, 77 Jeddo Road, London W12 (tel: 01-749 2013)

Jowett Car Club, Send an SAE to Ian Priestley, 626 Huddersfield Road, Bradford BD12 8JR.

Javelin performance and consumption (Series III)
"The Motor" April 8, 1953. Top speed: 82.4mph.
Overall mpg: 29.1 for 2290 miles.

Javelin body production
22,799 units

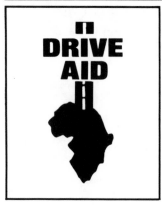

A Dash of Elan

Ian Ward writes on one of the great British sports cars of the sixties, the legendary Lotus Elan.

When Colin Chapman's new Elan was shown to the press for the first time in 1962, it was acclaimed with a single voice as possibly the most effective small sports car of all time. An inspired combination of sleek good looks, light weight, respectable power output and sure-footed nimbleness prompted often cynical journalists to eulogise about the little Lotus in a previously unheard of fashion. It was all the more remarkable that the Elan lives up to its promise to the extent that it is still cited, nearly ten years after its demise, as a standard by which to judge other machinery.

Construction

The idea of using a backbone chassis was nothing new, but this one was fabricated by pressing and welding sheet steel, rather than using girders. The central spine gained its immense strength from being $10\frac{1}{2}$ inches deep and 6 inches wide, and from being a complete box section with a bottom plate. The two ends of the frame were bifurcated, to form an elongated 'X' and to clear the engine at the front and the differential at the back. The four ends were equipped with towers, higher at the back than the front, to provide suspension mountings.

Front suspension was a double wishbone set-up with uprights coming from the Triumph Vitesse, while the steering rack and disc brakes came from the same source. A purpose-built anti-roll bar was fixed at its ends to the lower damper mountings and on its central section to the chassis.

At the rear, a Lotus-designed independent suspension system comprised a coil spring/damper strut, designated a Chapman strut, rigidly mounted in the upright in similar style to the Elite, with a flexible rubber mounting at its upper end where it joined the chassis. Unlike the Elite, however, lower location was provided by a wide-based transverse A-frame, alterations in driveshaft length and angle being taken care of by twin rubber Rotoflex couplings similar to those on the Hillman Imp and popularly known as 'doughnuts'. Disc brakes were also fitted at the rear, just inboard of the suspension upright.

The final drive was a standard Ford Classic or Anglia 105E unit, with a special Lotus light-alloy housing to convert it for independent suspension use. It was hung on rubber mountings from the rear chassis crossmember, with lower stabilising rods running forward to prevent twisting.

The Elan first appeared in 1962, although production didn't start until May 1963, by which time the engine had been enlarged. The first series is easily distinguished by its individual rear lamp lenses, while centre-lock wheels had yet to arrive. The sturdy pressed-steel backbone is shown inset on this illustration.

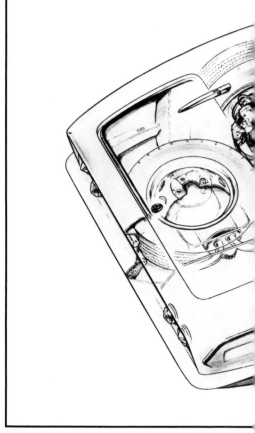

The chassis was plenty strong enough in its own right to obviate the need to stress the body. Glassfibre was used once again, but with only two mouldings required for the whole shell. Strengthening was incorporated for localised stresses such as passenger weight, door hinges and so on, but generally the glassfibre was of fairly even thickness, which simplified construction once more.

The Elan was strictly a two-seater, with some stowage space behind the seats (the battery was located behind the passenger seat in early cars). The rubber matting of the first cars was soon ousted by carpet, while the comfortable semi-reclining seats, although having a fixed rake, offered more than adequate fore-and-aft adjustment.

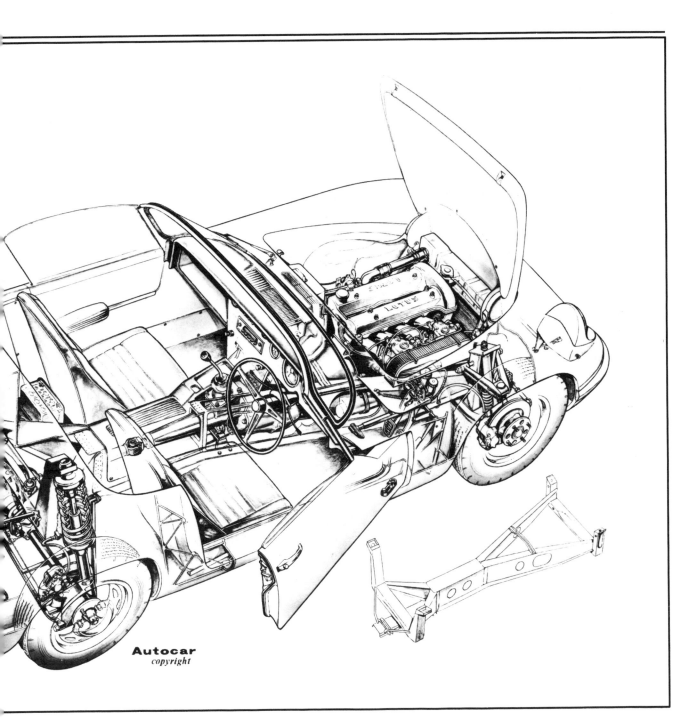

Autocar
copyright

Power

The Elite was powered by a highly-specialised Coventry Climax engine which was efficient but very costly, so for the Elan, Colin Chapman cast around for a production unit which he could adapt for his own purposes. Fortunately, Ford let it be known to Lotus that they were working on a five-bearing replacement for their small OHV four, to be used in the Classic and in the yet-to-be-announced Cortina. This was like a prayer answered and Chapman set Harry Mundy, designer and technical writer, to work to pen a twin-cam cylinder head conversion to suit.

Before long, Elans were complete and heads were being produced in light alloy by the famous JAP company. The units, with inclined valves located in hemispherical combustion chambers with the spark plugs between, dropped straight on to the standard iron blocks, which were equipped with special recessed-crown pistons to allow for full valve opening.

The twin camshafts ran in five bearings each, and operated the valves through inverted bucket tappets and clearance-adjustment shims. Originally, the tappets ran direct in the head, but high wear rates caused Lotus to fit cast iron sleeves. Double valve springs were more than capable of coping with valve closure at high speeds. The cams were chain driven from the nose of the crankshaft, the long single-row chain also turning the original Ford cam, which remained to drive the distributor and oil and fuel pumps. A sprung tensioner with an external adjuster kept the chain taut, and a plastic guide was fitted to the 'drive' side to reduce noise.

Fuel supply came from two twin-choke Weber 40DCOE carburettors, fitted to four separate inlet pipes cast into the head, with no balance pipes between the cylinders.

The original twin-cam retained the standard unit's 1498cc capacity, despite having a special cast-steel crankshaft, but after only 22 had been built the bore was enlarged from the 81.5 to 82.55mm, thereby increasing the swept volume to 1558cc. This was brought about by a

due to a final drive ratio of 3.9:1 rather than 4.125:1, the highest available from Ford, but Lotus did also offer their own close ratios as an option.

History

Although the car was announced in 1962, it did not go on general sale until 1963, and it was in May of that year that the larger engine was substituted and a hardtop offered as an option.

In November 1964 the Series 2 was introduced. Externally this was most easily distinguished by its Vauxhall Victor rear light clusters, which replaced the individual items of the S1.

In September 1965, a proper fixed-head

This is a Series 2 model, with non-standard S4 wheel trims and an optional-equipment hard top. It was not until the Series 3 appeared that electric windows replaced the different shaped manual items.

The boot aperture of the first two series is set into the rear deck, whereas that of the later cars wraps over the rear lip. This luggage bay contains the side cant rails which support the hood round the early models' frameless windows.

sudden change in the international competition regulations to allow a maximum capacity of 1600cc, to be achieved by overboring a production unit by not more than 1mm. Needless to say, a further 1mm rebore takes the engine out to 1596cc. This was most important to Lotus, as the twin-cam first saw the light of day in a victorius Lotus 23 sports-racer. From this point on, Lotus only used specially selected thick-wall blocks for the twin-cam.

All the small units were recalled in 1963 and replaced free of charge, the car becoming known as the Elan 1600. Incidentally, power output went up from 100bhp at 5700rpm to 105bhp at 5500rpm, although as both these figures were net, they were undoubtedly slightly flattering.

The diaphragm clutch was similar to that of the Classic, albeit with an uprated spring and driven plate, as was the all-synchromesh gearbox. The standard ratios seemed closer

coupe appeared. This was the first of the S3 models, which could be identified by several features other than the solid roof. Electric windows replaced the manual items and were equipped with permanent frames; the rear edge of these also sloped forwards rather than backwards towards the top. The doors were also substantially, but subtly, altered in shape, and new sealing arrangements cured the major leakage problems of the S1s and S2s. The flat boot lid was replaced by a larger cover which folded over the rear edge of the car and improved access, and the battery was shifted from behind the passenger seat to the offside of the boot. Inside, the doors were retrimmed, with remote door handles incorporated, and the dash was slightly altered once more. Finally, there was a new Triumph-derived radiator and an optional 3.55:1 final drive, and a few cars even had chrome plating on their glassfibre bumpers.

November of that year saw a new close-ratio gearbox option (the standard unit was by now that of the new Ford Corsair 2000E) and this became a standard on the Special Equipment S2 which was announced in January 1966. Power output of the engine was raised to 115bhp for this car, by virtue of new camshafts and carb jets, together with a different exhaust manifold – usually a fabricated confection, but sometimes a different kind of cast-iron lump. The centre-lock wheels were included and the package was topped off with a brake servo, together with harder pads, and flasher repeaters on the front wings. This car was short-lived, for in June the top was chopped off the S3 to include this

version's refinements in open-air motoring. The specification was much the same as that of the fhc, except that there was a new folding hood to replace the S2's complex lift-off cover, and the interior mirror slid up and down a central screen wire rather than being fixed. The SE conversion was also transferred to this model.

The exact date is uncertain, but some time during 1967, from engine number LP7799, the bottom end was modified. Tough 'C' type rods replaced the somewhat weak early items (identified by the legend 125E), and a new crankshaft required a different flywheel, with a six rather than four-bolt fixing, and a new sump. The Mk II pistons had modified cut-outs for the valves and the oil pick-up pipe was altered (the two are not interchangeable), but otherwise the engines were identical.

The next substantial change was to be seen in March 1968, when the S4 made its appearance. This was quite easy to spot, having flared wheel arches to accommodate 155 x 13 rather than 145 x 13 tyres, new rear lights from the Plus 2, a twin-pipe exhaust silencer and a bonnet bulge (anticipating the fitting of Stromberg carburettors in November to cope with US emission regulations). Headlamp operation was reversed, so that spring pressure brought the units up, and an electric cooling fan was fitted. In the boot, the fuel tank was made smaller ($9\frac{1}{4}$ rather than 10 gallons) to allow room for the slightly larger spare tyre, and the battery polarity was reversed to negative earth. Inside, there were new seats and trim, with flush door handles, and yet another new dash layout, with rocker

switches and face-level vents (later cars also had steering column locks).

The Stromberg equipment lasted only until August 1969, when Webers reappeared, although the unsightly power bulge persisted for some time and it seems that Lotus were still using up old stock of Stromberg-type heads and carbs long after this. It was not until the new Sprint went on the market in February 1971 that the back of the Strombergs was finally seen – and even then the first Sprints had bonnet bumps. The heart of the Sprint was a new big-valve version of the twin-cam, designed by Tony Rudd. With new cams and exhaust manifold and recalibrated Webers (or similar Dellorto DHLA 40's), together with an increased compression ratio at 10.3:1. this unit now turned out 126bhp at 6500rpm. To cope with this, the differential mountings were strengthened and tougher Rotoflex couplings, with metal inserts, were incorporated in the driveshafts. To give the car electrifying acceleration, the 3.77:1 final drive, first standardised during the life of the S3, and taken from the Corsair, was the only one offered. A two-tone paint scheme distinguished the early Sprints from afar, but otherwise they were similar to the earlier S4 models. This was the last of the Elans, production finally ceasing in August 1973 with 12,224 cars built. A five-speed gearbox, really intended for the Plus 2, was offered in 1972, but it appears that only four or five Elans were ever thus equipped.

For most of its life, the model was available either as a complete car or as a kit (the latter escaping purchase tax). In fact, very little work was required by the owner to complete the kit – mainly fitting engine/gearbox and front suspension – so the vast majority of Elans were sold in this form. Indeed, the Sprint was not offered complete. It was the application of Value Added Tax in

1973 that was mainly responsible for the death of the Elan, which was an event still widely lamented, although it provided an opportune impetus to Lotus's planned move up-market, which had begun with the appearance of the Plus 2S-130.

Buying Secondhand

It is some years now since the secondhand price of Elans ceased falling, although it is just about impossible to give an accurate guide to the amount that should be paid for any given type. Rarity value is such that this is more of a seller's market than a buyer's one, and the best advice is to make a careful check of all cars on offer in a particular area and then make an educated judgement of the relative worths. If offered a Sprint, try and ascertain its authenticity; it may be a beautiful S4. The surest check is to look for the strengthened differential mounting.

When buying an Elan, the most important rule is to make sure that the car is not about to fall apart. Contrary to popular opinion, the Elan is not generally especially fragile; however, there are a few areas which can be considered weak.

Starting with the engine, assuming that it is not emitting clouds of smoke or rattling like a child's money box (or worse!), check that there are no major oil leaks, particularly around the cam cover. Oil pressure at around 3,000rpm or about should be 40lb per sq in. One frustrating weakness is the water pump which, as mentioned earlier, is not easy to renew; if there is more than very slight play in the pulley, then the pump is unlikely to last much longer. A tip here is to leave the fan belt on the loose side and to fit a Ford plastic fan (assuming that the car does not already have an electric unit).

The long timing chain tends to stretch and

situ, and in any case it is easier to take off the distributor than the carb.

The transmssion is reliable enough – the clutch, although hydraulic, is adjustable, but it is worth jacking the car up and crawling underneath to check the condition of the Rotoflex couplings; if they are at all split they should be replaced. Don't bother to buy the old type; replace all four with Spring couplings.

Rear dampers do not tend to live to a very old age, so bounce the back of the car to test them. If it oscillates, one or both need changing. Also, check for fluid leaks, commonly caused by rusty operating rods. Rear wheel bearings are another weak point, particularly the inners. Late Elans had the wider bearings from the Plus 2, but these did not provide a real cure. Check by wobbling the wheels with the handbrake off.

At the front, the lower trunnion bushes

The engine bay of a Series 4 car. The twin Strombergs replaced the double Weber set-up for a short while, to comply with US emission laws. Despite tales to the contrary, the two-seat Elan was never equipped with an alternator for the home market.

Series 2 and 4 interiors. Things changed for the better, but basic layout remained much the same. The late models had the luxury of face-level vents, remote door handles and electric windows.

rattle, but this is easily tightened as long as the tensioning screw is not fully home. The starter often gives trouble, either sounding very sick or jamming, and this is not helped by Lotus using an incorrect 9-tooth pinion instead of the 10-tooth item which Ford specified for that bottom end. A new pinion is easy enough to fit, but the flywheel ring gear may be worn and replacement of this is a major operation.

It is worth checking that the carburettor mountings have not been over-tightened; Webers and Dellortos have spacers with rubber O-rings between them and the head to prevent frothing, and the carbs are supposed to wobble. At the same time have a look at the driver's footwell, beneath the carbs. Any sign of fouling here is a sure sign that the engine mountings are on their way out. Incidentally, it is not true that the front carb must be removed before the distributor can be serviced; it is in fact perfectly possible to adjust the points in

wear quickly, but these are cheap and easy to replace. Also, the pressed steel wishbones tend to rust and resultant failure has been known. All the suspension rubbers should be checked, because even a small amount of play can completely spoil the handling of the car.

The lower steering swivels are supposed to be filled with hypoid oil, but are often greased; along with other points. The trouble with grease is that it does not work its way through the internal threads properly and wear quickly sets in, preceded by stiffness. If the steering feels at all stiff, this is probably the cause.

Despite efforts at prevention, the brake caliper pistons go rusty with regularity, causing brakes to stick on and the car to pull to one side. The only cure, albeit temporary, is to fit new pistons – an expensive and lengthy task. The disc edges, too, seem to rust, but there is no way of preventing this.

When buying any second-hand Elan, it is essential to check the chassis as thoroughly as possibly for corrosion. Here, a substandard repair has been carried out near a rear A-frame mounting. Replacement chassis are galvanised and are readily available.

In basic design and construction, the Plus 2 is identical to the Elan. This is an example of the last series, known as the Plus 2S 130 and identified by its silver roof.

The chassis is usually protected by oil, but there are two common failure points, at the top of the rear suspension towers and the bottom of the front ones. Repairs are almost impossible with the body in place, so check very carefully here (if the rear seems to be sagging this is a likely cause). One clue to problems at the front can come from the headlights. The crossmember is used as a vacuum reservoir, and if rust sets in here, the headlights will quickly close when the engine is stopped. Also, the headlamp vacuum units themselves tend to corrode and leak and these are now quite hard to come by, so be sure to check properly.

Finally, the bodywork may well be showing its age in the form of cracks. Although these may seem to be only in the paintwork, they will be just about impossible to remove permanently without at least replacing the gel coat of the glassfibre. Later cars were thicker and suffered less than early ones. While looking at the body, make sure that there are no signs of major repairs. If there are then climb back underneath and search for chassis damage.

It is now very difficult to obtain some parts – trim etc. – through Lotus, but strangely, as the Elan gets older, more companies are turning to producing their own equivalents, so that there is actually very little that cannot somehow be acquired.

Tuning

With the racing history that the twin-cam engine has, it is very easy to tune it or, more correctly, to obtain the necessary parts. Of course, there are two obvious stages for the owner of a standard unit: Special Equipment or Sprint parts. If more power is required then there is a selection of wilder camshafts available to assist in this, and there are several companies offering special heads. Shop around for the best deals.

If you want an Elan, buy one now, because they won't get any cheaper. It is a fact that there is no other car to compare with the little Lotus in its class – not even another Lotus, at the moment, at least!

"A Touch of Elan" first appeared in "Hot Car" magazine.

Super Cooper

Buyer's Guide to the Mini-Cooper, by Graham Robson

How many of you, out there, are running round in an XR3i, a Golf GTi, or similar? Are you enjoying them? Good. Consider, then, that the car which really invented this breed of machine was the Mini-Cooper, built in big numbers between 1961 and 1971.

Of course, by modern standards, a Mini-Cooper doesn't feel all that quick anymore, but we promise you that by the standards of the day they were exciting enough. Furthermore, they were in a class of their own – quite literally, for at first they had no competition. Alec Issigonis had re-invented the front-wheel-drive car in 1959, and with the help of arch-racing-enthusiast John Cooper he went on to produce the sports saloons to follow.

In ten years, these 10 foot long boxes (not for nothing were they known as Mini-bricks ...) provided FUN for tens of thousands of owners, winning rallies, races, rallycross, and every possible permutation of each, by the thousands. Perhaps no car has ever handled the same way, or had such enormous character.

There was a period when the Mini-Cooper was a forgotten car, but not any more. Historic rallying has helped to rekindle the image, and of course Minis in racing have never been far away. The interest in well-kept standard examples is now on the increase. Read on ...

The choice

The original Mini-Cooper of 1961 was a long-stroke, 997cc, 55bhp car, with tiny disc brakes, and little equipment. Five years later, the definitive model was the 1275S, complete with beefy 1275cc, 76bhp engine, near-100mph top speed, twin tanks, and much more. It was a case of a competitions, and demand-led, evolution. In ten years, there were five different engine sizes, two distinctly different types of springing, and three 'Marks', not to mention two types of transmission, and a host of other changes.

There are two strains of cars to be considered. One, the most numerous, was the 'basic' Mini-Cooper, which ran through from 1961 to 1969, the other being the Mini-Cooper S model, built in three different engine series between 1963 and 1971. All were based on the same two-door saloon body shell, but the two sub-families were different in their own separate ways.

The founder of the family was the 997cc engined Mini-Cooper, built from 1961 to the end of 1963. This had tiny, 7.0in diameter, disc front brakes, and the engine was effectively a longer-stroke version of the ubiquitous 948cc unit (though the bore was slightly reduced). Like all subsequent models, this was badged as an Austin or a Morris, but that made no difference, as every car was built at the 'Austin' factory at Longbridge!

Naturally the hard rubber, all-independent, Mini suspension was retained, along with the inch-accurate rack and pinion steering. A sop to the sporting character was that there was a three-instrument panel, but no rev-counter. The remote-control gear change helped, but the seats were the usual back-breakers, and cross-ply tyres were fitted.

From the beginning of 1964, the 997cc engine was discarded, and a 998cc unit was installed instead. This reverted to the 948cc engine's stroke, with the bore (and re-cored cylinder block) of the 1100 engine, though there was virtually no external difference to be seen. The 998cc unit was much smoother, sweeter, and more ready to rev.

998s lasted for five years, and from the autumn of 1964, they were given 'wet' Hydrolastic suspension, interconnected front

The original Mini-Cooper, badged as a Morris, complete with tiny extra corner bumpers. Somehow, it didn't look like a sports saloon.

to rear, while in October 1967 they became 'Mark II' along with all other Minis, which mainly meant trim changes, and new grilles; an all-synchromesh gearbox followed within months. The last 998s were built in October/ November 1969, then 'replaced' (or so British Leyland insisted ...) by the long-nose 1275GT. Tell that to the Marines, for this wasn't as nice a car.

The Mini-Cooper S was developed with competitions in mind. The A-Series engine was thoroughly re-jigged internally, with re-positioned bore centres, bigger bearings, and Nitrided cranks, plus, more head hold-down studs. All three engines had the same 70.6mm bore.

First of the three was the 1071S, built in 1963 to 1964, with 70bhp. Most importantly, though, it had bigger front discs, a servo, and radial ply tyres.

The 1071S, however, was only interim, for two versions came on the scene in 1964 – the 970S 'homologation special' (with an ultra-short-stroke' 65bhp engine – only 972 cars were actually built), and the famous 1275S, which had 76bhp, really torquey delivery, and

was everyone's favourite. All three Mini-Cooper S cars shared the same chassis, brakes and tyres at first, but the 1275S was on its own from 1965 and evolved uniquely.

First, from the end of 1964, there was Hydrolastic suspension (also used by half the 970Ss), and then from the beginning of 1966 all were built with twin fuel tanks, an engine cooler, and wide rim wheels (plus a reclining seat option). In the autumn of 1967, the 1275S became 'Mark II', with new grille, bigger rear window, and other trim details, but the all-synchromesh gearbox did not arrive until mid-1968. Finally, from early 1970, it became 'Mark III', when the latest type of concealed-hinge body, with wind-up windows, and the Austin or Morris name dropped in favour of 'Mini', was introduced. The 1275S retained Hydrolastic suspension to the end of its run, in June 1971.

Where and how to look

Even though 101,242 Mini Coopers, and 45,438 Mini-Cooper S cars, were built in ten years, many have been scrapped since then. There

123

1961 and the Mini-Cooper launch: an Austin first followed by an apparently unregistered Morris.

are several reasons, notably the fact that the cars went though an 'unfashionable' period, that they undoubtedly corroded away if neglected, and were ignored because 'never mind, there are plenty more ...'

Fortunately, about one third of Mini-Coopers, and 20 per cent of Mini-Cooper Ss, were originally sold on the UK market, and there *is* still a reasonable supply on the market. Many, however, have been modified, and would need work to get them back to 'as new' condition.

The Bad News is that structurally they were always cheap-and-cheerful cars, with which a lot could (and did) go wrong. Here's what to look out for:

'Chassis' structure

In the case of these cars, this really means the big front and rear sub-frames. There can be problems! Start by seeing if the car runs straight, instead of crabbing down the road (yes – this is a common habit for bodged Minis), for this may tell a story.

Rear sub-frames suffer more than the front frames, but in both cases check that there are no rust holes – the good old hammer-taps and magnet checks all help – paying particular attention to where the frames mount to the body shell, and where the suspension members pick up to the frames. The frames themselves should never be patched (MoT testers fail such things, almost on sight!).

Unfortunately, trouble in these areas is very common, and in either case it is a very big, costly, and long-winded job to replace either frame, due to the amount of mechanical kit hung on to them.

Body shell

There are no basic differences between the three 'Marks', and all can suffer from really bad corrosion. One major problem is that almost every panel is welded, rather than bolted, into place, so replacement is not for the novice.

Firstly, check out the inner and outer sills, and the door steps, along with the floor pan. If the car has suffered serious water leaks, any or all of these sections could be in a sorry state. Next, look around the tail, particularly inside the rear wheel arches, the boot area, the spare wheel and particularly the battery recesses. Standing water (or battery acid!) may have caused havoc.

You will already have assessed the condition of the sub-frames; at the same time look at the integrity and condition of the body-work and the mounting holes to which they are fixed; there are no less than eight fixings at the rear, for instance.

Now look at the hinge panel condition – the external hinge types show rust here as soon as the rear of the shell starts to corrode. At the same time, check out the doors themselves, particularly at the bottom.

Now it is time to look at external panels, particularly those above and around the wheel arch cut outs, the 'A-Panel' between the raised external panel joints and the door pillars, the boot lid and the area around the headlamps. Fortunately, a lot of surface rust can be dealt with, rather than having to face panel replacement. A sure sign of trouble is for the external panel joints – front and rear – to look dreadfully corroded, for this usually means that the rest of the shell is in poor condition too.

We're sorry this is a discouraging story – but, then, all the Minis have always been like this.

Power train

The problem is that any major rebuild means a difficult craning job to get the combined engine/transmission/final drive unit out of the car. This is much more difficult than with a conventional front engine/rear drive car.

First, though, since all cars have oil pressure gauges, look for acceptable 'hot' medium-rev-range operating pressures – 40/50psi for Mini-Coopers, but up to 60/70psi for the Cooper S. Pressures are much higher when the oil is cold, and thick. Next, look for the smokey-exhaust syndrome, for these A-Series engines eventually suffer worn valve guides and piston rings.

The main wear points, which lead to noise, and a fall-off in performance, are in the valve gear – cam followers, rockers, and timing chains – though the cams themselves are usually OK. Incidentally, you may find the engines to be oily or leaky, externally. This is

usual and you may have to consider changing a lot of the cheap gaskets and seals. The gaskets between the engine and various transmission cases are a real pain to change.

The transmission – from clutch face to the drive shaft joints, may have taken a greal deal of punishment with hard-driven cars, particularly those which have been treated to power-tuned engines. First, check that engine mounts and tie-bars are in good shape, for though these are external, they might affect the feel and performance of the transmission. Clutches may slip, due to seals leaking from the engine and may suffer from judder, only curable by fitting a new unit.

Gearboxes wear out their second gear and third gear synchromesh when age and abuse sets in. The change linkage should be sweet, not sloppy. The real problem may be in the intermediate transfer gears (clutch to transmission), for if these whine or rattle at tickover, an expensive rebuild may be in prospect. The engine shares its oil with the transmission, so always beware leakage or other symptoms of loss.

You've heard all about the drive shaft problems? Forget the scares about locking joints, but do look for evidence of torn U/J boots, and worry about clicking outer joints on full lock turns; that will be costly, sooner rather than later; from 1966 on, 1275S models had solid (not rubber bushed) inner U/Js, which were much more robust.

The engine/transmission assembly of the early Mini-Cooper, which looked very much the same several years later, even though the engine size had grown from 997cc to 1275cc. Note the tiny disc brakes and the remote-control gearchange.

125

Suspension, Steering, Brakes

Once you've checked that the car runs straight, have a look at all the suspension mountings to the sub-frame (worn bushes are not difficult to change, except at the rear radius arms). Then look at front suspension ball joints, which wear, but can easily be renewed.

Most 1275S cars, and 998 Coopers, are Hydrolastic – check that the car is riding square, front to rear, and side to side. It *can* be pumped up by a BL garage, but if it sags again, there are leakage problems. 'Dry' cars (up to autumn 1964) should not suffer in this way. In any case, look for wear at the various knuckle and ball joints, and see that the

Coopers, have a hard time if flogged. Worn discs have to be replaced, not skimmed, and these are expensive. Check that handbrake cables are working well and not rusted up due to lack of use. On the test drive be sure that the car pulls up square, without wheel locking.

Trim and Furnishing

Firstly, is the car complete in all respects? This is important, for original pattern trim pads and the older types of strips and details are difficult to find.

Secondly, look for any signs of water damage, for leaks have been endemic to this car – windscreens, floors, wheel arches and

This is a 1963 model 1071S, with Austin badges, and wide rim wheels, but no name plates – the first of the real giant killers.

suspension units are in good shape, well-supported in the mountings and that the Hydrolastic fluid lines are not corroded. At the rear, be sure the trailing arms have not been bent out of shape by 'kerbing' accidents.

Shock absorbers are cheap and cheerful, and will sometimes need replacing; at the same time, you will need new bushes for their mountings.

The steering gear will be fine unless it has been damaged in a shunt, but look for signs of wear in the ball joints, and be sure the chassis mountings are still in good shape. It is not easy to change a rack (which is hidden away behind the line of the transverse engine).

Brakes, especially on the 'basic' Mini-

sliding-window doors.

Obvious horror spots on poor cars include the state of the boot, the condition of the fit-where-they-touch carpets, the headlining, and the trim around the instruments and parcel shelf. Door seals can be replaced, as can the door furniture, but be sure that plastic items like switches, knobs and latches are all present – replacement is sometimes impossible.

Front seats may be torn, sagging, or generally beaten up – replacement frames are available, but not cheap and original style fabrics are now rare.

The watchword here is not to skim over worries about missing components – ask

Quite a Mini-Cooper S bonnet-full of engine, with the semi-downdraught SU carburettors behind the engine, and all the electrical components to the fore.

From the front, there was no way of 'picking' one type of Mini-Cooper S MkI from another. This car could have one of three engine sizes.

yourself why the previous owners never found replacements? Will *you* be able to do so?

On the Road

You have to start by forgetting the true performance figures – the fact that a 998cc Mini-Cooper could be beaten-up today by a 1.1-litre Fiesta, and matched by a 1.0-litre Metro, and that a 1275S could be matched by an MG Metro is cruel, but irrelevant. *All* the Mini-Coopers, of whatever persuasion, were great sports saloons of their day.

The great joy of Mini driving, then and now, is that they were so very nimble. It seemed they could shoot any gap, turn on any sixpence, and out run any big car across country, all at a low first cost, in utter docility when not being pushed and while recording very good fuel economy figures.

The drawbacks were that, in all fairness, the seating position was uncomfortable for anyone of above-average height, the ride was very hard indeed on 'dry' cars, and quite hard even on 'wet' cars, and the internal noise levels at speed were quite intolerable.

But forget all about that. Consider the torquey joys of owning a 1275S, which could go anywhere in third and top gears, with great *elan*. Consider the roadholding, and the go-almost-anywhere ability of this amazing little front-wheel-drive package, and the cheeky character which has never been matched on any other car, before or since.

The Mini-Cooper was, and is, at its best on twisty roads, or rushing up and down hills, but much less happy on straight dual carriageways and motorways. Treat its brakes with respect (even those on the Mini-Cooper S),

Rear view of a Mini-Cooper MkII 1275S, launched in October 1967, showing the twin fuel filler necks. The car has a new grille and, from the summer of 1968, an all-synchromesh gearbox was standard, too.

and a Mini-Cooper can be one of the most reassuring and easy to drive of cars. Even today, we defy anyone to name a better car for elbowing its way through impenetrable traffic jams (remember *The Italian Job* film?).

To make a Mini-Cooper right for the mid-1980s, however, we'd have to recommend the fitment of a special seat, set well back, a re-raked steering column and some sort of sound-deadening insulation kit. Fascinating – all were available when the cars were current, and many can be found, even today.

Best Buys and Values

Perhaps we had better start by eliminating the least desirable types – the 997cc car because of its long-stroke engine and undeveloped details, and the 970cc 'S' because of its rarity and its high-revving 'homologation special' nature. Which leaves us with three types – 998, 1071 and 1275cc – to consider.

The 1275 'S' is one of the most commonly available, but suffers from a rather rough engine when pressed hard. On the other hand, the 998s and the 1071S are both sugar-sweet, versatile and fun to drive. The 1275S, however, is invariably the most highly specified, and of course was the only type to live on after 1969.

For all-round charm, then, a 998cc or a 1071cc car, but for the most urge (and probably the most choice, today), a 1275cc,

preferably post-1965, with all the 'extras' built in as standard, and with firmed-up Hydrolastic suspension.

How much to pay? Really, they are all still remarkably good value, which reflects the 'working-class' appeal, and the general availability. Expect only to pay £1,000 for a good, if not concours, 998cc car, maybe a bit less for a 997cc (pre-1964) example. On the other hand, a 1275S will be worth £2,000, more if in excellent condition, while if you found a 'mint' 970S or 1071S you'd have to pay up to £1,000 more than that.

Which, by way of standards, makes a 1275S a real value-for-money package today.

Where Built?

Assembly of all Mini-Coopers, no matter how they were badged, was at the Austin factory at Longbridge, the cars rolling down the assembly lines among more mundane models such as Minivans, Pickups and estate cars. No Mini-Cooper was ever built at Cowley, or by the Cooper Car Co. Ltd.

Body shells came from Fisher and Ludlow, engines from Longbridge, or the BMC Engines Branch at Coventry, and transmissions from other BMC factories in the Birmingham area. The cars usually had Dunlop tyres, always had Lucas electrics and the suspension units were produced by another division of Dunlop.

A typical Mini-Cooper interior of the 1960s; in fact, that of a 1968 model 1275S, showing the rather casual carpet fitting, and the very simple instrumentation. Nearly every surviving car has an accessory rev-counter, these days.

A lot of fun in a very small and still affordable package – the Mini Cooper. This is a 1966 Austin Cooper Mk I with 998 cc engine.

A beautiful old Beetle cabriolet in an interesting colour scheme. These Karm-ann Ghia-built convertibles are very sought after but can be difficult to restore.

Above: Ferrari's classic and elegant Daytona – here in spyder form. Thought by many to be the last and greatest of front-engined Supercars.

Far left: The dramatic and brutally powerful Lamborghini Countach was the undisputed leader of the Supercar pack until the mid eighties.

An early MGB roadster. Timeless lines and simple unadulterated motoring pleasure.

Main Picture: An early 'Series 1' Jaguar E-Type roadster showing the wonderful styling balance which ensures that the XKE will never be out of fashion.

Inset: Porsche 356A convertible. Simple uncluttered lines, amazing performance and handling for their time are all hallmarks of these great little cars.

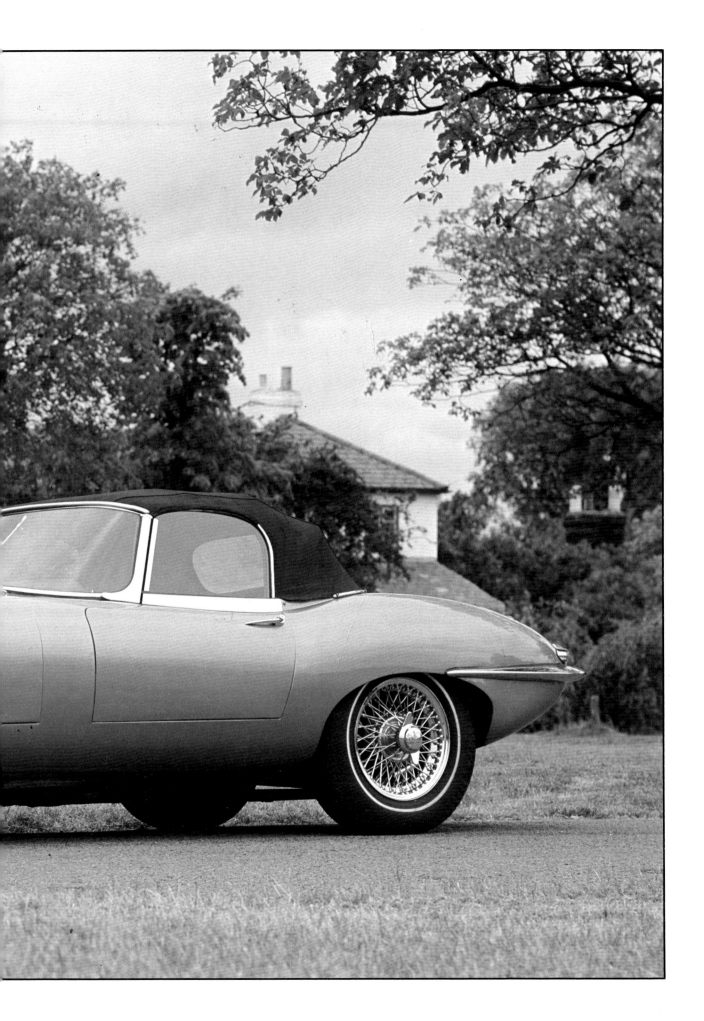

Has there ever been a prettier car than the MG TF? The last of the T-Series models, the TF was deliberately styled in a very traditional mould – this is a 1250 cc model.

A jewel from Lotus. Endowed with leechlike roadholding, ample power and Chapman genius the fibreglass-bodied Elan set a standard which other manufacturers could not hope to emulate.

Porsche's seemingly eternal 911. A real driving machine which will reward the sympathetic owner with endless pleasure. This is journalist, Chris Harvey's, SC with Chris at the wheel.

Parts Supply

The last Mini-Cooper S was built 15 years ago, so specialised parts are hard to find. Many parts of the shell, and suspension, are still common with current Minis, so be sure to have a Parts Catalogue to double check this.

Items like cylinder blocks are no longer available, but all the moving parts most certainly are. Don't expect a BL dealer to be very interested, unless his microfiche shows up a part number as still available, but there is a thriving parts tuning/preservation/industry in the UK to keep these cars going. Join the Mini-Cooper Club or the Mini Owners Club to get all the best advice.

As far as a 1275cc engine is concerned, beware – many non-S engines exist, and many parts from these cars will fit yours. But it isn't advisable to cut corners. Transmission rebuilds are costly, but can be done.

Join the Club?

In fact, you could probably get by, in terms of finding parts, restoration and rebuilding expertise without becoming a member of the one-make club, but we don't advise it. If nothing else, the fellowship of this organisation will point you in the direction of the best and most trustworthy specialists.

Accordingly, we suggest you contact: The Mini-Cooper Club, 1 Weaver's Cottage, Church Hill, West Hoathly, West Sussex RH19 4PW.

There is also a more general-interest club catering for all Minis: The Mini Owners Club, 15, Birdwood Road, Lichfield WS14 9UN – and a racing orientated club, which many Mini-Cooper enthusiasts also join: The Mini-Seven Racing Club, 33, Stoke Road, Slough, Berks SL2 5AH.

And the growing rally register which revives 'Historic' style rallies – and you don't need an ex-works car: Don Pither, Droys Court, Witcombe, Glos.

Also of interest is a book entitled "Mini-Guide to Purchase & DIY Restoration" which shows, using over 800 illustrations, what to look for when buying, and how to restore these cars in every detail, and is written by Lindsay Porter and published by the Haynes Publishing Group.

"Super Cooper" first appeared in "Sporting Cars" magazine.

Heritage

1951: A-Series engine, first seen in Austin A30.

1959: Launch of front-drive transverse-engine BMC Mini

Mini-Cooper family history
Autumn 1961: Launch of Austin and Morris Mini-Coopers, with 55bhp 997cc engines.

March 1963: Launch of original 1071cc Mini-Cooper S

January 1964: 998cc instead of 997cc engine for Mini-Cooper, by short-stroke engine. No power increase quoted, though some evident.

March 1964: Launch of 970cc and 1275cc Mini Cooper S models, with 65bhp and 76bhp respectively. 1071S dropped soon afterwards.

September 1964: All Mini-Coopers given hydrolastic 'wet', instead of rubber 'dry' suspension. No 970S after April 1965.

January 1966: 1275S given twin fuel tanks, engine oil cooler and wide-rim wheels as standard.

October 1967: In line with all Minis, Mini-Coopers became 'Mk II', with restyling touches including larger tail lamps and rear window, new grille, revised interior trim.

1968: Muddled, gradual, adoption of all-synchromesh gearbox, all cars.

Autumn 1969: 998cc Mini-Cooper discontinued.

March 1970: 'Mk III' 1275S introduced, having wind-up windows, and concealed-hinge body shell.

June 1971: Last 1275S of all produced, still with hydrolastic suspension.

Mini-Cooper production: 1961–1971
Mini-Cooper with 997cc engine (1961-1963): 25,000 approx.
Mini-Cooper with 998cc engine (1963-1969): 76,000 approx.
(Total Mini-Cooper production was 101,242)
Mini-Cooper S with 970cc engine (1964-1965): 972
Mini-Cooper S with 1,071cc engine (1963-1964): 4,017
Mini-Cooper S with 1,275cc engine (1964-1971): 40,449

Note: No attempt has been made to differentiate between so-called 'Austin' and 'Morris' examples, as they were mechanically identical in all respects.

Good points:
Small size, excellent roadholding, manoeuvrability.
Perky character.
Fuss-free performance, especially from 1275S.
Availability of most parts excellent.
Prices still very reasonable.
Good buying choice, all types except 970S.
Wide-spread restoration expertise.

Bad points:
In spite of claims, a small interior, and little stowage space.
Sub-frames and bodies rust badly if neglected.
Rubber-sprung cars have rock hard ride, 'wet' models can be sick-making.
Engine/transmission rebuilds made more difficult by front-drive layout.
Very sparse instrumentation on standard cars.
Not always easy to find 'un-customised' example today.
Not obviously 'classic' – too visually similar to other Minis.
None – not even 1275S – fast by modern standards.
And the noise.

DRIVE AID

The MG T-Series

F. Wilson McComb describes the development of MG's most famous series.

To most people, the T-series MGs are the classic example of that famous marque; indeed, to some, a T-type MG *is* the classic sports car, period. Which makes it all the more strange that they originated during a change of management that put MG's founder in a relatively subservient position and, he had little to do with their design, which was dictated from outside the confines of the Abingdon factory.

Although the highly-developed ohc MGs favoured by Cecil Kimber had proved immensely successful in competitions throughout the world by the mid-1930s, those successes had brought no dramatic improvement in the sales of ordinary sports models. This did not go unnoticed by Lord Nuffield, the man behind the MG Car Company, who was, in any case, becoming tired of Kimber's preoccupation with motor racing. In the summer of 1935, as part of a wider reorganization of the Nuffield empire, he sold the MG Car Company to Morris Motors Ltd of Cowley, and appointed his right-hand man, Leonard Lord, to be managing director with authority over the unfortunate Kimber, who now found himself merely the director and general manager of the MG factory.

The MG TA, the car that started the whole series off, though not, strangely enough, the most sought after in the range.

Leonard Lord lost no time in applying the sort of methods that were later to put him at the head of the mighty British Motor Corporation. He closed down MG's racing department in mid-season, discontinuing all further work on the new 750cc R-type that had been hailed as a brilliantly advanced design. He closed down MG's design department, leaving only two people there as liaison men, and the remainder were either transferred to Cowley or left to find new jobs elsewhere. As a temporary measure for the forthcoming Motor Show, the P-type Midget was given a larger engine and the N-type Magnette a new body, while the rest of the models were dropped. It was made clear to all concerned that Kimber's policy – designing high-performance competition cars on which future production sports models were based, using virtually the same components – would no longer be acceptable. Future MGs would be designed by Morris Motors at Cowley with the emphasis on low-cost production methods, and making the fullest possible use of the Nuffield corporate parts bin. If this meant they were unsuitable for competition work, that mattered not at all to either Nuffield or Lord.

The first of the new generation MGs was a 2-litre saloon, the SA, which had a Wolseley Super Six engine and was announced in 1936. A few months later the short-lived PB, last of the ohc Midgets, was replaced by the MG TA, whose pushrod-ohv engine was basically that of the contemporary Wolseley Ten. The TA two-seater, although still called a Midget, was appreciably larger than its predecessors. With a wheelbase of 7ft 10in and track of 3ft 9in it was, indeed, more of a Magnette in chassis dimensions and also in capacity, the engine size having gone up from 939cc to no less than 1292cc. It was indicative of Kimber's

now limited influence on design that hydraulic brakes, which he had always disliked and distrusted, were a feature of both the SA and TA models. The chassis frame still bore a close resemblance to those of previous MGs, having channel-section side-members that passed under the rear axle and swept up over the front one, with tubular cross-members and leaf springs all round. As before, there was no eye to the trailing edges of the main leaves, which passed through split bronze bushes carried in the ends of the cross-members.

The chassis frame was boxed-in for greater rigidity around the engine and gearbox, and its larger dimensions allowed for a roomier body, with more space for the occupants and quite a lot more for their luggage. Inevitably, the TA was heavier than previous Midgets, but the new engine gave a respectable 52.4bhp at 5000rpm, compared with the PB's 43.3bhp at 5500rpm, and road tests soon showed that, despite the increased space and comfort, the grown-up Midget performed quite well. At £222, the same price as before, it offered good value, and during the production life of the TA its sales easily outstripped those of the PA and TB together. Some cars were offered with Airline Coupé bodywork, a 'streamlined' alternative built by Carbodies of Coventry and previously sold on the PA/PB chassis, but at £295 this was rather too expensive for most folk. More popular than this was the Tickford drophead coupé, a handsome if rather heavy little car costing £268.10s.

Most magazines rated the acceleration of the two-seater as good at about 15secs, 0 to 50mph, covering the standing 1/2-mile in about 22secs, and most of them recorded a one-way maximum speed of almost 80mph. They were equally content with no more than 28mpg, but a new 15-gallon tank provided an adequate range. Of this, three gallons were held in reserve, with a two-way tap on the dash.

As indicated earlier, the TA was certainly not designed as a competition car, but the whole history of Abingdon demanded that the new MG should make some kind of showing in motor sport. Its predecessors had always performed well in that peculiarly British happening, the sporting trial, which was sufficiently widely supported to attract useful publicity. So the works built six special TAs for the Cream Cracker and Three Musketeer trials team drivers, with lightened bodies, lower first and second gears, and high-compression engines. In this form they won many awards, the Cream Crackers taking the MCC's Team Championship Trophy for the 1937 season. The Three Musketeer TAs were also entered for a 12-hour sports car race at Donington, where they carried off the team prize.

For the 1938 season the two teams had new cars; TA Midgets once again, but extensively modified to meet a growing challenge from other teams. The Musketeers used Marshall superchargers to provide the performance they needed, and gained many more awards. The Cream Cracker cars were at first fitted with 1548cc unblown engines from another pushrod-ohv MG of the period, the VA, but these were disappointing. Opened out to 1708cc, however, they went well and again won the MCC Championship in 1938. In the marketplace the TA Midget went through the same stages that every new MG has gone through over the years, being at first regarded with deep suspicion by the diehard enthusiasts, then accepted almost grudgingly, and finally treated with ever-increasing respect. MG sales had been very poor in the year of the Nuffield takeover, but they improved considerably in 1936 and hit a new record in 1937. In 1938 the Munich crisis caused another fall, but it was interesting to see how MG's export sales had started to grow, even in those pre-war days.

In 1939, completely unannounced, there came a new T-type which went into production only a few months before war broke out. The TA engine had been something of an oddball with its enormously long (102mm) stroke, the cork-lined clutch running in oil. The new one that became available in the spring of 1939 had a peak power output only 2bhp higher – 54.4 at 5200rpm – but it was a far better piece of machinery, destined to become one of the classic engines of all time, and still to be found under the bonnet of popular roadgoing cars in the mid-1950s. The ancestry of this new XPAG engine was Morris rather than Wolseley, for it was essentially the M-10 unit, but when given a bore of 66.5mm to a stroke of 90mm, it became an 11hp instead of a 10hp under the old RAC formula, which meant that a higher Road Fund Tax was payable. As the amount payable *per horsepower* also went up that year, perhaps this was why Nuffield omitted to tell the motoring world that the 1292cc TA Midget had been replaced by the 1250cc TB in May 1939. None of the motor magazines did a comprehensive road test of the TB, which was almost indistinguishable from the TA in any case, apart from the new engine and a dry clutch. Total TA production came to 3003, more than that of all previous MG models except the original M-type Midget, and the TB added a further 379 before car building ceased at the outbreak of war.

In October 1945, just five weeks after the official ending of WW2, the MG Car Company announced their first – indeed, for some time their only – post-war model, the TC Midget. If Cecil Kimber had rather mixed feelings about the first of the T-types in 1936, it is even more ironic to remember that he probably never laid eyes on the TC, the most widely renowned and respected MG of all time. He had been dismissed from his own company in November 1941 by Miles Thomas, a Nuffield director even more ambitious than Leonard Lord, and was killed in a railway accident eight months before the TC was announced in 1945.

It is difficult, now, to realize how desperately new cars were needed after six years of war. The only way that MG could even attempt to meet the demand was to do as all the other manufacturers were doing: get into production as soon as possible with an essentially pre-war design. It might have been thought, too, that an open two-seater sports car was not the ideal choice for a one-model programme in the midst of post-war austerity, when petrol was of low octane rating, strictly rationed, and most of the magazines believed that the popular choice would be a no-frills economy four-seater saloon. However, MG's own records showed that only four of their pre-war models had topped a production rate of 1000 cars a year, and all of them were two-seater Midgets. On that basis the decision was reached to take the TB Midget, simplify the chassis slightly by fitting conventionally shackled leaf springs, and to make the body a little wider across the cockpit. There were new instruments, new shock absorbers, and the wiring layout was improved, with a single 12-volt battery under the bonnet instead of two 6-volt batteries at the rear of the car. Otherwise, the post-war TC was virtually the pre-war TA/TB.

The Airline Coupé had disappeared with the TA, and the Tickford drophead followed it into limbo when the TB was discontinued, so the one-and-only body style for the TC Midget was the open two seater. It cost, when announced, £375 plus another £105 of purchase tax in the UK, but by the summer of 1946 the basic price had crept up to £412.10s. The performance of the new TC became something of a *cause célèbre* when the first road test appeared in the January 1947 issue of *Motor Sport*, for this announced that acceleration from 0 to 60mph had occupied a leisurely 27.25secs, the standing 1/4-mile had been timed at 23.45mph, and the highest attainable speed was a one-way 65.75mph: the two-way mean maximum, it said, was merely 63.5mph. Not surprisingly, the Nuffield publicity chief of that time, one Reg Bishop, invited the magazine's editor to explain how he had arrived at such extraordinary figures. His invitation was declined, and in retaliation he withdrew all Nuffield advertisements from the magazine in what other journalists dubbed the Bishop Ban. When the weekly magazines tested the TC later in the year, *Motor* reached their 60mph in 21.1secs, recorded a four-way average of 72.9mph with the screen up, and their best one-way speed was 77.6mph. *Autocar* put the maximum at 75mph and their 0 to 60mph figure was 22.7secs. These figures, of course, were achieved on the low-octane 'Pool' petrol of the post-war era. Overseas magazines published better performance figures, having access to fuel of reasonable quality.

The success story of the MG TC has been told far too often to need repetition here. Even in its native land the car was already an anachronism in the late 1940s, and very much more so overseas where, in some countries, the production and development of modern cars had continued until 1942 or even later. But in 1947 more TCs were sold overseas than in Britain, although it still had a separate chassis frame when the majority of cars had gone to monocoque construction; still had non-independent leaf springs when most had independent front suspension of one type or another, still had an exposed radiator with an unpressurised cooling system; still had separate mudguards, separate headlamps, a massive exposed fuel tank at the rear, and large-diameter wire-spoked wheels. It could not be bought with a radio or heater, there were no bumpers, and no matter where it was sold, every car was built with right-hand steering.

It was the American writer, Warren Weith, who expressed it better than anyone else when he referred to the TC simply as "A way of life. A wildly different car that you jazzed around in on weekdays and raced on weekends ... A moving spot of colour on a still-drab post-war landscape." But contrary to popular belief, the vast majority of TCs were sold in other overseas countries, not the USA, for the Americans remained conservative as always in their buying habits, and it was only a select minority that tasted the delights of the car when it first appeared. Of 10,000 cars built, only 2001 went to the USA, 4591 went to other overseas markets, and 3408 remained in Britain. And yet, although so few Americans actually bought the TC when it was new, the impact that it made upon them was something that persisted for many, many years to come.

The TC was raced with enthusiasm by the likes of Briggs Cunningham, John Fitch, and Phil Hill, the first American to win the World Championship. It was also raced in Australia, Africa, Ireland, Switzerland, Singapore, Spain, and heaven knows where else; France, for example, where a rebodied car ran twice in the Le Mans 24 Hours – even in the French GP of 1949, when it was held as a sports car event.

Outselling previous MG models three-to-one, the TC Midget sowed the seeds of its own destruction for in many countries where sports cars had previously been almost unknown, local salesmen demanded a new MG sports car that would be a little more comfortable, a little roomier, a little this, a little that. Abingdon took the chassis of the contemporary Y-type saloon, with its independent front suspension and pressed-steel disc wheels, cut 5 inches out of the wheelbase, and fitted a TC body. This was the prototype of the TD Midget, which in production form had the same wheelbase as the TC, a front track of 3ft 11 1/2in, and a rear track of 4ft 2in. The box-section chassis passed over the rear axle and the Y-type IFS was retained, together with that model's rack-and-pinion steering. The wheels were a mere 15in in diameter, more powerful two-leading-shoe front brakes were fitted,

This early model TD is shown here pictured with Michael Craig in a scene from the famous British film *"Life at the Top"*.

and a hypoid-bevel rear axle lowered the transmission line.

With more generous mudguards, and a wider and more rounded body and bumpers front and rear, the new TD looked surprisingly different from the lean and lithe TC. Once again there were loud protests from many enthusiasts, but it was a more practical car than its illustrious predecessor, because it offered at least the same performance with greater comfort, a substantial increase in weight having been countered by lower overall gearing. Because of this the acceleration was virtually identical, but the TD was a thirstier car. On the other hand, most magazines recorded a higher maximum speed for the new model. Priced at a basic £445 on the home market, the TD was for a long time virtually unobtainable in the UK, no less than 43 cars going overseas for every single TD sold at home. This was partly because the TD was designed so that it could easily be built with left-hand drive, unlike the TC, which in the end it outsold three-to-one. Total TD production was 29,664 cars, including the mildly-tuned TD Mark II which was really a 'homologation special' with reworked cylinder head, larger valves and stronger springs, 9.2:1 compression, larger carburettors and twin fuel pumps. Three works-prepared cars ran in selected races, scoring a class 1-2-3 in the 1950 Tourist Trophy at Dundrod.

But these were rapidly changing times. As the exciting new Jaguar XK120 two-seater was followed by other more modern sports cars in the early 1950s, the TD was increasingly criticized for its old-fashioned shape, and sales began to fall sharply – especially overseas. Abingdon designed a new two-seater based on the rebodied TD

that George Phillips had driven at Le Mans in 1951, and this was completed late in 1952. But in 1952 the Nuffield Group had merged with Austin under Sir Leonard Lord, as he now was, to form the British Motor Corporation. As Lord had also arranged to build a new two-seater designed by Donald Healey, the Abingdon project was turned down.

Hence the MG TF, which was a rather hurried 'facelift' of the TD for the 1953 Motor Show, using a lower compression version of the TD Mark II engine. The scuttle was lowered, and the bonnet (now with fixed side-panels) dropped to a sloping imitation radiator, with dummy filler-cap. The headlamps were partly faired into the front wings, the tail was sharply raked, and the dash was redesigned. Bucket seats were fitted, and wire-spoked wheels were an option because the hubs had also been redesigned.

In its day the TF was not a commercial success, even when fitted with a 1466cc engine that was available from July 1954 onwards, to counter the challenge of Triumph's much faster 2-litre sports car. When it was discontinued in 1955 to make way for the new MGA model, only 6200 of the 1250cc TFs and 3400 of the 1500cc cars had been built.

Nowadays, of course, the situation has changed completely. It is the TF that has become revered as the last of the 'square-rigged' MGs, commanding the highest prices among T-series models and, more recently recreated with modern mechanical components.

This article first appeared in an Orbis publication.

EX-175, the prototype MGA. Note the bonnet bulge to accommodate the T-type engine.

The MGA

The story of MG's first 'modern' sports car by F. Wilson McComb

It is only recently that collectors have started to become enthusiastic about the long-neglected MGA, the two-seater MG which was in production from 1955 until late 1962. Yet it was in its day one of the most significant models Abingdon even built. Apart from its obvious importance as the first modern-idiom MG sports car, it was the first MG in twenty-odd years to be designed specifically *as* an MG, by an MG design team located at Abingdon, and presided over by MG's own chief engineer. Moreover, it set a new record of commercial success by becoming the first sports car in the world to exceed a production total of 100,000.

Paradoxically, the T-series MGs which are now so sought-after and widely imitated, were designed by the Morris organization at Cowley, Oxford, after Morris Motors Ltd had taken over the MG Car Company in 1935 and closed down the Abingdon design office.

When war ended and the Abingdon works returned to car production in 1945, materials were so scarce and money so tight that the first postwar model, the TC Midget two-seater, had to be a very close relation of its prewar predecessor. Being such an anachronism even in its own land, it was not expected to sell well overseas – but it did, and this brought a demand for a roomier, more comfortable, sports car to take its place. Hence the TD, with its independent front suspension, pressed-steel wheels, bumpers fore and aft, and the option of left-hand drive. When the TD first appeared towards the end of 1949, it was undoubtedly what a great many enthusiasts wanted, which is why it outsold the TC three-to-one. But tastes were changing rapidly at this time, and within two or three years there were several other more modern sports cars available: the Jaguar XK120, the Triumph TR2 and the Austin-Healey 100, to name but three. Put an MG TD alongside any of these, and it looks like something from an earlier century. Compare performance figures, and you realize that although the angular little MG did remarkably well with its modestly-sized 1250cc pushrod-ohv engine, the body drag factor was such that a maximum speed approaching 100mph – which is what sports car buyers had begun to demand – was totally unobtainable.

So it was that MG sales, and especially the overseas sales on which Abingdon now depended most, began to fall rapidly. American magazines of the period were filled with gimmicks and suggestions for making the TD look anything other than what it was, with

imitation wire wheels, special paint jobs and the like.

MG boss John Thornley was well aware of the problem, and had already taken steps to overcome it. Those who raced MGs with any degree of determination would remove the angular body, sooner or later, and replace it by a lower-drag effort that also offered a lower frontal area. The TC and TD chassis being ill-suited to this kind of exercise, such racing bodies were invariably ugly, but they did achieve their purpose by improving the car's performance. One of the fastest and ugliest around in the late forties, it is fair to say, was the rebodied TC raced by George Phillips, chief photographer of *Autosport*, who had done well with it in the Le Mans 24 Hours of 1949, the French GP (a sports car event that year), and again at Le Mans in 1950. John Thornley decided that for the 1951 Le Mans race, Phillips should have a new car of impressive performance and decent looks, fit to wear the octagon.

Built on a TD chassis, this car, registration UMG 400, was an attractive two-seater with full-width bodywork, the effect of which was revealed when its mildly-tuned T-series engine was found to propel it at almost 120mph – a 50% improvement on the maximum speed of the ordinary TD. It dropped a valve early in the race, and to this day it is argued whether this mishap was due to excessive enthusiasm from the driver, or

the undoubtedly poor fuel supplied by the race organizers that year.

That was not important. What mattered was that the possibilities of modern-style bodywork had been demonstrated; here was an MG that went well, looked good, and – though designed for racing – was very close inded to being a practical road car. The one real snag was that the driver (and passenger, if any) sat high in the air above the narrow TD chassis frame. Syd Enever of MGs therefore designed a new frame, wide enough to seat the occupants between the side-members and the propellor shaft, and had a couple of them made up. The fact that he had two made, instead of one, was to prove useful in an unexpected way.

One frame was provided with a similar body to UMG 400, this time complete with windscreen, top, bumpers and other road equipment. It looked even better, and the occupants sat low; the only criticism this time was that the lofty T-series engine called for an ugly hump in the bonnet. This car, Project EX-175, was registered HMO 6 and tested in 1952. That, however, was also the year in which the Nuffield Organization was taken over by ex-Nuffield employee Leonard Lord, now boss of the Austin Motor Company and a man with a long-standing grudge against Lord Nuffield. The British Motor Corporation, as the new Austin/Nuffield combine was called, had just agreed to build an Austin A90-powered

two-seater designed by Donald Healey, revealed at the 1952 London Motor Show as the Austin-Healey 100. Therefore, Abingdon got a firm thumbs-down from Sir Leonard Lord when the Ex-175 prototype was presented as the sort of MG that MG *should* have been building, to maintain its leading position in the sports car market. In a fairly desperate

A group of roadsters and Coupes (and on the left a Midget) on show at an MG Car Club Concours in North California in 1962.

attempt to keep things going and stem the
downward trend in MG sales, the TD was
hurriedly remodelled as the TF, a rather
obvious 'facelift' job, for the 1953 Motor Show.

Surprising as it may seem now that the TF
is admired more than any other T-series MG,
it was a complete flop when announced, and
nowhere more than in the immensely important American market. Capt. George
Eyston, who had been associated with MGs
since 1930 and spent much of his time in
America, advised a new record attempt on the
Utah Salt Flats to boost MG's reputation in the
USA.

Unfortunately, Abingdon didn't *have* a
record car. Colonel Goldie Gardner had
fallen ill after his 1952 Utah attempt with the
famous Gardner-MG, following an injury
sustained at that time, and it was unthinkable
that anyone else should drive his car. EX-175
was kitted out as a record-breaker, tested,
and found unsuitable. So Syd Enever took the
spare chassis frame that had been made, fitted
it with an unsupercharged TF engine opened
out to 1500cc, and bodied it as a miniature
replica of the Gardner car. In August 1954 this
new machine, EX-179, was successfully driven

by Eyston and Ken Miles (an expatriate
Englishman living in the States) at speeds of
up to 153.69mph. And in this haphazard,
rather roundabout way, it happened that the
new chassis frame was not merely tested in
the normal way, but tried out at speeds far
beyond anything it might achieve in a road
car.

Faced by the continual drop in US sales,
Sir Leonard Lord finally got the message,
giving Thornley the go-ahead to re-establish
the MG design office at Abingdon under Syd
Enever and have EX-175 turned into a new
production MG two-seater as soon as possible.
More than that, he agreed to the establishment
of a BMC Competitions Department at Abingdon, and the entry of a three-car MG team
for the 1955 Le Mans race!

It was frankly admitted that the Le Mans
cars (then known merely as Project EX-182)
were the forerunners of a new production
model, soon to be announced, and Thornley
told the motoring press that the aim was
simply to finish the race at an average of about
80mph. It was also intended (though this was
not revealed) to demonstrate their versatility
by entering the race cars for the Alpine Rally

as well, and for this reason they were surprisingly close to normal road trim, except that the bodies were built in light alloy.

Two of the cars finished at average speeds of 86.17 and 81.97mph, the third being written off in a crash. This was excellent, but 1955 was also the year of the horrific Mercedes-Benz crash involving many spectators. All post-race advertising was withdrawn, and the Alpine Rally was cancelled. By a tragic coincidence, there was another multiple accident in the new MGs' next race, the Ulster TT at Dundrod. The BMC management decided to withdraw from racing altogether (although two cars were, in fact, entered illicitly for the 1956 Mille Miglia, finishing 2nd and 3rd in class to a Porsche).

The engine chosen for the new MG sports cars was the British Motor Corporation's 1489cc B-type unit, fitted to the MG Z-series saloon which had come out at the same time as the TF, and already responding well to tuning by the Competitions Department. Immediately after the Ulster TT the new MG was launched officially as the MG Series MGA, being given that label because MG had already run right through the alphabet with their previous model types.

Because of a delay in body tooling, the MGA did not go into full production immediately, and cars were not available for testing until late in 1955. They were greeted with considerable enthusiasm by the press, for although early cars gave only 68bhp compared to the 72bhp of later ones, it was found that the MGA would accelerate from rest to 60mph in about 15 secs, reach almost 100mph and achieve almost 30mpg, compared with the TF's 19 secs, 80mph and 25mpg. Abingdon production figures soared. The number of MGAs built during the new model's first full year, 1956, exceeded the total ouput of TC Midgets. In its peak year, 1959, MGA production in 12 months outnumbered the entire prewar production of *all* MGs!.

It was a car with a dual personality, although not everybody realized this. Being so much roomier and more comfortable than the T-series MGs, with ample luggage space, it was a very popular touring car that appealed to buyers who could scarcely be described as dyed-in-the-wool sports car fanatics. But it was also an exceptionally safe car that could be made to cover the ground very rapidly indeed. Thrown into corners at seemingly absurd speeds, it would break away completely predictably, and could then be throttle-steered with ease.

For the comfort-lovers, the 1956 London Show brought a fixed-head coupé version with winding windows instead of sliding side-screens, a larger windscreen and other refinements in what would now be called the GT style. For those who wanted to enjoy the MGA's excellent roadholding to the full, there came the Twin-cam in July 1958. The Lockheed drum brakes were replaced by Dunlop discs, front and rear, with peg-drive centre-lock wheels like those of the D-type Jaguar. The 1 1/2-litre engine had been enlarged to 1600 cc and carried a massive alloy dohc head with chain-driven camshafts. On a 9.9:1 compression ratio it gave 108bhp, exactly 50% more power than the pushrod car, which translated into an easy 115mph maximum and acceleration to 80mph in half the time.

This fast and responsive car was, in fact, a little *too* responsive for inexperienced drivers, responding so readily to the throttle that those who couldn't understand a tachometer could, and did, break it, simply by careless use of the right foot. It also required meticulous servicing, with particular attention to mixture strength and ignition timing, and 100-octane fuel was really essential. In practice, the result was a crop of service complaints, especially from overseas, and the Twin-Cam was discontinued after two years. Later it was discovered that most of the troubles could be avoided, with little loss in performance, by merely fitting lower-compression (8.3:1) pistons.

In May 1959 the ordinary pushrod ohv engine also went up to 1600cc, and although it was little faster at the top end, the new engine had more torque and gave better mid-range acceleration. At the same time the drum front brakes were changed for Lockheed discs, the pedal layout was improved, and this MGA 1600 model had a better hood and side-screens.

Finally, in April 1961, the capacity went up again to 1622cc for the MGA 1600 Mark II. Few people appreciated that this was not just a quick boring-out of the existing block but a new engine altogether, with a new big-valve head, a new block, pistons, con-rods, crankshaft and flywheel. Even the gearbox had a new casing, ribbed for greater strength.

MGAs fast, furious and filling the track!

A power increase from 80 to 93bhp was largely concealed by a simultaneous change in the final-drive ratio from 4.3 to 4.1:1, making for quieter cruising but no very noticeable improvement in acceleration. The Mark II was mainly distinguishable by a rather odd-looking front grille, and horizontal tail-lights mounted on the body instead of on the rear wings.

The Twin-Cam was dropped rather hurriedly on the advice of Marcus Chambers, the BMC Competitions Manager at that time, when he returned from the 1960 Sebring 12 Hours Race with reports of American service problems with the car. There were, therefore, a good many Twin-Cam chassis left over, and these, fitted with 1600cc pushrod engines, were sold as the MGA 1600 De Luxe – or, later, with the 1622cc pushrod engine as the MGA 1600 De Luxe Mark II.

Although the MGA had first appeared in public as a three-car Le Mans team, even before it had a model name it was, of course, primarily intended as a roadgoing production car, with the accent on safety and longevity rather than performance. Moreover, the accidents at Le Mans and Dundrod made the BMC management very wary of permitting full involvement in European racing, while recognizing that the marque had to be represented in an important American race such as Sebring. Lastly, sports/racing cars became so specialized during the late Fifties that when the Twin-Cam appeared it had little chance of achieving any notable success in such events.

An MGA 1600 Coupe in an English mud-trial, demonstrating the variety of sporting issues to which these cars were put in their heyday.

All of which explains why the MGA never won a major race or rally – but it certainly did not disgrace itself, especially in long-distance events. MGAs took the team prize in the Sebring 12 Hours of 1956 and 1957, recording a class 1-2 the second time. No MGAs were entered for the Florida race in 1958 (because the Twin-Cams were not ready), but in 1959 they had a class 2-3, and in 1960 they were 3-4 in class. De Luze MGA coupés secured first and second places in their class in 1961, and three similar cars completed the 1962 race without winning an award; it was the first and only time they came home empty-handed.

BMC having said no to official participation at Le Mans after 1955, an MG Car Club syndicate entered the same Twin-Cam for the 24 Hours in 1959, 1960 and 1961. The first run was ended by a collision with a large dog, and the third by mechanical failure, but the car won its class in 1960, beating or outlasting such machinery as Triumphs, AC-Bristols and Porsches. The class 2-3 in the 1956 Mille Miglia was repeated in 1957, with privately-entered cars, and four Twin-Cams filled the first four places in their class in the 1959 Silverstone GT Race. More impressive, perhaps, was the class third behind two Porsches in the 1958 TT by an MGA Twin-Cam described in *Autosport* as "probably the only genuine production car in the race." The ability of the MGA was already known to that magazine, whose first Production Sports Car Championshop was won by the Abingdon-designed car.

In international rallies the MGA was at first overshadowed by the Porsche 356, and later by the powerful Austin-Healey, but successes in the ladies' category of the RAC, Scottish, Alpine, Liège and Lyons-Charbonnières events helped Nancy Mitchell to win the Ladies' Championship in 1956 and 1957. John Gott, too, gained a Triennial Trophy for finishing the very difficult Liège event three years running, each time in an MGA. And when the model was nearing the end of its production life, a Mark II De Luxe coupé won the 2-litre class of both the 1962 Monte Carlo Rally (driven by Don Morley) and the 1962 Tulip Rally (driven by Rauno Aaltonen).

Having already broken records at Utah as EX-179 before it really existed, the MGA chassis returned to the Salt Flats in 1956 with an unsupercharged prototype of the Twin-Cam engine, there to exceed 170mph. A supercharged Twin-Cam engine was then installed in a new and revolutionary MG record-breaker, EX-181, for an attempt at four miles a minute – 240mph – at Utah in 1957. Driven by Stirling Moss, it achieved 245.64mph, and in 1959 the same car recorded over 250mph, driven by Phil Hill.

This article first appeared in an Orbis publication.

Living With A Midget

Lindsay Porter knows nothing about life with Toulouse-Lautrec. But he does know a thing or two about MG's Midget ...

It would be true to say that the entire history of the MG is full of fascinating sports cars and some sporting saloons, all of which have been full of character and have developed out of the spare parts boxes from some pretty ordinary, everyday motor cars. After all, the first MG was a rebodied 'Bullnose' Morris and the first Midget was a Morris Minor (the pre-war Austin Seven-like variety) with the MG treatment.

Ancestry

The modern MG Midget actually took the process of metamorphosis a stage further because it developed out of *another* sports car that had itself come out of the Austin and Morris companies' rag-bag. In the mid-1950s, BMC was headed by a dynamic and adventurous Chairman by the name of Leonard Lord, who is widely disliked and criticised by many motoring historians today, mainly, it would seem because of his working class background and language. Still, though he probably didn't give a damn, he did give the sort of lead that the industry seems to lack today. He also spotted that there was a gap in the market for a light sports car and he appointed the Healey family, who had already designed and developed the 'Big' Austin-Healeys, to develop a 'tiddler' sports car using Austin A30/A35 components. In the event, several Morris Minor bits, including the steering and rear brakes, spilled into the mixing pot along with the MGA-type combined brake and clutch master cylinder

Wind-up window Midgets were virtually identical on the outside, but other changes were developing under the skin.

arrangement, and the car emerged in 1958 as the Austin-Healey Sprite, known to all and sundry as the 'Frogeye' in the UK and 'Bugeye' in the United States.

You can look at the Frogeye today and see nothing whatsoever unconventional about it. But, in 1958 terms, it was actually a little revolutionary! For a start, it was the first ever sports car not to be fitted with a chassis, its strength residing in the rigidity of its floorpan and body panels. Secondly, its rear suspension was adventurous in that its springs were quarter elliptics: that is to say, they were held only at one end like a ruler held over the edge of a school desk. Furthermore, the dynamo doubled as the drive for the tachometer and the one-piece front end had frogeye headlights that gave the car its nickname.

MG Midget Mk I

By 1960, sales had begun to fall and the Frogeye was replaced in 1961. Its replacement was a typical piece of Lord

Hood up, the car looks just as perky while wire wheels do wonders for the sporting image. They're not easy to keep clean and they do need overhauling after a time.

badge-engineering; the MG Midget/Austin-Healey Sprite Mk II. The Frogeye's front end styling was controversial in its day and something more conventional was developed under Sid Enever at Abingdon. The rear end, *sans* boot lid, could also be annoying to those who didn't enjoy going pot-holing behind the rear seats to find that missing tin of baked beans, and so the newly bodied car had a 'proper' boot lid.

To start off with, there was little difference between the Frogeye and the Midget apart from the outer body panels. The Midget had no outside door handles and no wind-up windows, the bucket seats were Sprite-like, as was the dash and the engine, even down to the dynamo/tacho. drive, although the carbs were of the later 'plastic topped' type rather than the 'brass topped' variety and the 948cc engine was a little more powerful. Probably around 16,000 of these cars were built and, in my view, they're likely to become one of the most sought-after Midgets from the collector's point of view in the very long term, when all Midgets are considered ancient pieces of machinery. But how useable are they today? The ultra-stiff quarter elliptic rear springing makes things hard on the bottom on a longish journey and some spares are certainly a little harder to get hold of than those for later cars. On the other hand, for a fun, occasional-use sports car – well, suffice it to say that if anyone has got one that they want to dispose of ...

MG Midget Mk I¹/2

If the E-type Jaguar can have a 'Series I¹/2', we can have a Midget of the same designation! In October 1962, BMC decided to fit the 1098cc A-series engine in keeping with its use in the Morris Minor, the 948cc unit becoming redundant, I believe. The stronger 'ribbed case' gearbox also fitted to the Minor was used by the Midget, giving greatly superior synchromesh from its baulk-ring system when compared with crunch-with-every-change brass cone-type synchro previously fitted. Wire wheels were now offered as an option for the first time and disc brakes were fitted. The interior trim was slightly modified but the bodywork and suspension were left strictly alone. The spartan qualities were most certainly still there but the car was starting to look more 'liveable-with' from the modern point of view, at least as far as the car's mechanical components were concerned. Fortunately, body repair panels are almost all available for these early cars simply because most of them are the same as for the 1275cc engined cars, although it may be necessary to adapt the latch and lock holes found in later cars' door skins and the areas around the A-panels.

Midget Mk II

In March 1964 came the first of what you might call the Thoroughly Modern Midgets. A new 1098cc engine was fitted, very similar to the previous unit but, while the earlier engine was an unchanged Minor engine, except for tuning, the Abingdon magic had got to work on this engine and it was made much stronger and longer lasting with 2 inch main bearings. The two major differences were in the creature comfort departments, however, because wind-up windows replaced the earlier variety, quarter lights were fitted and (such decadence!) external door handles were used. The quarter elliptic springs were dropped in favour of (slightly!) softer half-elliptics and the dashboard was revised, while the steering wheel became similar to the MGB's but with only two spokes instead of three. An interesting point is that red cars were fitted (or maybe only offered) with red hoods, and were the only Midgets and Sprites to be fitted with other than black hoods as standard. Once again, the car can be seen as becoming ever more useable with the passage of time whilst still retaining the charm and interest of 'early' Midgets. Sprites, by the way, had settled into a pattern of being identical to the equivalent Midget except for the lack of external trim and the desirable 'MG' logos, of course. This model of Sprite sold for £20 less than the Midget.

Mk III Midget

In October 1966, the Midget 'Mark' number was updated for the last time, although the model itself was to be updated on several subsequent occasions. The 1275cc engine was fitted for the first time giving, in my opinion, the best power source available to the car from the performance and reliability points of view. At the same time, virtually the only bodywork modification to be made to the car was carried out when the cockpit shape was enlarged at the expense of the rear bulkhead top panel which became narrower and the rear wings were slightly altered at the top. The dash layout was greatly altered and the hood was of a different type that was much easier to put up and take down. For the owner who wishes to use his or her car every day and to *use* the hood, this is the first model of Midget which I would personally recommend. I know you can use earlier cars but that is true of any car – I know of a man who, until recently, travelled the 30 miles from Worcester to Longbridge and back every day in a Vintage Austin, 7, but that sort of feat is a tribute to stamina and determination and not necessarily something to recommend to others!

Over the years a number of other modifications were made, most of them of a minor nature, such as the use of a higher rear axle ratio in late 1968. But the next major changes were made in 1969.

October 1969 Midget

The whole car became more 'civilised' and modernized when twin silencer exhaust systems were used and a black recessed grille fitted, along with rostyle wheels and slimmer bumpers, the rear bumper being split into two halves. In essence, however, the car remained the same Midget as before; only the appeal became different and that is where the break-point between the most 'traditional' and more modern Midgets will probably be made in most people's minds. In practice, there's very little in it!

January 1972 Midget

When the first Midget was designed, Abingdon was given the job of redesigning the

engine was chosen by BL as the unit it could most easily adapt for the emission-conscious US market and, after it was adapted, it was fitted to both the Midget and the Triumph Spitfire. The Midget also received black energy-absorbing bumpers which some found distasteful at first but which I must admit to rather liking on both the Midget and the MGB. The gearbox was also changed for the four-synchro gearbox found in the Marina and all manner of modern 'goodies' were fitted as standard, such as hazard warning lights, and door mirrors. Later modifications were: headrests fitted as standard (January 1977);

The recessed grille 1275cc Midget was, like all the other cars, a big hit in the States and looked terrific with hood down. These are the rostyle wheels mentioned in the text.

rear end, while Healey at Warwick were told to concentrate on the front. For that reason, there was a prototype at Warwick which had a Midget front-end but a Frogeye round-wheel-arch rear. Ironically, the 1972 Midget copied that highly successful rear-end styling. Sadly, later in the decade when crash testing came in, the round wheel arch was found to be weaker that the square wheel arch shape reinstated when the 1275cc Midget was discontinued. Meanwhile, the Austin Sprite, so called from January 1971 when the Healey name was dropped, had been discontinued from June 1971.

Midget 1500

This was the last major face-lift that the Midget was destined to receive. The Triumph 1500

inertia reel seat belts as standard (April 1977); higher rear axle ratio (September 1977) radio console and aerial, 2-speed wipers, cigar lighter and brake failure warning light (April 1978); and dual line brakes (October 1978). In November 1979, BL in their infinite wisdom decided to drop the MG Midget and replace it with – precisely nothing, choosing instead to present a heaven sent opportunity to Reliant, the Japanese and to anyone else to try and build the type of car that had earned Britain millions of pounds in export sales and employed thousands of now-redundant workers. It's a mad world when 'those up there' don't listen to the common-sense views of 'us down here'!

All that's left now for the prospective owner of the best of the small British sports cars is to look for the model of Midget that

This well known BL publicity shot of the 'Rubber Bumper' Midget sought to confirm the car's heritage with the tantalising glimpse of an MG Midget from another era in the background.

If you're buying for restoration, don't buy one as rough as Practical Classics did when they carried out a Midget restoration. They needed everything to be done for the articles it gave them; you don't. The interior only looked scruffy; the bodywork was terrible!

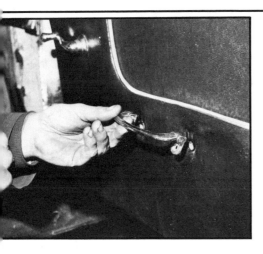

so there's no sense in complaining about the use of a different engine. The 1500 engine doesn't feel as tough as earlier units, it must be admitted and the big ends are a little vulnerable, so owners are strongly recommended to fit an oil cooler and to 'Slick' the engine oil (both available from the Club) to prolong engine life.

You can see that there's really a Midget for almost everyone and which ever one you buy, you'll be preserving another bit of MG history. I feel a bit uneasy mentioning my own books here but Club Secretary Roche Bentley says I should! *MG Midget & Austin Healey Sprite – Guide to Purchase & DIY Restoration* contains 250-odd pages and 700-odd photographs on how to maintain and restore a Midget, whilst *MGB (+ MGC & V8) – Guide to Purchase & DIY Restoration* provides similar information on the MGB; both are published by the Haynes Publishing Group and are available from the Club. Another book I've written for Haynes, *The Car Bodywork Repair Manual* contains around 1,000 pictures in almost 300 pages and shows how to weld, spray, panel beat and use all the tools on jobs from repairing a scratch to replacing a wing. This is also sold by the Club. Another two Haynes Restoration Guides are in print, *Mini – Guide to Purchase & DIY Restoration* and *Morris Minor & 1000 – Guide to Purchase & DIY Restoration* both written by myself and available from bookshops.

"Living with a Midget" first appeared in "Enjoying MG" – the magazine of the MG Owners' Club.

suits him or her best. The time has nowhere near come when all Midgets are regarded as antiques, or collectors' pieces and the majority are still put to very good use indeed. Undeniably the easiest to use would be the latest cars complete with all mod-cons. But if you can't afford one or don't like the Triumph engine (of which more anon), you may want to go for one of the just pre- or post- 1969 1275cc Midgets with many of the modern cars' features. (Well, all right, they've got a heater! But at least they handle and perform well, the hood is easy to use and spares are easy to buy.) The earlier you go from there, the more the cars become suitable for occasional use, although as I said before, there are no doubt thousands of enthusiasts proving me wrong! Now, back to that Triumph engine. I started the article off by saying that MGs have always used a motley collection of mechanical parts,

DRIVE AID

B for Buying

Lindsay Porter picks out the problems to be faced when buying one of the various models within the MGB, MGC and V8 ranges, and points out some of the delights of owning a car that is fast becoming acknowledged as one of the most collectable classics

The shape of the MGB has a clasically acceptable timelessness in my view; which exceeds that of any other car built. If that sounds like one of those statements erected to be knocked down, go ahead and try! The Beetle and Minor have lovable, cuddly shapes but they're undeniably of a bygone era; the Mini is still OK mainly because it's so anodyne, so nothing-in-particular. Even the E-type – well, have you seen a Series I FHC from the rear recently? It looks almost preposterously bulbous on top and hardly supported beneath by its spindly little tyres and narrow track. By contrast the MGB, designed almost three decades ago, still looks attractive from all angles even in an age when Porsches and the Slicka Celica are increasingly taking on the rounded appearance of one-man submarines.

Surprisingly, after all this time the MGB's attractions are not only skin deep. It is certainly true that none of the 1800cc cars accelerate at anything *like* the speed of light (does light accelerate?); their road holding doesn't permit the outrages that bang up-to-date suspension systems will allow (although it could be argued that this makes them safer because the driver is always quite clear as to where the limits lie – by the time you've found out in an Audi Quatro it can be too late!), while the noise and comfort levels are the areas in which the cars are most obviously looking outdated. But even these criticisms don't damage the MGB's greatest attractions of all – it's fun and it's easy to own! Just look around at other cars on the market under £2,000 (and most but by no means all MGBs come into that category) and see what else gives you economical, true-Brit, lazy-engined sports car motoring in a package that allows you to feel as though you are driving briskly at least. At the same time, the MGB is never 'exotic' in the sense of being temperamental or hard to repair or maintain. In fact, the reverse is true and MGBs are capable of being bodged up and abused well beyond the point where lesser motor cars would have given up. This means that we are lucky enough to be

surrounded by MGBs of all years and all types but that some of them – well, that's where the rest of this article comes in!

Definitely *not* Wysiwyg!

What-you-see-is-what-you-get is certainly not a term that could be applied to all MGBs for sale! Structurally, the cars are quite complex and therefore fairly expensive to restore thoroughly, and this means that bodywork will be disguised by the use of fibreglass and filler several times before the inevitable lack of structural strength makes further bodging impossible. Remember that the 'B was designed shortly after the 'Frogeye' Mk I Sprite which was itself the first ever sports car without a chassis. It may be that this makes the MGB the second-ever sports car in the chassis-less category and that accounts for the belt-and-braces way in which the bodywork was designed. The front bulkhead and inner wing areas, which take front suspension loads, are quite massively strong, as are the sills which run behind both front and rear wings. Sill replacement is quite a major exercise and should not be attempted by simply slapping a short cover sill between front and rear wings.

The bulk of the sill's strength lies in its three-section structure: the inner section forms a box which is clearly visible just inside the line of the doors running from front to rear of the cockpit; the outers are only visible between the wings but actually tuck behind each of them, extending some way both forward and aft, while there is yet another section which is invisible without dismantling – a vertical membrane which is slotted between the outer sill and the inner box section. At the rear, the massive over-strength is continued, the inner sill box section running right the way back to the spring mountings. As an aside, it is worth pointing out that this structure, including as it does a very strong cockpit section, seems to give the correct 'crumple zone' effect when the car is involved in a heavy shunt, the passenger compartment staying quite intact even though the front end may be deformed considerably. And in this respect later, post-1975 MGBs are even better than earlier cars because of their compliance with U.S. crash impact regulations.

Wings and things

The fact that replacing the sills is such a major job leads to that area being covered over when cheap repairs are carried out, and the same happens to the corrosion-prone front and rear wings. Rear wings are weld-on and may have been repaired in one of several ways. Perhaps the worst way is to chop the old wing off and to replace it with a complete fibreglass wing that neatly cuts out both corrosion and structural strength at the same time. (And remember that this is a unitary construction car where bodywork plays a major role in shell strength). Next worst is to fill or fibreglass the rotten area which just means that the damage is still festering away beneath the surface and will soon break out in even more virulent form than before. Both of these deficiencies can be totally disguised from the external gaze but feeling the inside of the wing will invariably indicate lumps of filler or the coarse texture of fibreglass, while holding a magnet against the surface of the wing will tell you for sure whether there is steel present because, as every smartipants schoolboy knows, magnets don't 'stick' to filler or fibreglass.

The third worst way of repairing the rear wing is only bad if the person doing the work is not an above average ability panel beater.

The last 1,000 MGBs were made as 'Limited Edition' cars. GTs were finished in Pewter Silver and Tourers were in Bronze. In the long run, they're bound to be worth most of all.

Repair sections are available to repair the whole of the rear wing from the beading down, leaving the top section which virtually never corrodes anyway. The problem is that this section is long and fairly flat and it buckles very easily when welded leaving ripples in the panel. Moreover, if it isn't properly sealed with seam sealer, rust will soon form in the new wing joint. If the repair has been done really well using this type of repair section, there will be nothing to worry about, but confirm by looking along the line of the rear wing beading, catching the light along it and also apply the magnet test there to ensure that the repairer hasn't overcome the problem with masses of filler.

The best way of repairing the rear wing is to replace the whole thing, including the wing top beading which comes attached to the new wing. The beading is formed from thin steel rolled to the shape required and is hollow inside making it prone to corroding and crumbling away. Check that the beading on a car you are thinking of buying is not just made up of filler. Its shape and the fluting along the top should be distinctly visible, although in fact the fluted shape can disappear under an excess of paint, especially where modern high-build primers are over-enthusiastically used. You should also check the fluting between the rear edge of the front wings and the top bulkhead panel.

Other panels susceptible to the filler-corrosion-more-filler cycle are the bottoms of the doors and the bottoms of the front wings, as well as a vertical area half-way between the front wheel arch and the door. First signs of door rust shows itself on the outside at the base, but rust may also be present on the

bottom of the door frame itself, and beneath the trim moulding along the tops of GT doors. The insides of door frames are prone to splitting where the quarter light frame bears up against them, too. All in all, MGB doors are not good news and when badly rotted out, can be expensive to replace. A new door skin won't set you back too much, but the door won't fit as well as it did before unless the work is carried out exceptionally well and you will often find that once the old door skin has been taken off, the frame looks far worse than anticipated.

Bolt-on panel problems

On now to front wings. You'd think the fact that they are bolt-on and nowadays not too expensive (they have actually dropped quite dramatically in price over the last few years) would mean that the condition of front wings was not too important. However, if you have to pay someone to fit new front wings, you may have to be prepared to pay for a whole day of labour for each wing! To say that they can be a swine to fit is to pay them a compliment! I suspect that their quality has dropped along with the price and it is usually necessary to do a lot of fiddling and filing-out of holes before bolts can be got in at all. On top of that, the Roadster's screen has to come out and replacement of the screen as well as replacement of some of the more difficult bolts can each be a pain of the highest order. On the plus side is the fact that the DIY-er doesn't

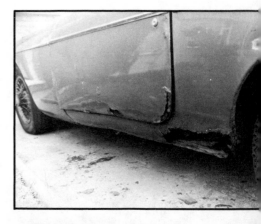

outer wing, however, and if you're tempted to buy such a car, remember that the top of the flitch/inner wing panel, the vertical mud trap and the fronts of the (normally hidden) sills will also require welding for sure and there may be other corrosion besides.

Before leaving the MGB's bodywork, don't forget that virtually every sports car is driven by someone with a sporting frame of mind, naturally, and that this has made the cars more likely to have had a shunt in the past. Carefully examine the inner wings from inside the bonnet for rippling and door gaps on each side for evidence of a major shunt, as well as any other panels at the front or rear, especially the semi-hidden ones where the panel bashings may not have been up to scratch. Check also the bonnet front and the fit

This outer sill, held up by John Hill, shows the true length and strength of the full sill and also the normally hidden inner sill vertical membrane. A collapsed jacking point will tell you that this has corroded internally.

It's good in some ways that MGB wings are bolt-on because at least you don't need welding gear to replace them, but they are time consuming to take off and even worse to replace.

have to pay those high labour bills and as long as he or she is prepared to dedicate the time, front wing replacement is definitely 'on'. Always expect to find rot behind a corroded of the grille for evidence of minor bumps which can nevertheless set you back a bob or two if replacement parts are necessary.

Checking the bits that whizz and roar

Turning now to the car's mechanical areas, you will find once again a large amount of over-engineering; something which enables the 'B to go on and on but which once again can be abused. It is here that you will find the only significant differences between the three different models in the range, the standard 'B, the MGC and the MGB GT V8. Starting at the back once again, and the rear axle: pre-April 1967 Tourers were fitted with a 'banjo'-type rear axle while all other models used the 'tubed'-type. None of them are especially troublesome although earlier axles seem slightly more prone to leaking oil into the brake drums, lousing up the rear brakes and handbrake. However, if the rear axle 'clonks', be prepared to overhaul it, especially when fitted to the MGC or V8. In those cars the axle is under so much more stress than in the 1800cc models and, worse still, their crown wheel and pinions are virtually unobtainable even second-hand. For that reason, only buy a 'C or V8 with a duff diff if you know where you can buy another good differential and if the

B's are prone to sagging rear springs. Check rear suspension height with a ruler ...

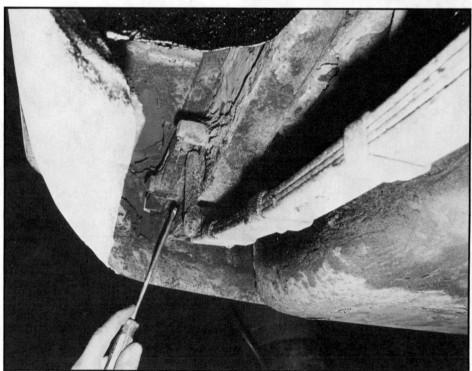

... but be prepared for the worst, which could be a collapsing rear spring hanger. Poke with a screwdriver.

price is rock bottom. On the other side of the coin, don't bother with a V8 conversion on a standard diff no matter how well it has been done, because the low ratio is totally unsuitable for the V8 engine and you will bump into the same problem of non-availability of the correct type.

Clonks are far more likely to be found in the 1800 MGB's drive shafts than in the diff – test them by levering hard with a screwdriver. Early three-synchro gearboxes are usually a bag of nails by now and are prone to wearing in every area imaginable. Later four-synchro boxes are relatively good units but test them for noise in the gears, jumping out on the over-run and ease of selection, not

forgetting reverse gear. Test overdrive for promptness of operation, especially when re-used several times and when worn. Bad electrical contacts (especially on early units) and low oil levels are far more common than severe wear but overhauls can be expensive.

1800cc B-series engines are either loved or hated – and I love them! I prefer any day an engine that gives you bags of torque so that gearchanging is done more often through choice than necessity, together with excellent economy and reliability, rather than a short-lived screamer that can only be driven with the aid of a whirling gearstick. You can check that the oil pressure, when hot, is over the 40psi mark at, say, 3,000 rpm and you must ensure that the water doesn't overheat after a few miles because that is almost certain to indicate a blown gasket and a warped cylinder head. A broken gauge, incidentally,

... while the front suspension, by torsion bar, is radically different from those of the rest of the cars in the MGB range.

The very first V8s were non-Leyland specials made by Costello. Complete with ugly bonnet bulge, a genuine Costello could be a historical find.

isn't a disaster because they can be overhauled by the specialist suppliers, although even that will cost you about the same as a new tyre. Tappet noise is fairly normal for a B-series engine and one completely free of oil leaks is quite unusual but beware of anything excessive in either area. Timing chain noise will necessitate renewal of the chain and adjuster, while an engine that blows smoke out of the exhaust pipe when revved or after a spell downhill on the over-run indicates that the head is ready for overhaul or even that bores are worn. Low down knocking means that the crank is worn out, but that will

certainly be accompanied by low oil pressure when the oil is hot. A full engine overhaul would be an expensive operation and, if you were to have the work carried out for you, engine removal is a fiddly, time consuming and thus expensive job – which is another reason for doing it yourself! Clutch renewal has to follow the same procedure: either the engine has to come out leaving the gearbox *in situ* or, and on balance I'd recommend this approach, the engine and box are removed and replaced together.

In general, V8 and MGC engines should be subjected to the same types of checks, but do remember that the V8 can run happily with lower oil pressures provided that there are no untoward rumbles from the bottom end. In addition, tappet noise from the V8 engine suggests that some fairly major expenditure on the hydraulic tappets will be imminent. Both engines are even less highly stressed than the 1800cc engine, of course, and if looked after could have an even longer potential life span.

Don't forget to check the front suspension very carefully for wear on all models. Replacement kingpins were just not available at all for MGCs until recently and they are quite expensive, but then so are those for the MGB and V8, which both share the same basic arrangement. Check with a stout lever for wear at both top and bottom of each kingpin in each direction.

Mirror, mirror on the wall ...

Whichever MGB is the fairest of them all is very much a matter of taste but there's no

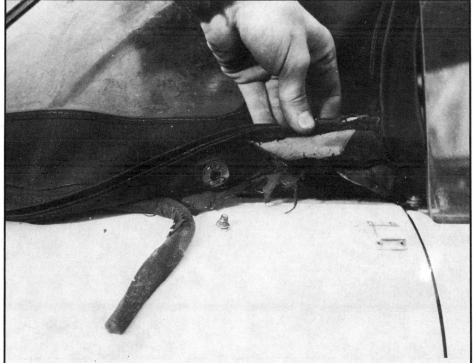

Leather interiors look and feel nice but are less comfortable than the better shaped later seats. Every item of trim can now be purchased from specialists.

Check soft-tops for clouded screens, cuts and for general disintegration. Top quality replacements, made by the original manufacturers, are expensive but cheap ones are probably not worth having.

doubt that any one of them can give sterling everyday service if that is what you want although, naturally enough, the later the car the truer this is and the latest 'rubber bumper' MGBs are certainly the most comfortable, quiet and well equipped of the bunch even if they have lost some of the sporty flavour of the earlier cars in the process. Earlier cars have less robust engines (3-main bearing), gearboxes and rear axles than those from the mid-60s on but the interior layout, leather seats and traditional grille were retained until the end of 1969 making these cars the best of the 'trad' MGBs, perhaps. If you just couldn't stand a rubber bumper 'B but wanted to go for better seats and rather more of the creature comforts with a much better Tourer hood, the '69 to '75 cars would be for you. MGCs are wonderfully 'lazy' cars to drive with a greater turn of speed than is at first apparent, but without neck-snapping acceleration! Even the V8 is not ridiculously fast although it could still be regarded as too fast for standard tyres, suspension that is anything past its peak and a wet road! In good tune, the V8 will give anything from 22 to 35mpg (depending on who is telling the story) but 25-plus would be a fair estimate. Unfortunately, the V8 only ever appeared in the GT bodyshell and that is so noisy at speed that you have to be quite determined to take full advantage of the car's potential.

There's no doubt that 'Bs of all shapes and sizes will continue to appreciate in value simply because there's nothing around to compare with them. But that doesn't mean that any old wreck is worth buying! The cost of restoration is higher than the value of just about any of the cars, unless you take a leaf, or even several leaves, out of my book *MGB – Guide to Purchase and DIY Restoration* and set about doing it yourself, following the approach outlined in this magazine in this and the following few months. And if what you want more than anything else is the greatest of all the 'affordable' sports cars, the MGB is the car for you!

"B for Buying" first appeared in "Sports Car Monthly" magazine.

There are relatively few 'chrome bumper' V8s as they were superseded by 'rubber bumper' models not long after production began.

Mercedes-Benz 300SL

A fascinating profile by the inimitable L.J.K. Setright

Sports cars? Too much sports in some of them, too much car in most. Throughout the several histories of Benz and Daimler and their joint history after amalgamation of 1926 as Daimler-Benz, there had been sports cars of one sort or another. Which sort was usually all too clear: the blend of iron fist and velvet glove, of track and town, even of Mercédès and Benz, was not always as smooth as might have been hoped. Yet it was not the most outright, forthright unexceptional clock-beater of them all – the W196/110, alias 300SLR, of 1955 – which captured the esteem and invited the covetousness of thirty years' worth of motoring enthusiasts, so much as a slightly earlier, much more compromised, if scarcely less successful, car so complex in its character as to invite citation as the most atypical of its age ever to be a sporting and commercial success.

This was the 300SL. It was conceived as a sideline, born as a stopgap, raised as a battlecry and thereafter allowed to mature as a boobytrap. It contained far too many bits from ordinary production saloons for it to be any good as a top-class racer, yet it did better in top-class racing than its pure-bred rivals. It could be driven in top gear at all speeds above 15mph without taking or causing any offence (indeed, it is likely that some surviving examples are so driven); it could run rings around most of its coevals without demanding anything more than a little muscular effort from its driver; but it has also reduced heroes to abject terror when they have gone too far and too deeply in its embrace, only to encounter the venomed fang beyond the tempting lips. It has, in fact, become a byword: it became famous as the Gullwing, once again proving that a little vice adds a lot of appeal to a character, for the drophead coupé version which eventually grew from it was altogether less vicious, necessarily conventional in its door arrangements, and much less memorable.

Had the 300SL never got that far – had it merely been built as a set of ten factory-owned racers to put Daimler-Benz back in, and on top of, racing in 1952, rather than going on to a production history of 1400 fund-drainers – it would still have been deservedly memorable. It had the first true spaceframe, the first true gullwing doors, the first production-line petrol injection, it essayed the first 'movable aerodynamic device' (to use the parlance of later racing regu-

lations), and just to make it really memorable it did not have the first low-pivot swinging half-axles!

The most important thing it had was Rudlolf Uhlenhaut as its designer. While still a young man, and while the ageing Hans Niebel was completing his life task in setting the high standards for which Mercedes-Benz engineering became renowned, Uhlenhaut was appointed racing service manager in recognition of his talents and in time for him to exploit them in the Grand Prix seasons run under the 750kg formula of 1933-1937. He grew scarcely less famous, and no less respected, than any of the stars who raced in his cars; in time for the resurrection of Daimler-Benz (it had ceased to exist, declared its directors, in 1945) after the World War, Uhlenhaut had his talents recognized again in due measure when he was appointed chief designer.

The fact that he had become Niebel's successor did not entitle him to design anything he liked. Times were hard, and real rehabilitation could only begin after the

currency reforms of 1948. His directors were wise enough to allow him a little latitude, however, a little scope for playing with ideas that would keep the exploratory modes of his formidable brain fit for a more expansive future. So he kept his hand in, during those years of austerity, with a series of design exercises; and it was as much in hope of a less utilitarian future as in memory of a fabulous past that the object of one of these was a sports-racing coupé.

Then, in the autumn of 1951, the directors decided that it was time for Daimler-Benz to return to racing. Because they were Daimler-Benz, they would have to be very strongly competitive, if not altogether overpowering: any attempt that was less serious would have been condemned by the world at large as being out of character. The deadline, the date by which a pridefully proper Mercedes-Benz standard-raiser would have to be ready for battle, was to be 4 May 1952, the date of the next Mille Miglia.

It was ready. Uhlenhaut took his design

study and turned it into a winner. It was entered in none of the mean and trifling events of the 1952 sports-racing season, only the important races in which it would have to bear the world's scrutiny. Only once did it fail to win, and that was surely pardonable on its first time out, considering that it finished second and third in the Mille Miglia behind the winning 3-litre Ferrari of Bracco. Clocking this, the fastest, circuit took longer than a circuit of the clock, so the 272 seconds by which he beat the 300SL of Karl Kling represented but a paltry 0.63%; and then in fourth place came veteran Rudolf Caracciola, at that time the only foreigner to have won Italy's great race in a foreign car (he did so in 1931 – in a Mercedes-Benz, of course) in another 300SL. A fortnight later, Carracciola had a nasty crash which finally ended his wonderful motor-racing career. The cars that were left, the SLs of Kling, Hermann Lang (another, perhaps *the* other, prewar star) and Fritz Riess, finished first, second, and third in the sports-car Grand Prix de Berne, run over the very fast and curvaceous Bremgarten circuit.

Another fortnight, another race. It was a race like no other, for this was the Grand Prix des 24h d'Endurance du Mans. Daimler-Benz fielded three 300SLs to be driven by Lang with Riess, Helfrich with Niedermayer, and Kling with Klenk. They even brought to practice a 300SL with an experimental airbrake, an hydraulically erected airfoil above the roof; not until three years later, at the same circuit, would we see its like again – on a Mercedes-Benz, of course. In the 1952 race, instead of looking like 'planes, the Mercs ran like trains: the Kling/Klenk car went out with a dynamo failure (no works-entered 300SL ever failed in a race through mechanical troubles) but the Lang/Reiss car won at a record 96.6mph, followed in second place by Helfrich and Niedermayer.

It could be said that Mercedes-Benz had won Le Mans a month earlier in the Mille Miglia. The sheer speed of the 300SL on the long Italian straights shook the Jaguar team rigid: urgent messages were sent back to Coventry even before the race was over, demanding that something be done to restore competitive speed to the C-type Jaguar that had so proudly won at Le Mans in 1951. Frantic redesign of the bodywork to reduce aerodynamic drag entrained serious cooling problems; the Jaguars did not last the French course. The 300SL had them beaten before they started.

If the speed of the gullwing coupé was a revelation, its agility (given the right drivers and, as we shall see, the right preparation) cannot have been too bad. The season held another sports-car Grand Prix of note at the Nurburgring, which was in those days no place for any car that might be wanting in the steering or stopping departments. The 300SL team finished 1-2-3-4, and one might think that was all that need be said; but somebody at the factory, strangely convinced that the 300SL

was lacking in the engine department, prepared a supercharged version (the 300SLK – K for *Kompressor*) for this race. The engine did not take kindly to this imposition on its thermal generosity, and overheated itself strenuously enough to put a stop to that particular line of development (and also, incidentally, the short-wheelbase chassis that went with it) safely before the day of the race.

There remained one more odd variant to be fielded before the season's racing was brought to a triumphal conclusion. As keen as any European manufacturer in pursuit of the US dollar. Daimler-Benz entered a 300SL team in the Carrera Panamericana Mexico. In addition to three familiar gullwing coupés they confected an open two-seater for the lanky American driver John Fitch. Kling and Klenk won the race, at over 102mph, with Lang second; but the K/K car was also modified before the race was over. In a sense it too had been made an open car: the windscreen had been smashed, and a grid of steel bars worthy of a jailhouse was hastily rigged in front of the hole. Somewhere in the wastes of Guatemala, it transpired, some four-footed creature had passed away and, not wishing to pass unnoticed, had done so in the middle of the road. The neighbourhood vultures, not at all put out, dropped in for the customary feast, but one of them was a bit dilatory in getting airborne again when the SL coupé intruded upon the party at around 130mph. The hapless bird came straight through the windscreen, and the impact knocked Hans Klenk unconscious. By a convenient circumstance, it was Karl Kling who was driving at the time: maybe the vulture's *kamikaze* intentions had been frustrated by seeing too many other transatlantic cars, but the fact was that all examples of the 300SL were left-hand-drive. With the engine offset as it was they could not be built any other way.

How was it built, then, this sudden masterful arrival on the quickening motorsport scene? Firstly, remembering how short was its gestation, it was built quickly; secondly, remembering its impeccable reliability, it was built skillfully; thirdly, considering how everybody raved about its appearance (even when, as looked least natural to it, it was standing still) it was built beautifully; and fourthly, looking at the design features which have yet to find an authentic echo, it was built like nothing else. Everyone who raved about its streamlined two-seater body with the gullwing doors recognized at once how they promised ease of entry and exit in a narrow garage or parking slot, or the means of a glamorous arrival at some gathering of the élite; only later did people debate the accompanying threat of imprisonment after a roll-over accident. Those doors were so designed for a good reason: the sill height imposed by the lateral trusses of the car's unique spaceframe chassis made conventional doors quite impractical.

There were in 1952 two cars which pioneered the true spaceframe, that properly triangulated structure of slender tubes subjected only to axial loads and giving the car a foundation of exceptional lightness and rigidity. The other was young Colin Chapman's Lotus 5, which was no more a production car than the Mercedes-Benz factory racer. Compared with that of the Lotus, the structure of the 300SL was much more complex and a little nearer perfect. The welded lattice of square-section steel tubes, dozens of them, located all the major components, accepted and distributed all the loads they imposed, and withal weighed only 181 lb – about 55lb less than a full load of fuel. It was a most elegant structure, especially around the sides where other designers had always capitulated into dependence on sheer mass of metal to hold the front and rear sections together. The triangulated trusses around the sides of the cockpit preserved the torsional stiffness of the chassis, its beam stiffness, and its lightness.

There was rather of weight of iron in the engine, though, and rather a dearth of novelty. It was not much more or less than the in-line six-cylinder affair taken from the type 300 saloon, tilted 40° on its left side to lower both the bonnet line and the centre of gravity, and tuned by conventional methods. It was already a high-performance engine by current production standards: it propelled the elegant and comfortable six-seat saloon, which had made its debut at the 1951 Frankfurt motor show, at 100mph. Being an in-line six, and especially because it had seven main bearings rather than four (which would have been cleverer but more difficult). It was prey to the dreaded three-per-revolution prod pattern which makes torsional flutter a crankshaft designer's nightmare. Sticking a damper on the nose of the shaft allowed the output of this touring engine with its single overhead camshaft to be raised from 115 to 125bhp; for the 300S two-seater roadster of 1952 a higher compression ratio and three downdraught carburettors raised this to 150bhp. As installed in the 300SL for the races of 1952, with an 8:1 compression ratio and a trio of downdraught Solex carburettors from whose throats the mixture simply fell into the ports of the tilted engine, the engine yielded 175bhp at 5200rev/min, with another 10bhp being found by the end of the season.

That represented a brake mean effective pressure of 154lbf/in², which may be rated as scarcely better than respectable by the standards of the time. But then, the 300 engine did not even have a crossflow cylinder head, which certainly made it no easier to route the exhausts away under the bonnet. It had a curious head indeed, the joint face of which was as flat as that of an Heron type today but was clamped at an angle of 18° onto the correspondingly slanted top surface of the cylinder block. This arrangement left a lopsided wedge of combustion space at the top of each bore, the shape being modified by sculpting of the block and moulding of the piston crown. Bosses for the spark plugs were set in the top of the block, leaving plenty of room for two large valves to stand in line and parallel in the head and accept rocker operation from the chain-driven camshaft up above. It was a curious engine, then, but it worked pretty well, and it kept on doing so for ages on end. That iron block had a lot of integrity – and it did not have quite so much iron as in the 300, for where the flanks did not have much to do (designing and casting iron blocks was not a very precise business in those days) holes were cut, to be sealed by thin steel plates which could readily be removed for inspection of the the interior. There were also passages whereby cooling water could be carried right down to the vicinity of the main bearings; and at the bottom of it all was a suitably angled sump to match the 40° tilt of the block.

This, such as it was, sufficed to propel a fully enclosed two-seater at speeds so high as to reduce Jaguar, champions at Le Mans a year earlier, to a state of shock. The obvious deduction is that the smooth-flanked and curvilinear fully-enclosed bodywork was impressively efficient in air penetration. It was pretty good, certainly, but it was not quite fully enclosed enough. There still had to be, and was, a hole in the front for cooling air to reach the heat exchanger; but after passing through that, where could it go? Doomed to buffet about under the bonnet, the cooling air accounted for far too large a proportion of the car's total aerodynamic drag.

When the 300SL next made a significant showing, its appearance had changed in the course of aerodynamic improvements. The new look was paraded, albeit in a half-baked state that was to undergo some revision pretty soon, before the directors at about the turn of the years 1953/4. The intervening time had been devoted, at their behest, to other more pressing things, such as the preparation of the 1954 Grand Prix single-seaters and the company's most modern production car, the new type 220a; but Uhlenhaut had not wanted the 300SL to go to waste, and had pursued his ideas for its development to the point where he had a pre-production prototype to show to the Board. They must have been impressed, for in February 1954 it was shown to the New World at the New York Auto Show, where everybody was very impressed indeed.

If the directors had expected, or even hoped, that the gullwing coupé would be dismissed as nothing more than a dream car or a publicity catcher, they were soon forced to think again. American dealers, led by one Max Hoffman '(perhaps the most prominent east coast importer of European cars) bombarded Daimler-Benz with demands for the car to be catalogued and to carry on in the showrooms what it had started on the Show floor. They won, and in a matter of months the 300SL was on sale to the public.

What had been done to relieve the underbonnet pressure was to provide an exit path through large coarse-grilled apertures in each flank, behind the front wheel arches. The prototype had similar vents behind the rear wheel arches too, but airflow around all the wheels was tidied in the production car by long horizontal strakes above and behind the arches. The forward vent was relocated to suit, the aft vent was deleted, and the net effect was to lend emphasis to the car's length and look of speed: the slabsided heaviness of the works-racer jowls had been beautifully relieved. Much more dubious was the restyling of the nose: the purity of the original elliptical air intake was lost in a more angular display of brightwork and bumper, both presumably demanded by America.

All the other concessions to the private car market were welcome in the production SL. The trim, the surface finish, the facia detail, the hinged steering wheel (for easing entry and exit, not for reach or height adjustment) and the contours of the seats all attracted praise; but none of it was as fulsome as what came gushing forth in exaltation of the car's engineering and exultation in its performance.

Amazing things had happened to the machinery. In a dazzling refutation of conventional behaviour patterns in the motor industry, the production car had been made more powerful than the racer, by more than 16%! Eighteen years after they had led the world with direct petrol injection in production aero engines, Daimler-Benz had done it again for the production car. Those blockborne plug bosses had been shifted to the cylinder head, their places being taken by a row of injector nozzles all served by a high-pressure Bosch jerk pump. There were people who feared the complexities of injection, but as a matter of course it proved to be eminently reliable and easy to maintain. There were actually only two adjustments, to idling speed and mixture strength, and both could be done with the edge of a small coin. True, small coins might not figure in the lives of such wealthy men as could afford a 300SL, but the mechanical equivalent could always be sought in the comprehensive toolkit.

The injection apparatus allowed some strange side-effects, the oddest of which was more like a reverse-effect. Switching off the engine at any speed above idle was strongly discouraged, as was switching it off immediately after a bout of high-speed, high-load operation; ignoring this warning could result in the engine bouncing itself backwards into a flurry of counter-rotational running-on (would that, in other words, be running-off?) such as had hitherto been the unique idiosyncrasy of the Scott two-stroke motorcycle engine – which earlier device could, to give it its due, accomplish the reversal at idle without being switched off! Stuttgart's recommended remedy (mark that well – no Scott owner would ever have been so daft as to enquire at Shipley!) was to engage a gear and let the clutch in against the brakes.

For what boons it brought, injection would have been worth far more trouble. A fair bit of trouble was taken over the installation, as may be imagined, but all the little alterations fitted most neatly together. For instance, the new inlet manifolding required more space if the tracts were to be as long as they now should; this meant tilting the engine over by another ten degrees (at 50° slant, the cylinder were now more nearly horizontal than vertical), but that meant an even lower centre of gravity, which was fine. It also meant a new sump, but the lubrication system was being revised to a dry-sump system anyway, so the job would still have had to be done. As for the two inches of offset of the crankshaft to the right of the car's centreline, that was splendid in making more room for all the driver's pedals and feet, at no real cost to his passenger who would still have ample room for straining against the floorboards in times of stress.

Compared with these details, the great thing about injection was that by ridding the inlet tracts (now equalised at 17 inches length, for optimum induction-boosting resonance) of venturis and similar structures, it allowed the engine to breathe much more freely. This was exploited by very large valves (of austenitic steel), the exhaust 41mm in diameter and the sodium-cooled inlet no less than 49mm, a very healthy proportion of the 85mm cylinder bore. Dual concentric valve springs and a bigger better torsional damper allowed the engine to run up to much higher rotational rates, thus piling on even more power, the bhp tally rising to 215. Under such impulsion, and with comfortable gearing wrapped around the ZF limited-slip differential in the final drive, this 2600lb roadburner could romp through its four synchronized gears (the gearbox was built in unit with the engine, but had its own integral oil pump) from standstill to reach 60mph in 7.75 seconds, a quarter-mile in 16, 100mph in 17.75 seconds, and so on up to a maximum speed of about 140mph. Much more could, however, be made available.

All the customer had to do was to be willing and able to empty some very deep pockets. In return he could be furnished with a whole host of options, and while some of these were meant to bring comfort to the eyes, ears, or bottom (non-silver paint, radio, leather upholstery), most were meant to raise the car's performance potential. There was a lightweight aluminium body, for instance (and why not, since that elegant spaceframe carried all the significant stress?) which pruned a good 350lb off the total mass. There were centre-lock wheels, and non-standard gear ratios. Then – or, as was more usually the case, first – there was the competition camshaft. Its timing was still not outrageous (20°/58°/56°/18°) but it was wider and had more overlap than the standard cams, and it also gave the valves much more lift. With so much more area under the lift/time curve, the engine's volumetric efficiency rocketed, as did the power curve – to 240bhp at 6100rpm.

A peak-power b.m.e.p. of 170lb/in² was very respectable indeed. So was the speed of the car in this form. Geared to give, at 6000rpm in each successive ratio, 47mph in bottom gear, 79 in second, 116 in third and 149 in top, a good 300SL could reach 166mph. That meant about 6800rpm, which in turn meant a mean piston velocity that, at 3927ft/min, came within jeering distance of the 4000 figure which most designers regarded as the dizzy limit. Not that it was likely to be reached often, nor sustained for long; the best of drum brakes – and those in the 300SL were girt with copious lateral finning, shod in front with twin leading shoes, aided by an Ate servo, measured 10$\frac{1}{4}$ inches in diameter and were no less than 3$\frac{1}{2}$ inches wide – were not really up to that sort of thing.

Neither was the gullwing's handling. To be faced with the need for sudden avoiding-action when travelling at such high speeds as came so readily within the provenance of the 300SL, and to realise that whatever the combination of speed and trajectory one must not lift off the accelerator pedal until a ruler-straight course has been resumed, is a circumstance almost guaranteed to induce chronic impairment of the zeal. Alas, unless your exercise of options included the competition springs and dampers, which so stiffened the wheel rates that actual wheel motion was usefully reduced, the gullwing simply had to be running straight when the power was eased. If it were not, the probable consequence would be a vast and incorrigible spin.

Uhlenhaut really should not have put swinging half-axle rear suspension into the 300SL for public consumption – unless consuming some of the public was the intention. In truth, he almost certainly did not want to: he knew better than anyone, from the lessons learned with the ill-mannered GP Mercedes-Benz cars of 1934-1936, how many and various were the vices in the system's repertory. In 1937 the cars his team's aces drove to dominate the season, while swinging half-axles drove the Auto-Union rivals to distraction or worse, had revived the elegant De Dion rear suspension. Alas, the original notion behind the 300SL was that it should be composed of existing hardware: Mercedes-Benz saloons were built for comfort rather than agility, and fully independent rear suspension was demanded. What cheaper or sturdier way was there than the swinging half-axle, a type of suspension that had proved itself effective on the terribly rough roads of the Tatra Mountains where Joseph Ledwinka had made it work well enough for Porsche and others to pinch it?

For low-speed comfort on rough and steeply cambered roads, the system was very good. For conferring stability and road-holding on fast cars, it was very bad: such things were not then understood, but it imposed a very high rear roll centre, superimposed severe variations in wheel camber, and was often so located by radius arms as to define a conical path of wheel travel which introduced variations in toe-in as well. Add the notorious 'jacking effect' which prompted the outer wheel to tuck under and roll the car when cornered hard, and the system should have been the last thing to be allowed within sight of a high-performance

car, or even of a VW Beetle on a wet roundabout. However, in the 1930s most people did not know these things, and even in the 1950s most commercial directors would not be told them. Of course, the 300SL was perfectly sound in its road-holding and handling: look how well it had done in the races of 1952. And, of course, the production car must have softer springs. And what was all this technical blather about a roll axis being too steeply inclined upwards from ground level between the paired wishbones at the front to somewhere up above hub level at the rear? Strictly for mechanics, that sort of jargon!

We know that Uhlenhaut knew better. The evidence is there, plain to see in the new system with a single low pivot which made its first appearance in the brand new 220a chassis at the beginning of 1954. That was before the 300SL went into production; so was the dazzling debut of the revolutionary W196 GP Mercedes-Benz at the French Grand Prix, and that car had low-pivot half-axles too, even though the details (like everything else about the machine) were very different. The principle could have been applied to the 300SL, if the directors had been prepared to wait for their dollars; but it was not. Accordingly, steering by throttle, braking into a corner, and most of the other arts applied by a skilful driver through accelerator or steering wheel, were emphatically not to be cultivated in a gullwing SL being driven fast. The only way through a corner was to finish all braking on the previous straight approach and then go through with the throttle progressively opened, so that the natural inertial response of tail-squat would keep the rear roll centre down and the wheels' camber negative. So long as the approach to the corner was straight, and so long as you knew and recognized the corner, all was well. Otherwise ...

The low-pivot system would come. There was a Mercedes-Benz tradition that the touring car of today produced the racing car of tomorrow, and the 220a's rear suspension would surely follow that trend. The 300SL already embodied an earlier example of the tradition: longitudinal compliance had been a feature of high-performance Mercs since about 1930 and after the advent of independent front suspension a beautifully engineered arrangement of pivoting wishbone assemblies, exquisite in their steering geometry, had been devised to endow the 500K and 540K sporting tourers of the mid-1930s with compliance. Radial-ply tyres had not come on the scene, but racing bias-ply tyres had similar cord angles to a radial's belt, and the GP Mercs inherited the compliance system of the tourers. Indeed, the 300SL inherited the same arrangement in turn, via the type 300 saloon; but think of the irony of the situation in which the vapid and feeble 190SL roadster, vaguely styled in emulation of the nobly ferocious gullwing 300SL and generally despised as a gutless wonder, should have a

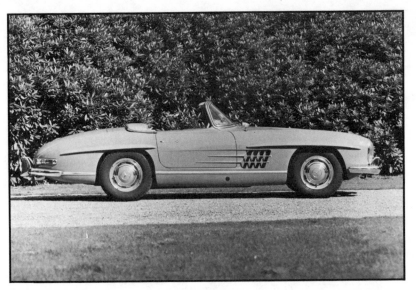

Later, from 1957, the 300SL Roadsters were built with conventional doors. This one hails from 1962, the last-but-one year of production. (Courtesy National Motor Museum, Beaulieu.)

Famed for its extremely high top speed the 300SL may have been but this one was seen enjoying Prescott in May 1958. (Courtesy National Motor Museum, Beaulieu.)

chassis derived largely from the 180 and 220a with the rear suspension of the latter!

When the factory's racing team were in Italy practising for the 1955 Mille Miglia, most of the drivers used the 190SL for familiarisation with that memory-daunting route. The car mustered only 105bhp, so that the top speed in each gear was successively 29,50,79mph and whatever you could get after a suitably long wait in top. Hardly the sort of performance, one might have thought, for growing used to corners appearing at racing speeds all the way across Italy. On the other hand, the car had inherently safer handling: the time to drive the 300SL over the route would be when the driver knew it.

Most of those drivers were entered in 300SLR sports-racing two-seaters, those wickedly clever 3-litre adaptations of the 2½-litre Grand Prix single-seater. That was the year of the most famous victory, when Moss and Jenkinson won in record time and style for Mercedes-Benz, two hours faster than Bracco's time three years earlier. Somehow, hardly anybody noticed that the touring category was won, at an 86.18mph pace that gained it fifth place overall, by a privately entered production 300SL driven by that American friend of long standing, John Fitch. Two other SLs came seventh and tenth; the following year, the gullwings would once again win the class, taking 6th, 7th, 8th and 10th places in the general classification. There was no more Grand Prix racing, no more official racing of any sort by the factory; the memory of the disaster at Le Mans in 1955 was ineradicable. Instead, the firm turned to rallying, and in this new field the 300SL shone. It won the Sestrières, Acropolis and Iberian rallies, and best of all it won the Marathon de la Route, the exhausting Liège-Rome-Liège rally, in the hand of Mairesse and Genin. In a 300SL, Schock and Moll became European Rally Champions.

Thereafter the successes tapered off, as was only to be expected, but the cars continued to do decently in lower levels of

competition for years to come, always privately entered and driven. In the end it might be nothing more arduous than a *concours d'élégance* in California, but in its own way that too can represent quite a challenge.

Perhaps that is as it should be. After all, the Americans always exercised the most influence on the looks and fates (and, to some extent, the specifications) of the production Mercs. It was to satisfy their cravings that an open (for which you may read 'drophead' or even 'roadster' according to your predilections) version of the 300SL was eventually produced – and at long last those accursed swing axles were discarded.

The drophead could not have gullwing doors, that was clear. It followed that it could not have those elegant trusses where ordinary doors might open; so when the spaceframe was pruned away to allow the passage of American legs, the lost structural stiffness had to be restored by new bracing tubes rising from the transmission tunnel back to the trelliswork above the final drive casing. In fact, the whole chassis frame had to be revised, and in that case there was not the slightest objection to adopting the low-pivot rear suspension. This was done; the car was cured; and the effect was generally overlooked.

What people did notice was the increased abundance of brightwork on the body, the subtle assumption of stylistic features from other cars in the Mercedes-Benz range, such as might eventually lead to the 230SL of 1963. Buyers may not even have noticed that in the drophead version the high-performance camshaft was standard!

With its revised suspension, the car could better deploy the power. The rear roll centre was now at the central pivot point, some inches below hub level. The roll axis was now more nearly horizontal. It followed that camber variations and oversteering tendencies should be less troublesome, but the latter were reduced further by means of the ingenious central auxiliary spring scissored between two arms projecting above the axle-halves. This was arranged so that the effective spring rate in bump was higher than in roll: in other words, the roll stiffness of the rear suspension had been reduced, which is tantamount to playing games with torsion bars to alter a car's roll couple distribution. The difference is that in the Mercedes the supplementary spring was damped in action, whereas anti-roll torsion bars seldom are; certainly the one at the front of the SL was not. Who cared? The car was glamorous. It was easy to drive, given a bit of strength at the pedal and behind the wheel, so high-geared at 1.7 turns between locks and yet so smooth. The secret was a damper on the central piece of the three-part trackrod, and a recirculating-ball steering box; but, really, who cared? It was a car to clean and polish and drive slowly in the sun with the roof and windows down and your popular esteem sky-high. It was no longer a car in which to race for international honours; it was past that. It was a car in which to show off.

And quite right too. In later years, when the once-proud driver has been withered by the sun and humbled by the calendar, when mature judgement has supplanted youthful fervour, then it will be time enough to drive the 300SL as it was surely meant to be driven. Thirty years ago, when the machine was newly on the market, it was a very, very fast car. Today it is still a very fast car. Tomorrow should not be too late.

This article first appeared in "The Car". It was revised for this book.

Porsche Portrait

In the beginning there was a sawmill in Austria, a family name, and a deep knowledge of cars. From this there came the Porsche 356, the model that made the company famous. Mike McCarthy reports.

The number '356' is hardly memorable. It doesn't roll of the tongue, it doesn't sound poetic, it could be the most anonymous number you could think of between 1 and 1000. Yet to motoring enthusiasts generally, and Porscheophiles in particular, those three digits have a very special significance. They were applied to one of the greatest sports cars the world has ever seen.

Its origins are quite prosaic. It simply meant Porsche project Type 356, a design for a small, light tourer based on VW Beetle mechanics. But it was the culmination of the lifetime's work of one man, a genius called Ferdinand Porsche, who would not live to see the 356 and its successors cover themselves with glory.

After the war the Porsche works at Gmünd had taken on any and every job they could, first under Ferdinand's daughter, Louise Piëch, then under his son Ferry.

By 1947 however, the company had grown, and an idea that had been brooding at the back of Ferry's mind became more concrete: Porsche would build their own car, bearing their own name. On June 11, 1947, project Type 356 was officially born.

Not unnaturally, proprietary parts had to be used – the company was too small to invest in tooling to manufacture such costly items as engines, transmissions and suspension. And, since the car they knew best (more than anyone else in fact, for had they not designed and developed it?) had miraculously, and against all predictions, gone into production, it was only natural that it would form the basis of the Porsche – it was, of course, the VW Beetle.

The first prototype was very much a one-off. It was a three (abreast) seater, open, with a space-frame chassis and – uniquely – a mid-engine configuration, with the power unit between cockpit and back axle. This was a modified VW air-cooled flat-four with bigger valves and ports and a daringly high (considering octane ratings of the day) compression ratio of 7.0:1 to give between 35 and 40bhp, a vast increase on the standard offering of 25bhp. VW independent suspension, by torsion bars all round, was fitted, as was a standard VW gearbox turned back to front. Covering all the mechanics was a very

The Stuttgart-built coupe of 1950 had a form that continued right up to the 1955 model year. The two-piece windscreen was curved at the outer edges but flat in the centre.

sleek aluminium body, with minimal ornamentation or excrescences, designed by a name famous in Porsche folklore, Erwin Kommenda. Across the nose the name Porsche was spelt out in distinctive, square lettering of a form that is still with us.

Concurrent with the original prototype, another was being constructed which was in fact the definitive 356. It was a coupé, and it differed radically from the open car. For a start, the engine was in the normal VW position, overhung behind the rear axle. Then the chassis was constructed of sheet steel fabrications, not tubes. And it was, of course, a hard top, visually almost identical from the waist down to the open car. Kommenda's shape was, once again, utterly smooth, full of wide radius curves, with nary a straight line in sight. Today such curves are accepted as the norm for good aerodynamics (cf the Audi 100/200 and the Ford Sierra): in the late forties opinions varied from ugly to sensational, but there was no doubting the shape's effectiveness. In what must have been one of the first experiments in aerodynamics, wool tufts were attached to Porsche's demonstrator to check airflow, with very satisfactory results.

From these unlikely beginnings, a legend would grow. The 356 is not one but a multitude of models, some, such as the Speedster and Carrera, so different as to be regarded as unique in their own right, and requiring separate treatment. Throughout its 18-year lifespan the 356 underwent a continuous, constant, bewildering process of development, refinement and proliferation, recounted under 'Production history'.

There were concrete constants. The name, the basic configuration with an air-cooled flat four in the tail, independent torsion-bar suspension, efficient streamlined bodywork. Then there were the less concrete constants. The insistence on superb quality: a performance out of all proportion to engine capacity; cost – they were never cheap in the sense that the Austin Healey or Triumph TR2 were, particularly in the UK; Porsche's determination to go its own way and not just follow fashion; but, above all, perhaps, was the 356's addictiveness. Speak to a 356 aficionado and he will brook no criticisms. Quirky handling? Never! All other cars are boring by comparison.

Few who have ever driven a 356 in anything like reasonable condition can come away unimpressed. For a fifties car it hides its age remarkably. The steering is light, direct, and *so* responsive. The ride is astonishing. The feeling of tautness, of rigidity, even in the open models, is outstanding. Here is a highly civilised, highly enjoyable, jewel of a machine, quite unlike anything else of its own period or any other.

If there is one facet of the car which creates more controversy than any other (looks apart) it is the handling *in extremis*. Primitive swing axles at the rear plus an engine in the tail add up to oversteer, no matter how you look at it (which is why, in later models, Porsche kept adding understeer to the chagrin of enthusiasts). There is even a phrase used by Porscheophiles to describe the handling of the early cars: *'wischen'*, the German for wiping, a graphic description of the car's cornering attitudes. It was counteracted by *'sägen'*, or sawing, which is what the driver had to do to stop ends swapping. If you did overstep the mark you performed what Denis Jenkinson, and arch-enthusiast if ever there was one, calls the 'ground-level flick-roll', to the detriment of car and driver. The world, though, is divided into two species: those who revelled in such antics (flick-roll apart!) and those who were frightened by it. What the latter didn't realise was that the speeds at which the 356 became 'uncontrollable' were usually considerably higher than those at which more conventional machines would long since have exited stage left! *Wischen* then just hopin' was *not* the way to conduct a 356.

It is said 'they don't make them like that any more'. Offically, the 356 disappeared in 1965 – but is not the 911 Turbo, one of the ultimate Supercars of today, a genealogical descendent of that little alloy-bodied coupé that first saw light of day in 1948?

Production History

Between 1948 and 1951 official records show that 51 Type 356s were sold from Gmünd, though more than this were actually made. They consisted of coupés and cabriolets, with

VW engines of either the standard 1131cc capacity or with reduced bores to give 1086cc and thus allow the cars to enter the 1100cc capacity classes in competiton. Distinguishing features include the all-aluminium bodies, flat two-piece screens with curved quarter lights in the doors on the coupés and – from 1949 on – a special cylinder head. Cabriolets (convertibles) were made both at Gmünd and by Beutler in Switzerland. Of all the production road-going Porsches, these original Gmünd cars are the rarest and, like the alloy-bodied XK120s, have a mystique unto themselves.

Few survive, and are worth a small fortune.

Gmünd, though, was an out-of-the-way place, and Porsche's roots were in Stuttgart. A return was always envisaged, and became imperative in 1949 and 1950. However, the Americans were occupying the Zuffenhausen site, so a return there was temporarily out of the question. Then Porsche killed two birds with one stone: since the most time-consuming part of car construction was the bodywork, they contracted for an old-established German coachbuilder, Reutter, to make the bodies for them. And, to assemble the cars, they hired their floor space.

Easter 1950 saw the first German-built Porsche completed, a light grey coupé nicknamed *'Windhund'* or greyhound. With the move to Stuttgart, the opportunity was taken to refine the 356, a process that was to continue almost non-stop until it went out of production. The major change was the use of steel for the body, this being both cheaper and easier to manipulate. Styling was modified, too; the edges of the windscreen panes now wrapped around, thus doing away with the distinctive Gmünd quarter lights. Both nose and roof were slightly altered and there were minor trim revisions. The power unit was the standard 1086cc, 40bhp flat four, which would be an option until 1954.

Hydraulic brakes and tubular shock absorbers – and the 1300 (actually 1283cc) engine arrived in 1951. This was made possible by Mahle, the piston people, who had perfected a way of coating aluminium with chrome to give a hard wearing surface. This material was used for the 1300's cylinders, thus not only allowing an increase in bore but also providing better cooling. Power went up to 44bhp, and refinement was improved.

By this time, of course, Porsches were beginning to be seen regularly in competition, both on road and track, usually taking their class. To prove the 1300, three were entered for a strange event in June 1951, the Baden-Baden Rally. This was nothing more than a high-speed blind between Munich and Stuttgart, and, running on Porsche's experimental plates to ovecome the American-imposed 50mph speed limit (sound familiar?), they averaged 75mph for 30 hours, recording a fuel consumption of 24mpg. The best 'lap' was covered at 85.4mph, and one car was timed at 96.3mph. And by August 1951 the 1000th German-built Porsche rolled off the line.

That same year saw some more Porsche milestones. In October three cars, two coupés and a cabriolet, were displayed on Connaught Engineering's stand at Earls Court, their first appearance in the UK. The general consensus was that they were good but pricey. It wouldn't be until 1954 that AFN Ltd would import Porsches seriously. In America, too, sales began, prodded on by the entrepreneur *par excellence,* Max Hoffman, in spite of the fact that these tiny cars cost the same as a Cadillac convertible!

But probably the most significant event was the appearance of a singleton entry by the French importer, Auguste Veuillet, at Le Mans. It was a modified Gmünd coupé, with full wheel spats and increased tankage. It finished 20th overall and won its class, thus recording the first success at a race which, in the seventies and eighties, Porsche could almost call their own.

A Roller-Bearing Crankshaft

However, as early as 1950 it had become obvious to the Porsche management that yet more performance was required, and an

Porsches galore on the starting grid with, far right, a 356A.

increase in engine capacity was the logical step. The use of Mahle aluminium cylinders allowed an increase in bore, but the proximity of the camshaft to the crankshaft, believe it or not, prevented an increase in stroke. The solution was the Hirth roller bearing crankshaft, an intricate piece of machining, which meant that a one-piece conrod, minus big end bolts, could be employed, thus giving the greater clearance between crank and camshaft that an increase in stroke required. The result was the 1500 engine, actually 1488cc, which was first offered for sale in autumn 1951. Producing initially 55bhp, this soon rose to 60bhp then, with a special camshaft, to 70bhp. It quickly became the darling of the race tracks thanks to its ability to rev, and was joined by a 1300cc version. Roller bearing crank engines would remain a Porsche offering until 1957.

A momentous year for Porsche was 1952. For one thing, the Reutter assembly plant was bursting at the seams, so a new one, still in Zuffenhausen, was built. One-piece wind-screens were phased in and – the most dramatic visual change – the bumpers were moved away from the body. The interior was updated too.

And there was yet another 1500cc engine, this time with plain bearings: this was arrived at by modifications to the big ends and the position and size of the camshafts. The power output was 55bhp, but the engine itself was much more refined and less of a racing unit. The poky roller bearing engined cars became the 1500 Super, 'The first of many legendary road machines from Zuffenhausen' as the historian Karl Ludvigsen put it, while the plain bearing engine cars were named *'die Dame'* (the lady) because of their softer, more civilised behaviour.

Another important event that year was the introduction of a new gearbox with syn-chromesh. This worked extremely well, and the 'Porsche system' synchro would eventu-ally appear on all sorts of cars, earning Porsche a tidy sum in royalties over the years. Finally, to cope with the extra speeds of which the new Porsches were capable (maximum of the 1500 Super was now well over 100mph) bigger, more powerful brakes were introduced.

With all these changes, 1953 became a year of consolidation with relatively few mods but 1954 saw another burst of activity. First there was the introduction of the Speedster, a model that was initially intended as a 'cheap' Porsche, instigated by Hoffman who wanted something to compete with the Austin Healey and Triumph TR2. It was stripped of inessen-tials in the interest of cost – but that also lightened it considerably. It was fitted with a minuscule windscreen and a top which, when up, destroyed visibility in almost every direction. Hood up it was as ugly a machine as was ever made – but it went like the proverbial scalded cat, thanks to its lightness, and acceleration-oriented gearing, and soon became *the* Porsche for the tracks. The

Speedster is a very special car, however, and will not be dealt with here.

The same year the 1100cc engine was dropped, and a switch was made from two-piece magnesium (ie VW) crankcases to three-piece aluminium ones. And in March the 5000th 356 rolled off the lines.

September 1955 saw a whole host of changes introduced – so many, in fact, that the models were given a new name: the 356A. The most important of these modifications was an increase in bore of the aluminium block to give 1600cc and thus two new models: the 1600 and 1600S. There was also a new star in the firmament: the Carrera, which combined the 356 running gear with the 550 Spyder's four-cam engine. This was, and is, such a different car, however, that, like the Speedster, it will have to be treated sepa-rately. Other significant mods were made to the suspension, such as an anti-roll bar and wider, smaller diameter wheels. Visually there wasn't much change, however, the identification pointer being the constant radius curve of the windscreen, thus removing the distinctive vee of the earlier cars.

Another relatively quiet year on the alteration front was 1956, though Porsche being Porsche they couldn't leave well enough alone and mods were introduced almost continuously, if not publicly an-nounced. However, the Frankfurt Show in 1957 saw yet another round of technical changes revealed: the Hirth roller bearing crank was dropped, and in the interests of cost and quietness the aluminium cylinders were replaced by cast iron in the 1600 Normal engine, though they were retained for the Super. One change for the worse was the routing of the exhausts through the rear over-riders: this gave better ramp clearance but was not otherwise popular. Clutch and gearchange also came in for attention.

Another new model joining the line in 1957 was the Hardtop which, as its name implies, was a removeable glass-fibre affair for the Cabriolet, while 1958 saw the 'ugly duckling' Speedster replaced by a more attractive Speedster D (from Drauz, the body builder), with a bigger windscreen and more headroom. Die-hard Speedster enthusiasts promptly scorned it: a change in name to the Convertible D allowed the Speedster purists their one-upmanship.

The Frankfurt Show in 1959 saw what was, perhaps, the most startling visual change to the 356. The whole nose was raised and was fronted by a massive bumper – a genuine 'facelift'. The rear bumper was raised as well. Enter the 356B. Along with it, of course, came the invariable multitude of smaller mods, most hidden, like the improved synchromesh, others, like the styling, more obvious – more rear seat room, for example.

The 1600 and 1600S engines remained, but yet another new one was added: the 1600S-90. With typical Teutonic logic, it was so named because it gave near enough 90bhp which was sufficient to propel the Coupé to a

---

Specification (Porsche 356B 1600S)

Engine: Flat four, air cooled
Capacity: 158cc
Bore/stroke: 82.5mm x 74mm
Valves: Pushrod OHV
Compression: 8.5:1
Power: 75bhp (DIN) at 5000rpm
Torque: 86lb ft at 3700rpm

Transmission: Four speed manual
Final Drive: 4.43:1
Brakes: Drums back and front
Suspension (F): Ind. by transverse torsion bars, trailing arms, anti-roll bar
Suspension (R): Ind. by transverse torsion bars, swing axles
Steering: Worm and peg
Body: Steel floorpan, pressed-steel body
Tyres: 5.60-15

Length: 13ft 2in
Width: 5ft 6in
Height: 4ft 4in
Wheelbase: 6ft 11in
Dry Weight: 18.4cwt

Max speed: 107mph
0-60mph: 13.5sec
Standing 1/4 mile: 18.8sec
Fuel con.: 30-35mpg

Years built: 1960-1963
Nos built: 30,963
Price when new (inc tax): £2063

top speed of 115mph and the Roadster, as the Convertible D had been renamed yet again, to 110mph. Cornering with the Super 90 was improved by the use of a compensating spring at the rear which acted in the opposite way to an anti-roll bar and thus forced that end to do more work, and the adoption of radial-ply tyres for the first time on a Porsche as standard.

pressure, and make sure there are no visible oil leaks. Areas that can leak (and frequently do) are the rocker box gaskets, the oil cooler, and the seal on the gearlever shaft. Rectification is simple, however, and the leaks are niggling rather than serious. Engine parts are relatively easy to find if you are contemplating renovation.

The only area of worry with regard to the

The 356B, in 1960 and '61 had higher bumpers, raised centre hub-caps and higher mounted headlamps. This is a Cabriolet.

In 1961 the basic 356 bodyshell was given its last major modifications. The windscreen and rear window were enlarged, more space was found under the front 'bonnet' which featured a squared-off lower edge. September of the same year also saw the 2 litre version of the Carrera, called – wait for it – the Carrera 2 ...

By 1962 Porsche were heavily involved with the 356B's replacement, the 901, and the days of the 356 were coming to an end. But not before one final thing: in 1964 the 356C was announced. To look at there was little difference, for the 356B body was carried over, but a clue was given by the wheels hiding disc brakes which Porsche had finally adopted. The range, too, was simplified, with just three engine options. The 1600 'Normal' engine was dropped, leaving the 1600S or Super 75, the 1600SC (replacing the Super 90) and the Carrera 2.

The last 356, a white cabriolet, rolled off the Zuffenhausen assembly line in September 1965, the 76,303rd of the model. Well, not quite: ten more were built 'to special order'. Some people just couldn't bear to see it go ... Of this figure, there were 7,627 356s, 21,045 356As and 30,963Bs.

Buyer's Spot Check

The good news for prospective 356 purchasers is that the mechanics of the car are remarkably long lived. The engine requires the usual checks – look for steady oil

rest of the running gear is that the link pins in the front suspension can seize; this is checked by jacking the car up and rocking the wheels. Similarly, ball joints can be checked in this way. Steering is by worm and peg, and there's an inspection hatch in the front 'boot' compartment. Once uncovered it's easy to check for play in the steering assembly. Again, parts are easily obtainable, either from the States or through Stuttgart, although they don't come cheap.

The major troubles with the car are usually structural and bodywork; it pays to check just about everything meticulously, as to replace panels and chassis parts is costly,

Subtle dash changes continued to be made but the same functional philosophy persisted.

simply because nearly everything has to be made. If there is one fault with the cars, it's that they're prone to rust, and that can mean MoT failure.

On the chassis front, the vital areas are the suspension mounting points, the area around the front and rear of the floorpan, and the longitudinal chassis members. The mounting points are easily checked. Effectively, you can see these in the area immediately behind the wheels, forming, for want of a better example, the inner wheel arches. On really rotten examples, it is possible to flake the rust away by hand, but judicious use of a sharp object (if the vendor doesn't mind) will pinpoint just how good or bad these areas are. If they are far gone, then bear in mind that it'll be expensive to repair.

The area at the front of the floorpan often goes; a warning is sodden carpets, a sure sign that water has been trapped in the footwells. Similarly, the rear floorpan joint rusts badly; a quick look underneath will tell you if all is in order. Cabriolets are worse than coupés for this problem.

The longitudinal members also rot badly; as they form the sills, you can't really prod them, but if the jacking point can be moved, then they need replacing. Use of a magnet will detect if there is a lot of filler patching this part up. All these disorders are going to be expensive to repair properly; it's no use just patching up, you'll need whole areas re-placed, and they have to be made.

One other vulnerable spot is the rear suspension bump stop; brute force is the only check here, so grab hold of the stop and waggle it around to ensure its security.

Bodywise, the car suffers from the demon rust badly, too. Look at the wings, the door bottoms, boot, and, on cabriolets especially, the inner doors and door pillar rears.

Where the wing is turned over onto the chassis, there is a water trap; check for rust here. The door bottoms and inners are prone to go, and it can be difficult to check these if filler has been used in quantity. The same applies to the front boot ... make sure you look *everywhere!*

To ensure that the door pillar rears are sound, take a look at the trim behind the doors; if it's out of shape that's a sure sign that water has got in. And that invariably means rust and a general weakening of the body's strength. One other place to check is the area between the grille apertures at the front – again, it's expensive to refurbish. Take a careful look at the spare wheel compartment, which is where the battery lives, for corrosion.

It's worth remembering that many of these cars have suffered crash damage in the past, so it's well worthwhile checking all the above points very carefully; when the cars were worth a lot less, fastidious repair might not have been thought cost effective. And if the car needs structural repair, it will not come cheaply.

Rivals When New

The 356 was one of those difficult cars that, for various reasons, didn't really have any 'rivals' (in the sense that, say, the TR2 and Austin

At the 1961 Frankfurt show, a body modification for the 356B was announced: twin rear grilles were introduced and the rear window enlarged. For some reason, this short-run model is not regarded as being quite as 'desirable' as earlier 356Bs.

Healey 100 were rivals) when it was new.

Take, for example, 1955. The standard 1500 cost £1786 (all prices include purchase tax, by the way), the Super £1956. By comparison, the MG TF cost £780, the Austin Healey 100 £1063, the Triumph TR2 £886, and the Jaguar XK140 fixed-head £1616. On the other hand, such exotica as the Aston Martin DB2-4 sold for £2728, the HRG 1500 (were any actually sold in 1955?) for £1269, the Keift 1100 (a real rarity) for £1559, and the Swallow Doretti for £110.

Thus, for a 1¹/₂-litre, the Porsche's only competition came from the likes of HRG and

Hardtop for £949, and the TVR with MGA engine for £1040.

None of these, however, had all the Porsche's unique qualities, and you had to look for 2-litres or above to come near to its performance, particularly in Super form.

Clubs, Specialists and Books

There is no club *per se* for 356 owners – they come under the umbrella of Porsche Club Great Britain (Ayton House, West End, Northleach, Glos. GL54 3HG, tel: 04516 792).

When it comes to specialists, most

Keift, while bigger, faster machinery (Jaguar, Healey *et al)* cost less. And there were *no* British rear-engined sports cars during this era.

By 1963 the 1600 was up to £1900, the 1600 Super 90 to £2277, and the competition had increased, though again, much of it was bigger engined. The AC Ace Bristol went for £1873, the Alfa Romeo Giulia 1600 Sprint for £1597, the Healey 3000 for £1045, the E-type for an incredible £1828 in open form, the Lotus Elan for £1317 and the Elite for £1662 (the latter with Special Equipment rose close to the Porsche for £1862), the MGB for £834, the TR4

Porsche dealers shy away from 356s, preferring to concentrate on later models. Fortunately, 356 owners are a tight-knit group, and if you go through the Club you can get most jobs done. The Club has picked out two experts, however: for bodywork only Ernie Gregory in Farnham (0276 32490) is your man, while for ground-up rebuilds – not servicing or panel repairs – contact Nick Mayman (08242 3986) in Wales. In addition, the Club has a list of engine and servicing specialists: Tony Standen (01-828 9501) and David Edelstein (01-723 5626) will point you in the right direction.

356Cs were visually only distinguishable from earlier cars by their flat hubcaps, but behind them lay highly desirable disc brakes. (23/7)

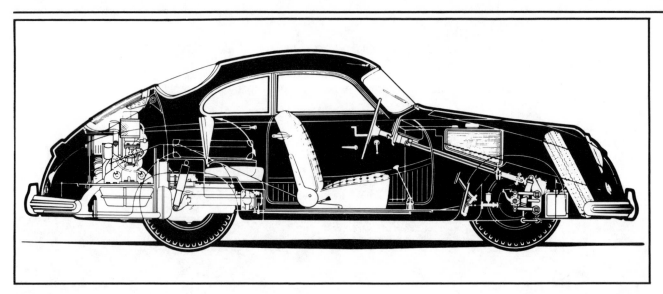

356A in 'X-ray' profile.

The good news, though, is that Porsche are themselves becoming involved, having just bought out Stoddards (*the* 356 specialists) in the USA, so 'new' spares should soon be available via Reading, while one member of the Club has a franchise from PB Tweeks in California, another source of parts.

Book-wise, the Porsche owner is almost inundated, but those dealing specifically with the 356 tend to be a little rarer. The bible on all matters Porsche has to be Karl Ludvigsen's *Porsche – Excellence Was Expected* (£39.95), probably one of the most detailed one-marque books ever, followed closely by Lothar Boschen's and Jurgen Barth's *The Porsche*

Book (£22.50), recently reprinted, while Denis Jenkinson's *Porsche 356* (£6.95) is required and joyful reading for any enthusiast, not just Porsche buffs. Other books which concentrate purely on the 356 and its history and technicalities are Harry Pellow's *The ABC's Of Porsche Engines (356/912)* (£6.95) which covers the 356/912 (1500cc and 1600cc) engine family, *Porsche Brochures And Sales Literature 1946-65* (£15.95), two reprints of German road tests, *Porsche 1948-1958 Tests* and Porsche 1959-1965 Tests (both at £5.50), three in the Brooklands Books magazine article reprint series (*Porsche Cars 1952-1956, Porsche Cars 1957-1960 and Porsche Cars 1960-1964,* at £3.95 and £4.95 respectively) and Henry Elfink's *Porsche 356 Technical Manual* (£6.95), all of which are on Albion Scott's list. And then, of course, there's a splended all-purpose coffee table book, *The Classic Porsche* (Bison Books, £7.95) by, ahem, Mike McCarthy.

Prices

Had we profiled the 356 a year or so ago, the chances are that we could have said you could pick one up relatively cheaply. Not so now, though: our price guide has shown some dramatic increases in asking prices (13 per cent in October, 15 per cent in November) and an indication of how the 356 has become a cult car came at a recent Christie's auction when a Super 90 Cabriolet was sold for £7000. Mind you, the purchaser was none other than the Porsche company itself.

However, being more down to earth, 'basket cases' can be picked up for a few hundred pounds as with most cars. In order of desirability and therefore asking price, the normal coupés with the 'Damen' engine are the most available, and our 'Price guide' shows that the average asking price is rising from £2500 towards £3000. Cabriolets fetch more, and Super 90s more than – but not much more than – Cabriolets, fully restored examples of the latter fetching £6000 to £7000. However, when it comes to Carreras and

Speedsters, the sky seems to be the limit. Even assuming you can find one, start looking at £10,000 and go on up.

"Porsche Portrait" first appeared in "Classic & Sports Car" magazine.

Model	Engines	Outputs	Years
356	1100	40bhp at 4200rpm	1950-1954
	1300	44bhp at 4400rpm	1951-1955
	1300S (R/B)	60bhp at 5500rpm	1953-1955
	1500	60bhp at 5000rpm	1952-1955
	1500S (R/B)	70bhp at 5000rpm	1954-1955
356A	1300	44bhp at 4200rpm	1955-1957
	1300S(R/B)	60bhp at 5500rpm	1955-1957
	1600	60bhp at 4500rpm	1955-1959
	1600S (R/B)	75bhp at 5000rpm	1955-1957
	1600S	74bhp at 5000rpm	1957-1959
356B	1600	60bhp at 4500rpm	1960-1963
	1600S	75bhp at 5000rpm	1960-1963
	1600S-90	90bhp at 5500rpm	1960-1963
356C	1600	75bhp at 5200rpm	1964-1965
	1600SC	95bhp at 5800rpm	1964-1965

(R/B = roller bearing)

The Sting in The Tail

Unique among sports cars, the earlier Porsche 911s are attracting growing interest. Mike McCarthy and Richard Sutton are your guides.

Has there ever been a car quite so astonishing as the Porsche 911?

Now in its 21st year of production, it has grown from a 130bhp 2-litre to a 300bhp 3.3-litre *mit Kompressor* – and those are just the road versions. It has won, in one form or another, just about every major competition event of any significance for which it was eligible, from the Monte Carlo Rally to Le Mans. It has a mechanical layout that was fashionable when it was introduced but is now regarded as thoroughly obsolete – but don't tell 911 owners, who blithely go their own way, enjoying themselves. It has been called a triumph of development over design, probably the most accurate statement ever made about it. You could go on eulogising about it for hours – it is the ultimate sports car.

The models being considered here are those with unblown engine capacities below 3-litres, basically for three reasons; first, to keep the story to a reasonable length; secondly, the change in capacity gives a good break point; and, thirdly, these are the models that are currently most affordable.

The 911 was the second generation Porsche road car, succeeding the 356, and the product of the third generation of the Porsche family. Though Dr Ferry Porsche was still in overall charge, the 911 was styled by his son Butzi, and the distaff side of the family provided Ferdinand Piëch, who had a considerable hand in its mechanical development.

By 1959 it was becoming obvious that the 356 was coming to the end of its life, excellent though it was. Its replacement would have to be more refined, more luxurious, more spacious and quicker. Which also meant more expensive, but then Porsches were never cheap. It had to be rear-engined and air-cooled: no other configuration was even considered.

Initially a Four-Seater

Initial plans called for a four-seater, and Butzi designed a prototype called the T7 (the T6 had been the last of the 356 shapes). The bottom half is instantly recognisable as 911, but topping it off was a large greenhouse, more notchback than fastback. The T7 was a foot longer in the wheelbase than the 356, but

by 1962 there was a fundamental change in attitude; the new car would be a 2 + 2. Thus the wheelbase was brought down to a little over 4 inches more than that of the 356. For the new size of car Butzi kept the T7's bottom half but added a sleeker, slimmer, lower roof line, sweeping in one glorious line from the base of the windscreen up and back to the rear bumper. Thus was born the definitive 911, as timeless and beautiful and distinctive today as it was in the beginning.

Meanwhile work was continuing on the underpinnings, the engine, suspension and chassis in particular. Taking these in order, Porsche had considerable experience with

pushrod fours, twin overhead cam fours (in the Carrera) and twin overhead cam eights (in racing cars). None of these was suitable for production, though: the pushrod wasn't powerful enough, and the twin cam fours and eights too complex. A six was an ideal compromise.

Initial ideas revolved around a pushrod layout, with two camshafts, one above and one below the crankshaft, operating the valves via pushrods and rockers. The carburettors were placed outboard of the heads, with intake ports between the valves. Cooling was by two axial fans, and it developed 120bhp at 6500rpm from 1991cc. However, it was very wide, thanks to those outboard carbs, and pushrods limited revs which, for an engine which was going to be raced whether Porsche liked it or not, was not a Good Thing.

Thus the decision to place the camshafts above (or should that be outboard of?) the heads was taken; as one Porsche engineer put it, ''If we're going for two camshafts they may as well be in the head'' The carbs were in a more usual position, above the heads, and a single axial fan was chosen. In this form it produced 130bhp at 6100rpm.

The suspension design, too, represented a radical departure for Porsche. Gone were the traditional trailing arms and transverse

In 1963 the 911 replaced the 356: the first models had a clean, sharp, uncluttered appearance that was never to be regained. This actual car was badged as a '901' but the central '0' had to be changed to 'l' when another manufacturer pointed out that they had established a right to such nomenclature as 304, 305, etc.

torsion bars at the front, replaced by MacPherson struts. The reason was simple: space. The 356 system took up too much room, whereas the struts could be placed as far apart as possible giving the largest volume possible in the nose. For the same reason torsion bars, running longitudinally and incorporated into the lower wishbones, were used as the springing medium instead of coil springs, which operated the torsion bar, and an angled arm attached to a bracket on the torsion bar carrier tube at one end and the hub at the other. Steering was by rack and pinion, and there were disc brakes at each corner. There was a five-speed gearbox in the standard Porsche position, ahead of the engine and axle centre line.

This, then, was the configuration that appeared on a car, given the designation 901, at the Frankfurt Motor Show in 1963. It is still the quintessential layout that survives to this day, though it is unlikely that a single part has remained exactly as it was on that prototype. Nevertheless, the basic layout, the body shape, the flat-six engine and suspension have remained constant in concept if not in execution.

The car at Frankfurt was very much a teaser, and production didn't start for nearly another year. In the meantime Peugeot stuck their oar in, claiming that they had the copyright for designations which consisted of three numbers, the central one being zero (as in 104, 204, etc). Ferry Porsche shrugged, and the name was changed to 911. A rose by any other name smells as sweet.

There were, of course, teething troubles. One in particular involved the old Porsche bug-bear, handling. When it first appeared the 911 was on narrow section (165) tyres and 4^1/$_2$ rims, intended to combat changes in camber, and the engine was heavier than expected. In addition Porsche engineers were still learning about the problems that can arise when MacPherson strut suspension is in volume production instead of careful assembly in development departments.

The net result was that the early cars understeered quite considerably under moderate cornering loads but would flick into the dreaded oversteer if the driver lifted off at high cornering speeds. In addition, sensitive drivers noted that some cars had different cornering characteristics depending on whether they were turning left or right, and straight line stability was not all it should have been. To achieve consistency, incredibly tight tolerances were specified on the line and complex production techniques introduced. Neither really worked, and at least one odd solution, involving lumps of iron in the corners of the front bumpers which affected both weight distribution and polar moment of inertia, was tried! Eventually Ferdinand Piëch took over this department as well, and under his guidance the problems were ironed out (no pun intended!)

The development history of the model will be more fully covered in the section headed 'Production history', but it can be summed up quite easily: more power, better handling and greater aerodynamic stability. Porsche are at their most brilliant when it comes to steady, progressive, clinical, effective development, and it is as much for this reason as any other than the 911 is the machine it is today.

Once the road testers got their hands on 911s, the eulogies started flowing. 'Jenks' of *Motor Sport* said in February 1966 that the 911 was 'the best car Porsche have yet built for road use' and 'this is one of the best cars I have ever driven'. John Bolster, a month later and in the same car that Jenks drove, recorded a 0-60mph time of 8.7secs and a top speed of 131mph, his impressions of the car being succinctly summed up: 'Enjoyment, that's the word!'

Most testers raved about the roadholding and handling, which goesto prove that you had to be trying very hard indeed to discover the limits of its dynamic envelop – or be driving under slippery conditions, when the lack of the usual early warning signs could mean a rapid rearward trip into the undergrowth. As *Autocar* said in late 1966, 'the 911 is not a car for the novice and even the experienced fast driver must slow down when the road turns wet ... In the dry, the adhesion is little short of phenomenal ... (but) in the wet the power available is too much ... One needs to feed the throttles open carefully and progressively to prevent the tail twitching about, and to treat the polished surfaces in town with considerable discretion'. In general the 911 has always been praised for its performance, steering, ride and precision of controls, and in that respect nothing has changed in the last 21 years.

Remarkable Engine

We have driven a number of 911s, though nothing with a capacity of less than 2.7-litres, and all display characteristics that can only be called pure 911. There is that remarkable engine, happily pottering along at 1000rpm or howling away, its note a combination of fan whine and exhaust growl, at the red line. There's that astonishing steering, light, direct, and full of feel yet without any trace of kickback. Brakes that work magnificently. A feeling of total solidity. By today's standards the gearchange takes some acclimatisation (though the higher the mileage the better it is) and the awkward heating and ventilation system has never been as good as those cars with water cooling, but those are about the biggest criticisms you can make of the 911. Above all, a 911 is a near perfect car for fast, cross-country trips with the minimum of fuss or drama, and the maximum of speed. A 911 is not fun in the sense, say, that a Mini Cooper or Golf GTi is: it is much too good to be simply fun. To understand the 911 mystique, you have to live with one for a while, and, if you do, you find you become automatically a better driver. You can't say much better than that.

But good though the 911 is, it is doubtful if

it would have the charisma that it has today were it not for its competition record – not even in their wildest dreams would the Porsches and Piëches have envisaged a 700bhp version winning at Le Mans when the 911 was first considered!

The first competition entry for a 911 came in the 1965 Monte Carlo Rally, when engineers Herbert Linge and Peter Falk took a works prepared car to an excellent fifth place. In fact, all initial efforts were concentrated on rallying, and in 1966 Gunther Klass finished up as European GT Rally Champion. For 1967 Porsche ran their first ever official rally programme, with Vic Elford driving and David Stone navigating. Elford and Stone won the Lyon Charbonières, Tulip and Geneva Rallies outright on their way to the European GT Rally Championship – while the Polish driver Sobieslav Zasada took the European Saloon Rally Championship. In racing, too, the 911S was making its mark, with GT class wins on such diverse tracks as Daytona and the Targa Florio.

In 1967 the 911R (for Racing) appeared. Stripped to the bare minimum, and with considerable weight saving, plus some 210bhp, only 22 were made. Its debut came in the Marathon de la Route, an 84-hour blind around the Nürburgring, and the ubiquitous Vic Elford was one of the drivers, along with Hans Herrmann and Jochen Neerspach, who brought one home first. It was also notable for the fact that it was fitted with the Sportomatic semi-automatic gearbox which Porsche were pushing at the time ...

In the late sixties homologation was a complex process, but Porsche read the rules properly and the 911 appeared in almost every category. There was the 911 and 911L for touring car racing, the 911T for Grand Touring events, and the 911R for the prototype class. You paid your money and took your pick.

Elford and Stone chose a 911T for their attack on the 1968 Monte Carlo Rally – and promptly won it, with Pauli Toivonen second in a similar machine. Elford then turned to racing, so it was Toivonen who won the Geneva, East German, Danube, Spanish, German and San Remo rallies. To nobody's surprise he finished up as World Rally Champion. The same year saw 1-2 in the Marathon plus GT class victories in the Nürburgring 1000kms, Watkins Glen 6 Hours, Le Mans, Monza 1000kms, Sebring 12 Hours and the Targa Florio, while Messrs Kremer, Kelleners and Kauhsen took the Spa 24 Hour saloon car race. Some season!

For 1969 the 911T continued to dominate the rallying world, with a first and second in the Monte again, while Toivonen won the Acropolis, but it was Ford who finished up as champions. On the tracks the list of GT class wins grew even longer, while – just for added interest – a 911R took the recently rejuvenated Tour de France, and 911s filled the first four places at the Spa 24 Hour event. From then on the 911 was banned from saloon

racing, much to almost everyone else's relief!

Porsche's rally efforts with the 911 peaked in 1970, when they won the European Rally Championship, via, among other events, a hat-trick win in the Monte. The early seventies, however, saw most of Porsche's efforts going into racing with the 908s and the magnificent 917s; and the only significant result on the rally front in 1971 was a second in the RAC. By then, however, the 911 was almost completely dominating the GT racing classes, and this was to be the pattern until the arrival of the turbo models. One notable achievement in 1972 was John Fitzpatrick's win in the newly created European GT Touring Car Championship; another was Hurley Haywood's similar result in the IMSA Camel GT Championship.

However, 1972 also saw the introduction of the Carrera RS, and its racing derivative the RSR, at the Parish Motor Show late in the year, to combat the possible opposition from Ferrari's Daytona, and these would prove to be Porsche's most successful non-turbocharged cars ever. To list their successes would take a book, but first overall at the 1973 Daytona 24-Hours and the Targa Florio, plus the European GT Championship will do for starters.

In 1974 and 1975 the Carrera RSR 3.0 swept all before it, taking the IMSA Championship, the European GT Championship and the FIA GT Cup both years, though the writing was on the wall as far as the future was concerned with the appearance in 1975 of the 911 Turbo 2.14-litre, to be followed in 1976 by the 935. But that's another story ...

Production History

One of the first changes to the 911 came in early 1966, with a switch from Solex to Weber carburettors to overcome a flat spot, but the real news came in August that year, and in two parts. The first was the introduction of the S

Announced in 1969 were the 911S and 911E, both with Fuchs five-spoke forged alloy wheels while, from 1970, the 'straight' 911 could also be ordered with the same wheels in place of the steel variety.

Engine:	Horizontally opposed 'six'
Capacity:	2341cc
Bore/stroke:	84mm x 70.4mm
Valves:	Sohc per bank
Compression:	8.5:1
Power:	190bhp @ 6500rpm
Torque:	159lb ft @ 3200rpm
Transmission:	Five-speed manual
Final drive:	4.43:1
Brakes:	Servo discs all round
Suspension front:	Ind by wishbones and torsion bars
Suspension rear:	Ind by semi-trailing wishbones and transverse torsion bars
Steering:	Rack and pinion
Body:	All steel unitary construction
Tyres:	185/70VR-15
Length:	13ft 8ins
Width:	5ft 3.5ins
Height:	4ft 4ins
Wheelbase:	7ft 5.5ins
Weight:	21.2cwt
Max speed:	144mph
0-60mph:	6.1secs
Standing 1/4 mile:	13.9secs
Fuel consumption:	18mpg

The 1972 911S came equipped with a front 'spoiler' or 'air dam'; but again, the spoiler was offered as an option on the T and E models and was very shortly offered on all Porsche 911s.

version, with more power – 160bhp – and a top speed of 140mph against the standard car's 130mph. To go with the added power came ventilated disc brakes, clearly visible behind meaty forged five-spoke alloy wheels, their pattern becoming a Porsche hallmark.

The other news was a brand new bodyshell, basically a convertible but with a heavy roll-over hoop. Like the Carrera 356 before it, it was given the name of a famous race with strong Porsche connections, the Targa, after the Targa Florio, Butzi had wanted

a full convertible, but impending American legislation knocked this on the head, and it added strength anyway. Porsche played on the roll-over hoop theme so successfully that the term 'Targa top' is now generic ...

In 1967 the original O Series 911 became the A series. The main changes were slightly wider wheels and the announcement of the 911T, basically a down-market model with 110bhp. The 911 became the 911L, and the 911S topped the range. There was also the optional 'Sportomatic' semi-automatic trans-

mission, consisting of a normal four-speed gearbox but with both a torque converter and a clutch. It could be used as a pure automatic – with dismal performance – or as a clutchless manual; a switch in the gear lever knob caused the clutch to disengage, plus dispensing with a pedal, but still leaving the driver to decide when to change gear (and curing him of the habit of resting his hand on the knob!) It was mildly popular, but being neither fish, flesh nor fowl, was eventually dropped.

August 1968 saw some major revisions to the range, the most significant by far being the extension of the wheelbase by just over 2 inches. This was achieved by moving the rear wheels back but leaving everything else where it was. To accommodate the new angle of the driveshafts Löbro units (incorporating Rzeppa constant velocity joints) were used, and the semi-trailing arms lengthened. The purpose behind this was to achieve a more equal weight balance, and thus better handling. Magnesium replaced aluminium for the crankcase and twin batteries were mounted in the nose, improving matters even further. For the most powerful S versions, rim widths were increased to 6 inches and the result was what was hoped for – a reduction in the understeer at low speeds and the instant oversteer at high speeds.

For the 1969 model year the T remained more or less the same, the L became the E with the adoption of Bosch mechanical fuel injection and 10 more bhp, and the S was given the same treatment with the same results, power rising to 170bhp at 5500rpm.

As night follows day, the C and D Series followed the B for the 1970 and 1971 model years. The most important modification was an increase in capacity, via a 4 mm larger bore, from 1991cc to 2195cc. The reason for this was quite simple: an improvement in bottom-end torque, mainly to satisfy the Americans who were more used to the pulling power of a big lazy V8 than to the high revs of a small 'six'. Naturally power went up, so that the T was giving 125bhp at 4200rpm, the E 155bhp at 6200rpm, and the S 180bhp at 6500rpm.

But the 2.2-litre engine was only a brief stepping stone to the next in the series, the E and F models, which expanded capacity to 2.4-litres (accurately 2341cc) via a longer stroke. In spite of a drop in compression ratio

so that the engine would run on low-lead fuel, power rose again to 130bhp, 165bhp and 190bhp for the T, E and S models respectively. As power and torque had risen quite considerably since the introduction of the original 2-litre, a new gearbox was introduced which also had a more normal pattern with dog-leg fifth instead of first. The first steps towards the use of aerodynamics appeared in 1971, too, with an air dam under the nose of the S: the next year it was fitted across the board.

But the big news in 1972, for the 1973 model year, was the introduction of the Carrera. This was intended to be a Group 4 (Special GT) homologation special, for which a production of 500 was envisaged. The sales staff were considerably worried as to whether or not they could shift such a considerable number: they needn't have worried. Within a week of its appearance they had sold their 500, and by April 1973 the 1000th had been produced, which allowed homologation into the Group 3 (Production GT) category. One of the greatest and most charismatic Porsches ever had been born.

The biggest change was yet another increase in capacity, to 2687cc, making it eligible for the 3-litre class, and bringing the power output up to a rousing 210bhp at 6300rpm. The extra capacity called for special cylinders, using a nickel-silicon carbide compound called Nickasil to act as the wearing surfaces of the cylinder walls. There were 7 inch wide wheels at the back, covered by wide, flared arches, heavier anti-roll bars and Bilstein gas-filled dampers at each corner. Visually there was a deep air dam under the nose and an astonishing appendage at the rear – it looked like, and was promptly nicknamed, a 'duck's tail'. The Carrera looked stunning, and had performance to match: it would reach 150mph, took $5\frac{1}{2}$ sec to reach 60mph from a standstill, and could generate 0.9g lateral acceleration when cornering. For those who took their racing seriously, there was the Carrera RSR with even wider wheels and wheelarches and some 300bhp ...

And here's the same again – or is it? The 'whale tail' and plain bumpers indicate that it's a Carrera, a lightweight and very quick motor car not made available for road use in the USA until 1974.

In actual fact, it is somewhere between difficult and impossible to place any 911 purely on the evidence of its body panels: this range sold by Autofarm, for instance, as well as the availability of 'factory' panels, mean that any amount of disguising is both possible and extremely popular among owners.

The 1973/74 model year saw a contraction in the 911 model range. All models received the 2.7-litre engine, but in different states of tune and therefore output. The straight 911 replaced the 911T as the base model, and gave 150bhp against the T's 130bhp. The 911S replaced the 911E with 175bhp instead of 165bhp, and the Carrera topped the line, replacing the earlier 911S (yes, it *is* confusing!) with that 210bhp instead of 190bhp. The new 911 and 911S were fitted with Bosch K-Jetronic fuel injection, the Carrera retaining a mechanical layout. The big news visually for the 1973/74 G-Series, though, was the appearance of heavier bumpers front and rear, to meet American safety regulations. These were integrated most harmoniously, thus giving the lie to the Americans (and the people at MG) that they had to look ponderous, hefty and ugly.

There was also, in 1974, an 'interim' Carrera, the RS3.0 which is significant only insofar as it introduces the first of the 3-litre engines, and therefore signals the end of the tale. It was followed later in the year by the 911 Turbo, but that is definitely another story! The 2.7-litre was finally dropped when both it and the Carrera were replaced in 1977 by the 3-litre 911SC.

Buyer's Spot Check

The main thing to remember when buying an older Porsche 911 is that it is not a cheap car to run by the standards of sports cars such as the MGB. But it can be a very cheap car by the standards of supercars like Ferrari.

The only way you can save money when running a 911 is to be able to do much of the maintenance yourself, which is not difficult if you are reasonably competent. The engine and transmission can be removed, for instance, in only an hour or so, after which work on these components is much easier. But Porsche standards of service are as high as the quality of the car, which means that a major service – every 12,000 miles – is likely to cost around £350.

The older 911s belong to the era when practically everything could be taken to pieces and reassembled – quite unlike modern machinery where the electronics are likely to give nightmares in years to come. So if you are capable of dismantling and reassembling beautifully-made machinery, an older 911 can be cheap to run because everything is so well made it lasts a long time. The only real advantage the modern electronically-injected 911s have over the older mechanical cars is that they are far more fuel efficient. Tyre and brake wear, on the other and, is higher, because the more modern cars have put on so much weight.

One of the wonders of owning an older Porsche is the relative abundance of second-hand parts, which is fortunate because new ones – still marvels of engineering – are expensive. This practice of using second-hand parts (providing they are in really good condition) is made all the more practical by the fact that so many of them are interchangeable throughout the 911 range. It would, for instance, be possible – although hardly economical – to convert one of the earliest 1964 cars into a modern Turbo! The ready availability of used parts also makes an older 911 so much more practical to run as there should be nothing that goes wrong that can keep the car off the road if a near-identical substitute can be accepted for the time being.

The only problem other than lack of money that can be terminal with an older 911 is the dreaded corrosion, and then it is simply a question of how much you can afford to spend on specialist treatment, providing the rear torsion bar tube is not about to collapse. A bare-metal respray with new rubber mouldings and so on is likely to set you back £3500. Remedial work on the metal beneath the paint, which is likely to be necessary, adds to a bill which can reach £8000 in a typical rebuild in which all four outer wings, sills and aprons need replacement and the doors need treatment. Again, the ultimate quality of the rebuild depends on how much you can afford. The basic 911 hull is so strong that it is quite practical to use glass-fibre panels – which can be obtained in abundance – and save yourself a fortune with a cheap respray. Corrosion in the roof of a 911 is virtually unknown and the main floorpans were galvanised from 1971, which offers not only protection against corrosion but great security of mind. Targas, however, are far more prone to corrosion than fixed-heads, because the body flexes more and opens up the seams.

The best thing about the front wings is that they are bolted on, which makes replacement far easier than those at the back, which are welded in. The fuel filler flap box, light boxes and so on are prone to rot, but they can be bought separately. The sills are vital to the car's strength and have to be replaced in total – both inner and outer sections – for security. Otherwise, it is like trying to gloss over the onset of a cancer that can eat away the car from the inside. And then expensive paintwork, applied to new outer sills when the inners are rotting, will have been wasted. The doors rot in all the usual places and the shutfaces are particularly prone to corrosion; in extreme cases, the doors can fly open as the metal collapses. This makes it all the more imperative to wear seat belts in an older 911! Early 911s – pre-1968 – suffered from front crossmember corrosion. Initial warning spots can be carpets dampened by the moisture that seeps in through corroded front wings and then attacks the floorpan. Rusting oil tanks and oil coolers – which are carried in the wings – can also cause expensive engine trouble as dirt from them gets in the bearings. Stainless steel replacement tanks are readily available.

The most common 911 engine fault is with its hydraulic timing chain tensioners. These are designed to work over a wide range of temperatures, which tends to limit their life to between 40,000 to 50,000 miles. Replacement bills run at about £300 or £400 if the chains are changed at the same time. Run the engine at about 2500rpm and listen for noises – which disappear in any case above those revs. Valve guides last about 60,000 miles on average, but can go on smoking their way through litres of oil for ages! Piston rings are likely to need attention at about 80,000 miles.

Early gearboxes – on the 2-litre cars – suffered from input shaft weaknesses, and premature bearing failures were not eliminated until after the 2.2-litre cars. Pump replacements on the mechanically fuel injected cars are expensive.

Heat exchangers generally last only about two years because they are subject to such extremes of temperature. Early replacement is all the more essential on the mechanical fuel injection cars because they rely on a supply of hot air to turn off their automatic choke. If they do not get it, the fuel consumption soars and the bores become worn with the over-rich mixture. It is a wise policy also to leave a cold 911 running on the hand throttle at around 1200rpm until an oil temperature of 180 degrees has been reached to minimise engine wear.

Pre-1968 cars suffered from wishbone corrosion, and the self-levelling struts fitted to the 911Es are prone to collapse. It is easy to convert them to the normal suspension, but the parts needed are extensive and expensive. Porsche were particularly generous with the early brake disc thickness, however, and these can often be skimmed quite safely.

One of the main points about which to be wary when buying an older Porsche 911 is accident damage. This is quite common, such is the unforgiving nature of the handling in unsympathetic hands. Check the door gaps for pillars that might have been put out of alignment in a major accident and avoid a crab-tracked car like the plague. Bent suspension arms from kerb-walloping exercises are easily repaired, however, and minor items, such as worn wheel bearings, can cause a car to pull to one side or the other.

But such is the potential cost of repairing a really bad car that there can be no greater bargain than paying a Porsche specialist for a few hours' work in checking a possible purchase.

Clubs, Specialists & Books

There is only one club in this country catering for Porsches and therefore early 911s – the Porsche Club Great Britain. Formed in 1961 the club is now a highly professional and highly regarded organisation with a 4000 strong membership. For the £16 annual membership fee (£18 for the whole family) a member receives, among other things, the club's quarterly magazine *Porsche Post*. Always the best part of a hundred quality pages, the magazine is a thoroughly good read with a wide variety of features from Register news to Porsche celebrity interviews. Four newsletters a year are published to complement the magazine.

Around six national events are organised each year and the 20 local regions organise their own smaller occasions, with monthly pub meets.

Club membership can realise substantial savings at a number of Porsche specialists and the club receives preferential treatment from some insurance brokers. The club's own race championship, sponsored by office seating manufacturers Giroflex, has been heavily subscribed and promises to be both competitive and exciting.

The club address is: Ayton House, West End, Northeach, Glos. GL54 3HG

Porsche 911 owners are well catered for on the specialist front although there are few companies who will be prepared to take on *all* types of work, or tackle a full ground-up restoration. Among those that will cater are: Dage Sport, la Bessemer Crescent, Rabens Lane, Aylesbury, Bucks (tel: 0296 33200); Charles Ivev Ltd, 160 Hurlingham Road, Fulham, London SW6 (tel: 01-731 3612): Tognola Engineering Ltd, 32 Montagu Road, Datchet, Berks (tel: 0753 45053); Autofarm, 5 Hill Avenue, Amersham, Bucks (tel: 02403 28196); Dick Lovett, Official Porsche Centre, Ashworth Road, Bridgemead, Swindon, Wilts. (tel: 0793 61500) (some restoration); Motowerk, 120 High Street, Offord, Cambs (tel: 0480 811799); Stewart Kelsey Cars, 1-7 Colville Mews, Lonsdale Road, London W11; Millswood Coachwork, Blackwater Way, Blackwater Trading Estate, Aldershot, Hants. (tel: 0252 310471); Club Automobile Services, Victoria Works, Fallows Road, Sparbrook, Birmingham 11 (tel: 021 773 3631); and Tony Bianchi Porsche Specialists, 53 Hastings Road, Bromley, Kent (tel: 01-462-8265) (not restoration).

For the purely mechanical restoration and servicing contact: Turner Automotive, Unit 49, Sapcote Trading Centre, 374 High Road, Willesden, London NW10 (tel: 01-451 6000); D K Engineering, Unit D, 200 Rickmansworth Road, Watford, Herts (tel: 0923 55246); Paul Edwards, Unit P, New Crescent Works, 3 Nicoll Road, Harlesden, London NW10 (tel: 01-965 1058) mechanical repairs; Ronnoco Engineering, 199/201 Pooley Green Road, Egham, Surrey (tel: 0784 65293); AFN Limited, Falcon Works, London Road, Isleworth, Middx (tel: 01-560 1011) (also sells new and second-hand Porsches, accessories etc); and Michael Gleeson, Porsche Specialists, Beechill Garage, Headley Down, Bordon, Hants (tel: 0428 712171).

Bodywork restoration specialists include: Graham F.F. Richardson, Grange Way, Whitehall Road Industrial Estate, Colchester, Essex (tel: 0206 576543) and Bill Taylor, Station Garage, Station Approach, Shepperton, Middx (tel: 0932 222007).

Accident repair specialists are Autotech Motor Engineers, Units 34 and 35, Nash Works, Belbroughton, Stourbridge, West Midlands (tel: 0562 730035); and Roger Clark (Cars) Ltd., 45-49 Coventry Road, Narborough, Leics. (tel: 0533 848510)

Machtech tuning (J. McHale Autos Ltd) are a specialist Porsche tuning firm and experts at fuel injection trouble shooting.

Service specialists are Parker and Parker, Longpool, Kendal, Cumbria (tel: 0539 24331), and Stafford Garage, Gloucester Road, Thornbury, Avon (tel: 0454 411214) who also buy and sell classic Porsches.

Other sales specialists, likely to stock early 911s, include Nick Faure, Crossways Garage, Witley, Surrey (tel: 042 879 47089), and Motortune, 250 Brompton Road, London SW3 (tel: 01-581 1234).

It is important to mention at this stage that most general restorers of 911s will also sell the cars (aforementioned Autofarm are a good example) and that general restorers and mechanical specialists will welcome routine service and tuning work. Similarly general restorers will be happy to undertake accident repair work.

High Road, Chadwell Heath, Romford, Essex (tel: 01-590 8412); Noel McGinn Ltd, 3 Poplar Court Parade, Richmond Road, Twickenham; Parrock Brokers Ltd, Veryan, Parrock Road, Gravesend, Kent (tel: 0474 52224); and Hyde Park Insurance Consultants, 191 Westbourne Grove, London W11 (tel: 01-221 2222).

Mention must also be made of two principal spares specialists; Hubert Schellbenge, BP Station, Gladbecke St 266, 4250 Bottrop, West Germany (tel: 02041 33384), and Autocavan, 103 Lower Weybourne Lane, Badshot Lea, Farnham, Surrey (tel: 0252 27627).

Finally, if converting your car either to Cabriolet or Turbo specification appeals, two companies can cater: Motowerk and Club Automobile Services – both previously listed. Club Automobile Services will also undertake converting cars from left to right-hand drive and vice-versa.

There's one thing for sure: Porscheo-

Driving a 911 quickly – and particularly an early one – is not for the faint-hearted. This sort of contortion would be extremely eventful on a public road!

Some of the listed specialists also undertake competition car preparation. These include; Dage Sport, Turner Automotive, Tognola Engineering, Autofarm, Paul Edwards, Dick Lovett, Charles Ivey, and Michael Gleeson.

At least three companies specialise in supply of Porsche exhaust systems: J.S. Exhausts, Queens Road Mills, Gibbet Street, Halifax, West Yorks (tel: 0422 51314); High Legh Filling Station, Warrington Road, High Legh, nr. Knutsford, Cheshire (tel: 092 575 6830); and Jaystock, 71 Michleham Down, London N12 (tel: 01-445 6821).

Tyre specialists include: Quickstop Tyres, 198/200 London Road, Kingston-Upon-Thames (tel: 01-549 2855), 31 Raymill Road West, Maidenhead, Berks (tel: 0628 20543) and at 88 Leatherhead Road, Chessington (tel: 01-397 3075), and Thompsons, Ettingshall Road, Wolverhampton, West Midlands (tel: 0902 44495).

Owners will be pleased to learn of at least four insurance brokers offering competitive rates for 911s; MRB Insurance Brokers Ltd, 313

philes won't be short of reading matter! There can be few companies whose history has been so thoroughly covered, so we'll just mention those we recommend here. On the 911 front, the definitive tome is Paul Frére's *Porsche 911 Story* – the author is a Porsche *aficionado* of note, and an ex-works driver. Mike Cotton's *The Porsche 911 and Derivatives* is one of the excellent MRP Collector's guides, while Chris Harvey's *The Porsche 911* (Oxford Illustrated Press) takes an entertaining and rather more personal look at the model.

On the more general front, two in particular stand out: Karl Ludvigsen's bible on the marque, *Porsche: Excellence was Expected* (An Automobile Quarterly Publication) which gives an in-depth report on the life of the company, and Lothar Boschen's and Jurgen Barth's *The Porsche Book* for those who want detailed technical specifications. Mention must also be made of *Porsche* by Anders Clausager (Haynes) and *The Classic Porsche* (Bison Books) by someone called Mike McCarthy ...

Rivals When New

Throughout the model's life the 911 has enjoyed, and continues to enjoy, a unique position in the market place, offering a combination of performance, build quality, reliability and economy which has never been seriously threatened by a rival manufacturer, Jaguar and the E-type momentarily excluded.

By the time 911 was properly established, the car's most direct rival was probably the Jensen C-V8. The C-V8 MkIII was around £200 more expensive than the top of the line 911S and was substantially quicker to 60mph, managing the figure in 6.7secs compared to the Porsche's 8.0secs. But at the top end the Porsche won hands down at 137mph to the Jensen's 129mph.

The Mercedes-Benz 230SL may have won over some potential Porsche customers, but purely on 'chic' appeal. Similarly, Lancia's Farina Coupés and GT3C would qualify on an aesthetics and glamour basis, but would have lost out badly on the performance front at 911S money.

By 1968 the choice was wider for the enthusiast, with between £3228 (911T) and £4385 (911S) to spend. At the cheaper end of the scale the pretty BMW 2000CS was a weak challenge with far inferior performance. The Lancia Flaminia suffered similarly.

If only the Fiat Dino 2.4 Coupé had been properly marketed in right-hand drive form it may have made an appreciable impression on the Porsche market at similar money to the mid-range 911s. It cost £3737 when Porsches ranged from £3228 to £4385. Top speed was around 130mph and 60mph could be reached in 8.5secs.

The Jaguar E-type fixed-head coupé, by this time in 4.2-litre form, was a true competitor in all respects but price – you could buy nearly two for the price of a 911S. But the 'E' wasn't quite as quick as the 2.4-litre Porsches.

For the less sporting, the Jensen Interceptor and Mercedes-Benz 280SL may have tempted, both costing much the same as a 911S. The Aston Martin DB6 was also similarly priced and offered, at least in Vantage form, arguably superior performance.

Perhaps the man who would have had to stretch himself financially even to afford the base 911T might have been persuaded to settle for the lovely Fiat 2300S – you could, after all, get those Abarth tuning bits for them. But the 2300, like the 130 Coupé that followed it, was not successful in this country. Neither was nearly quick enough to compete with the contemporary Porsches.

Renault-Alpine have always produced cars which might threaten Porsche, but the Dieppe-based company has never distributed its products this side of the channel. This also rules out the Ligier JS2 and Lancia Stratos. All these machines were very much homologation specials, making little pretence at being comfortable cars.

The early seventies saw competition of a refined sort from Citroën with the SM and from Alfa Romeo with the bizarre Montreal. Other likely alternatives were the Mercedes-Benz 280SL, BMW 2800 coupé and the underestimated ISIO Rivolta GT.

With the introduction of the 2.7-litre Carreras, Porsche launched themselves into the supercar bracket. By 1973 the basic 911 cost £4562 and the top of the range Carrera Touring £7193. Discounting GT cars like the AC 428 (£6914), Jensen Interceptor III (£6981) and Mercedes-Benz 350SL (£5725), the classic comparisons came from Italy in the form of the Ferrari 246 Dino (£5915), De Tomaso Pantera (£6596) and Pantera GTS (£7627), Lamborghini Uracco (£6545) and from Germany with the BMW 3.0CSL (£6899).

Two other enigmatic machines which must be considered as should-have-been rivals to the Porsches were the Trident V8 Clipper (that furious 427 Cobra-powered machine killed by the energy crisis) and the Chevrolet Corvette Stingray. The Chevrolet was nearly £5000 in 1973 – about the same money as the 911E and 911S – and the Trident was similar money to the base 911T.

Prices

To state categorically that there is a 911 for everyone's pocket might be a little rash, but during the winter months of 1985 enough cheap 911s were advertised to justify that statement. Restoration jobs are available for just a few hundred pounds (£250 recently for a 911T being a case in point) and a similar model in mostly sound taxed and tested condition can be bought for around the £3500 mark.

Make no mistake, the majority of early 911s advertised in regional trade newspapers and journals for around £3500 are a bundle of trouble, but with careful inspection bargains are there to be had. As a general rule, any car advertised under £4000 should be treated with the greatest of suspicion.

Excluding 2.4S and Cerrera models, overall condition is far more important than the car's age or model. 'Ss' will always be more desirable among enthusiasts, early sixties cars are rapidly acquiring a cult status and 1969 fuel injected cars are probably best avoided – otherwise there are no pros or cons for any individual model. Targas are also generally worth less than the coupé variants.

In summary then, £3500 is bottom 'roadable' money for a pre-'73 911, £4000 is safe and £6000 should buy a superb example of any of the non-Carrera cars from a dealer.

RS Carreras also vary enormously in value. A good '73 car will fetch nearly £20,000 whereas a '74 car, in spite of being virtually identical, is worth half that. Such is the value of the definitive collectable machine!

''The Sting in the Tail'' first appeared in ''Classic & Sports Car''.

DRIVE AID

Porsche 924 ———

The Porsche 924 is listed at over £15,500 new these days, but you can find a tidy used example for around £4000. Is this the Porsche for you? Paul Clark investigates ... ———

Porsche's 924 presented an entirely new image for the Stuttgart company when it was introduced in 1975, and was destined to pave the way for the firm's new generation of front-engine, rear-drive models for the eighties and nineties.

The original Porsche 356, back in 1950, had used many VW parts in its construction but was, without doubt, a Porsche and was sold as such. That model had acquired a fanatical following for the marque which was enhanced by the arrival of the 911 series in 1965.

As early as 1970, the VW-Porsche VG (Vertriebsgesellschaft – the organisation formed to market the ill-fated 914) realised that the 914 was not going to become anybody's favourite and consequently started looking at the possibilities of building a new car to be designed and developed for VW-Audi by Porsche but sold as an Audi sports car. This was the idea of Ferdinand Piëch who had recently joined VW-Audi from Porsche and who, indeed, was Porsche's nephew. His restructuring of the company excited the management which badly needed a new car to enhance its image and move it up-market.

In practice, however, things didn't quite work out that way. True enough, VW-Audi did approach Porsche to commence the design and development of the new car: a set of design parameters was laid down which included the criteria that the new 924 (as it was to be called) should utilise as many volume-produced VW-Audi parts as possible, that it should be front-engined using a water-cooled, four-cylinder unit of VW design (but Audi's building), that it should be a $2+2$ with at least as much room in it as the 911 series, and that it should bear a family resemblance to the 928, which by then was already in the design stage.

In 1973, when Porsche had completed the design of the 924, a total change in the management of Audi prompted them to drop the project. The OPEC oil crisis was in full swing at this time and it seemed uneconomical to contemplate the idea of producing an up-market sports car such as the 924 when the fortunes of the industry were not at their best. Accordingly, a deal was struck with VW-Audi for Porsche to produce the car at the old

Neckarsulm NSU plant, one that was, in fact, due to be scrapped in a 'tidy-up' operation of VW's eight car-producing facilities. The same workforce, which had previously been managed first by NSU and then VW, would be used to build the 924.

So the 924 was born, Body styling was the responsibility of Dutchman Harm Lagaay from Porsche's design studio and it incorporated a number of features that had never before been seen on a Porsche. At the front, concealed headlamps popped up electronically, but separate spotlamps were incorporated into the bumper. A one-piece glass rear window hinged upwards to reveal a large luggage area and seating was indeed $2+2$. A Cd figure of 0.36 was recorded for the body which was the best of any car in the world at its introduction.

Under the bonnet was a Porsche-developed version of VW's 1984cc single belt-driven overhead camshaft engine, canted at an angle of 40 degrees to the vertical so that it could be accommodated under the sloping bonnet line. It was fitted with a Bosch K-Jetronic fuel injection system and developed 125bhp (DIN) at 5800rpm. This engine, in carburettored form, was the one destined for VW's LT van but, despite these humble origins, gave the 924 a spirited performance.

The transmission was mounted as a transaxle at the rear, the Porsche-designed casing containing Audi internals and thus, for the first time on a Porsche, having cone-type synchromesh on the four forward gears rather than the patented Porsche type. The clutch, however, was mounted on the back of the engine and was connected to the transaxle by a 20mm propeller shaft revolving in a steel torque tube of 85mm diameter.

Independent suspension all round was of Volkswagen origin with the front comprising MacPherson struts derived from those of the Beetle, and lower A-arms from the Golf and Scirocco series. At the rear, a trailing arm layout pivoting on the tubular torque tube featured together with 22mm torsion bars. Front shock absorbers were from the Beetle and either Boge or Fichtel and Sachs units were used at the back. Anti-roll bars, 20mm front and 18mm rear, were optional on the first cars. The brakes too, had VW origins, the front discs being from the Beetle and the rear drums from the K70, split diagonally and servo-assisted.

This was the initial specification of the 924: at first, production was planned at about 100 cars a day when the first ones came off the production line in November, 1975. Although this figure wasn't met immediately, it had risen to 60 cars a day by April 1976.

Response to the 924 was lukewarm. Most people felt it was not a Porsche at all but simply a glorified Audi or Volkswagen. Indeed, the very first cars were not representative of what a Porsche should be, albeit well made and finished. The engine was notably gutless and harsh and the handling did not make the car the true driver's machine it should have been.

Yet Porsche's response to this was rapid and the company's policy of continual development began to show.

The first rhd models appeared at the British Motor show in October 1976, but some dealers in the UK had had lhd versions for demonstration purposes before then. The first rhd models were available for sale in March, 1977. This was followed in late 1976 by the three-speed automatic form. The rear axle ratio on automatic cars was 3:445:1 or 3.727:1 on US-spec cars, first delivered in 1977.

At the Frankfurt Motor Show of 1977, Porsche introduced the Getrag ..ve-speed manual gearbox as an option which enhanced driver appeal considerably and made the car instantly more usable. First gear was on a dogleg to the left and back, opposite reverse, while the others, all indirect ratios, were in the normal H pattern. This was accompanied by a final drive ratio change from 3.444:1 to 4.714:1. At this stage a revision was made to the rear suspension mounting which reduced road noise quite considerably.

Porsche Cars (GB) Ltd worked out a 'Lux' package for the 924 in 1978 which offered tinted glass, headlamp washers, rear window wiper, electric windows, 911-series steering wheel, electrically heater door mirror and leather gearlever gaiter as an extra cost option, and it should be noted that 99% of cars sold in Britain are Luxes. In 1979, the five-speed 'box was made standard and a 'space-saver' spare tyre was employed on all except UK spec cars, where these were illegal. Pressure cast alloy wheels, tinted glass, a vanity mirror on the sun visor and stereo speakers were also included.

This was, however, overshadowed somewhat by the introduction of the 924 Turbo which differed in external appearance in that it had front and rear spoilers, a NACA duct on the bonnet, different alloy wheels and four grilles above the bumper at the front. Mechanical alterations included the fitment of four-wheel disc brakes on European-spec cars (US versions retained the disc/drum set up) and substantial changes were made to the cylinder head, though the block remained the same as that of the standard 924. Briefly, the changes involved reducing the compression ratio to 7.5:1 by utilising a different shaped combustion chamber within the head, which, when coupled with the dished pistons, gave a flattened hemispherical chamber. Platinum tipped spark plugs were moved to the intake side of the head and the head gasket was made of copper. Two electric fuel pumps were used to maintain pressure, and the turbocharger was a KKK (Kuhnle, Kopp and Kausch) unit with a wastegate fitted downstream of the exhaust manifold. Mounting the turbo on the exhaust side meant that the starter motor had to be moved to the left hand side of the engine. At the same time, the Turbo's propeller shaft was increased in diameter to 25mm to cope with the extra

power and the final drive was altered to 4.7:1. Power output of the Turbo was 170bhp (DIN) at 5500 rpm, with 180lb/ft of torque at 3000rpm.

1980 saw the introduction of a new five-speed transmission based on the old Porsche four-speed box with fifth to the right and forward opposite reverse. The Turbo retained the Getrag gearbox as the four-speed unit couldn't handle the extra torque. Four-wheel disc brakes became standard in 1981.

Production of the Turbo ceased in 1981 as did export of 924 models to the US. The introduction of the 944 in 1981 suited the emission control regulations far better than the 924 ever did and it is this model which is now selling best in America.

Bodywork

As might be expected with any Porsche, the quality of materials and build of the 924 is of the very highest order, and consequently there are few, if any, rust problems.

Even early cars had galvanised rear wings, floorpan and sills but watch for corrosion on the front wings above the bumper and on the lower edge behind the arch. Look also for paint flaking around the top of the arches front and rear as stone chips are most pronounced. The earthing on the spotlamps in the front bumper can also be affected by mud accumulation.

Check the catches for the rear window as these wear with time, causing the ingress of water and noise to the cockpit.

Engine and Gearbox

The most significant problems concerning the engine of the 924 are to be found in the cylinder head as head gaskets are known to be a weak point and valve guides and seats wear rapidly if neglected. Reconditioning the head is expensive – think in terms of £350-£400 basic with valves themselves an extra £86 and seats costing £50 or so. It is essential to check the fuel system and in particular the state of the fuel tank. Dirt or water getting into the fuel injection pipework may necessitate renewal of the complete system – and that's extremely expensive! Early cars were noted for being a problem to start when warm due to lack of fuel pressure but this was later modified by the fitment of an electro-magnetic valve. Typical operating pressure should be around 60-70psi.

The turbo is really a completely different kettle of fish: maintenance costs can be extraordinarily high, and abuse of the turbocharger can lead to premature failure. A new one costs about £485 and parts such as the special platinum spark plugs are about £11 a set. It is essential, if viewing a prospective purchase, to examine the service records very carefully. Porsche does not give any special instructions relating to driving methods for the Turbo, so it's quite possible that it has been treated as a normal 924, which isn't

Based on the Volkswagen LT van engine, Porsche's version of the 1984cc slant-four develops 125bhp (DIN) in injected form though is it notably gutless and thrashy when extended.

sive: around £41 for the front set and £43 for the rears. They wear quickly, too, so check them frequently as discs are not cheap should the pads go through to the metal.

On other 924 models, four-stud alloy wheels of a simpler pattern are fitted, except for very early models which had pressed steel wheels. Pads and shoes for standard 924s work out at around £30 for the front set and £24 for the rears. They wear quickly too, so the same careful treatment applies here as for the Turbo.

Interior and Trim

Interior trim on Porsches has always been regarded as being slightly spartan for the

really on. It's quite possible to have turbo failure after fewer than 25,000 miles in the wrong hands. Be warned!

Synchromesh on first gear in the Getrag 'box can become sticky with age so check this for wear. Otherwise the transmissions on the 924 are very robust.

Steering, Suspension, Brakes

Early cars had optional anti-roll bars front and rear, so check to see whether they are fitted to your proposed buy. The dampers on these cars were of dubious quality also, but Konis were optional so check for these as they will make a significant difference to the handling and roadholding.

Five-stud 'honeycomb' alloy wheels were fitted to Turbo models together with disc brakes all round. Pads for these are expen-

Rear seats are strictly of the 2+2 variety with a large transmission hump in the middle.

Check the interior trim conforms with the car's specification: Lux variants have tinted glass and electric windows not fitted to standard cars.

price. Nevertheless, it is functional and comfortable accommodation for two adults and their luggage in the 924. It is strictly a 2 + 2 as the transmission hump intrudes significantly in the back. Razzy black and white check upholstery may not please, but comfort almost certainly will!

For the driver, the steering wheel may encroach on knee room as it is very low set and non-adjustable. The boss is also offset from the centre which aggravates the problem when on lock.

When looking at a prospective purchase, check the interior specification very closely as the car might have been the subject of a 'personal import' from the Continent. Remember, 99% of all 924s in this country are 'Luxes' so be suspicious of cars not conforming to this specification (see earlier). The 'Lux' pack was devised in Britian and cars were not supplied with these 'extras' as standard direct from the factory.

This article first appeared in "Thoroughbred & Classic Cars" magazine.

Early cars had pressed steel wheels. Pictures courtesy of Autofarm, 5 Hill Avenue, Amersham, Bucks HP5 5BD, (02403 2112) Porsche specialists.

Special Editions

A number of 'special' edition 924s have been offered with special trim packages. These are:

Martini – 1976, all-white bodywork, white alloy wheels, tapering Martini colours down the sides, black interior, red carpets, blue seat inserts, sunroof, four-speed gearbox, 100 built.

Doubloon – 1979, pale gold metallic paint, black and polished alloy wheels, tan pinstriped interior. 50 built.

Le Mans – 1981, white paintwork, German colours running around body, Turbo-style wheels (four-stud), Pirelli P6 tyres, black seats with white piping, Koni dampers and anti-roll bars. Turbo rear spoiler, sunroof, 924 Turbo steering wheel. 100 built.

Steve Kevlin stands by his racing 924 which he campaigns successfully in the Production Porsche Championship, frequently winning his class by considerable margins. Thanks go to Steve for his help in preparing this article.

Robin Levey

© HAYNES
H8527

DRIVE AID

Buying a Rover?_

*John Williams conducts you through the ritual of selecting a P4 Rover – a quality classic that's still affordable.*_____

One of the biggest tributes to the Rover P4 series is the quantity you see about in active use today – production ended in May 1964, over 20 years ago, yet quality construction and durable bodywork has ensured many survivors. 'Quality' certainly sums up the P4 – it may not have been the fastest six-cylinder car of its period, but it was certainly one of the best put together and has a beautifully engineered feel to it when driven, even to this day.

Much of the mechanical side of the original P4 of September 1949 – engine and suspension for example – was directly inherited from its predecessor, the pre-war styled P3. The new Rover 75, with its characteristic 'cyclops' central spotlamp, thus used the same overhead inlet/side exhaust six-cylinder power unit, albeit with an aluminium cylinder head and twin carburettors, and coil sprung independent front suspension with the unusual feature of radius arms which anchored on mountings under the gearbox. Re-circulating ball steering was used, and the then fashionable column gear change (it went back on the floor in 1953).

There are rather a bewildering number of individual models which make up the 130,000-odd P4s which left Solihull during the car's 15 year production run – no less than nine in fact, and even these can be further sub-divided to an extent, so to sort them out refer to our Production chart. The various types have their own merits and enthusiastic following, though as a general rule there seems to be a mild preference for later models, the reasons including better performance and brakes (discs arrived in 1960), and, possibly, better

condition mechanically and inside the car. However, later cars seem to have been made of lighter or poorer steel and did not have aluminium panels so a thorough body and chassis inspection is important.

Engine

A variety of engines were used in the P4 series, though really only the Rover 80 (1959-62) was the odd man out with a more normal *overhead* valve engine of 4-cylinders and 2286cc capacity, as fitted to Land-Rovers for many years. Although strong and reliable this engine is considered by some to be rather harsh to be installed in the Rover saloon, and is no more economical than a six-cylinder engine. All other P4s had overhead inlet, sidevalve exhaust engines, all of which were six-cylinder engines except for the Rover 60 of 1953-59. The 60 had the P3's single-carburettor four-cylinder engine of 1997cc, and was correspondingly short on performance, if good on economy, with a fuel

Some P4 Production Changes

1954: Synchromesh became available on 2nd, 3rd and top gears (previously 3rd and top only).
1956: Laycock overdrive became optional on the 90, and later available on all cars except the 95. The Rover Freewheel device was fitted to all cars prior to 1956 when it was phased out, as the 105 models and later 90s were fitted with brake servos.
1960: Front wheel disc brakes were fitted on the 1960 cars and continued to the end of the service.
1963: Aluminium panels were discontinued in March 1963.

Rover P4 Production

Model	Production years	Number built	Cyls.	Capacity (cc)	Engine bore x (mm)	stroke
75	49-54	43677	6	2103	65.2	105
	54-59		6	2230	73.025	88.9
60	53-59	9261	4	1997	77.8	105
80	59-62	5900	4	2286	90.49	88.9
90	53-59	35891	6	2638	73.025	105
95	62-64	3680	6	2625	77.8	92.075
100	59-62	16621	6	2625	77.8	92.075
105R	56-58	3499	6	2638	73.025	105
105S and 105	56-59	7201	6	2638	73.025	105
110	62-64	4612	6	2625	77.8	92.075

Rear end body styling and chassis alterations were necessary in later models partly to accommodate larger tyre sizes. Radial tyres should not be used on P4 Rovers. The rear skirt, below the bumper, is prone to rust.

consumption of up to 30mpg, if the overdrive or free-wheel are put to good use.

Although some people choose to criticise the four-cylinder cars it is worth mentioning that with less weight over the front wheels than the six-cylinder cars the steering was lighter and the car probably handles better.

All the other P4s used six-cylinder engines which were basically similar, although there isn't space to list all the changes which affected these engines over the years, The 75 started life with the engine carried over from the P3 series as mentioned, and in 1954 the capacity was increased from 2103cc to 2230cc – in effect this became a short stroke version of the 90 engine. The 105R and S had twin carburettors. For the Rover 100, a short stroke version of the seven-bearing Rover 3-litre engine was produced, having a stronger crankshaft and roller bearing cam followers. This engine was also used in the 95, and, with a Weslake head, in the 110.

The post-1960 engines are reputed to have a longer life than their predecessors and to be a great deal quieter in their old age. Crankshaft oil supply and pressure should not be a major problem provided that a suitable oil is used, the oil level is checked frequently, and the oil and filter changed at 3000 mile intervals. Problems are more likely to arise in the top end of these engines and, although the

The 110 interior is typically neat and impressive, with comfortable seats and plenty of timber. Bear in mind the very high cost of restoring a quality interior these days and examine it all carefully. Look under the carpets, too, and especially around the outer edges of the floors.

A lot of thoughtful engineering went into the P4 cars. For example, the 110 has this neat chromed bracket on which each wiper arm rests, clear of the screen when not in use ...

... and side windows which wind down complete with part of the 'window frame' was a feature of all P4 cars. Note that the interior woodwork was french polished; not the toughest of finishes, especially when dampness is present. The wood on the driver's door is likely to be the worst affected.

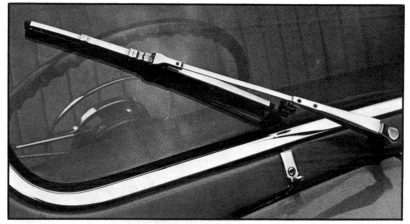

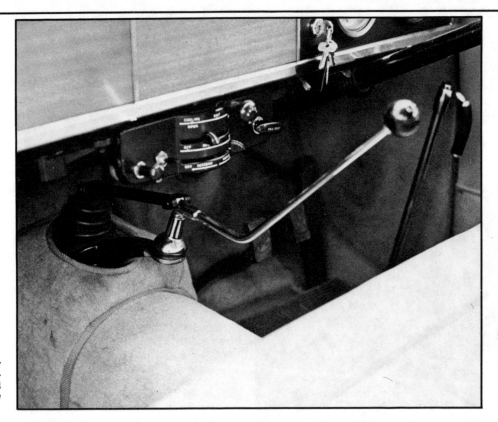

Another nice feature of many models is the adjustable gear-lever. This can be moved from side to side to suit the driver's seating position.

problems are by no means inevitable, they are all too often caused by inadequate servicing or unskilled overhaul work. These engines respond remarkably well to expert attention and will cover very high mileages between major overhauls if the work is carried out correctly. In this connection I can certainly recommend DAK Autos. Hillview Lane Garage, Billington, Leighton Buzzard, Beds., tel: (0525) 382944 whose work I have witnessed on a number of occasions when gathering information and pictures for *Practical Classics* articles.

New chrome parts are unobtainable now so you may have to consider rechroming where possible. The front wings are particularly prone to rust around the indicators and sidelights and below the headlights. Look under the wings, too, and prod the inner panels with a screwdriver to check that they are solid. Note any significant build-up of mud etc, which retains moisture and salt and does a lot of damage, and don't assume that all is well just because there is a nice fresh coat of underseal.

Remember to look at the bottoms of doors – which are often neglected.

The chrome bezel over the rear number plate is unobtainable now but may be remanufactured soon if there is sufficient demand. Examine the rear bumper and rear apron, and look inside the spare wheel compartment which is under the boot, where rust may have taken a hold.

The rubber sealing strip which attaches to the edge of the step beneath each door may be well worn or even missing. These are becoming available again but only through owners' clubs.

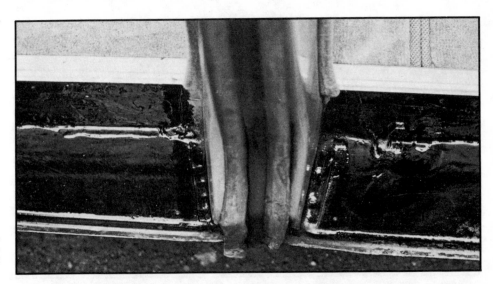

As on so many four-door saloons, the base of the centre
door pillar is a favourite spot
for rust ...

... and the area around the
bottom hinge of each rear
door deserves special attention too ...

Make a special effort to look
under the wings and check
the conditon of the tyres, too.
If you have not owned a car of
this size previously you may
be surprised to find that good
quality tyres will cost around
£45 each.

corrosion in the outrigger upon which it is mounted.

For a blow-by-blow account of where to look for rot, see our picture sequence. When it comes to spare parts, second-hand items from scrap cars still constitute a useful source of supply, including the aluminium panels which last well. Doors, with minor alterations, are interchangeable throughout the range, and because of the substantial saving in weight, many owners of 95s and 110s have fitted their cars with alloy doors from earlier models.

The P4 Rover is surprisingly affordable especially when compared with, say, contemporary Jaguars, and in quality gives away very little to any make. Once you've acquired the taste, this sort of Rover motoring may be very hard to give up!

Chassis

A sturdy box section chassis was used throughout the series, but chassis corrosion may be present, particularly in cars produced from 1960 onwards for some unaccountable reason. The points to watch are the outriggers which carry the body mountings, especially

Look in the petrol filler compartment and note that the door tends to rust.

Having noted the general condition of the boot, lift the covers and inspect the floor, especially around edges and in corners. The boot can be full of unpleasant surprises in otherwise tidy cars, particularly if a leak in the rear window seal has allowed water to find its way into the boot. This is not uncommon.

Body

Doors, bonnet and bootlid were of aluminium until early 1963 when there was a change to steel for the last year of production. This affected the remaining 95s and 110s but many of these may since have acquired the aluminium panels. On the other hand, earlier cars which have been accident damaged may have had some of their original aluminium panels replaced by steel! Most of the panels and chassis sections which are likely to be needed for these cars are obtainable again either off the shelf or to order (DAK Autos), these are being remanufactured in aluminium or steel to meet the original specifications. The condition of chassis outriggers (also available) is important and it is worth noting that an inefficient handbrake may well be due to

Paint lifting off aluminium door panel. Paint condition is important – a quality re-spray will be expensive.

the front pair which are located just behind the front wheels. Check the handbrake mounting and the area around the anchor points for the front dampers, and also those sections of the chassis which curve over the rear axles.

Gearbox

All the P4 cars except the 105R had manual gearboxes which were relatively trouble-free. High mileage gearboxes (80,000 +) do have a common fault in the form of worn layshaft bearings (especially the front one) which produce a rattle when the clutch pedal is depressed, so keep your ears open. A certain amount of noise in the indirect gears is quite normal.

Newcomers two Rover motoring may be unfamiliar with the free-wheel device which was used on many of these cars. This allows the car to coast on the over-run (thus saving fuel) and enables gearchanging to be carried out without using the clutch (although the accelerator pedal is used in the normal manner). There are two important points about the free-wheel which are worth noting here; firstly, it can be engaged and disengaged with the car in motion provided that the engine is under load, and secondly it must not be engaged whilst reversing.

The 105R was fitted with the rather unusual Roverdrive semi-automatic transmission. This was discontinued when the 3-Litre was introduced with its Borg Warner transmis-

Later cars were particularly prone to rust around the indicator and sidelamp.

The wheel arch edge and the point where the rubber seal on the bulkhead meets the wing are prone to rust.

sion. It has been argued that Roverdrive was unsuccessful, and cannot be particularly recommended now due to scarcity of spares. In fact, it was an extremely smooth transmission system, if somewhat sluggish, and apart from any problems which may arise with a few switches and relays the only part likely to need replacing is the overdrive section, and this was common to other models so is still obtainable. Incidentally, if you find a 105 (without the R or S), it is exactly the same as a 105S, and will be a 1959 model, because the letter S was dropped as it was no longer needed for identification when the 105R was discontinued.

Suspension & Steering

Some steering links and bushes are difficult to obtain, and kingpin assemblies are expensive. Check these areas carefully, and note that kingpins should be oiled and *not* greased, otherwise they will tend to seize up and cause extra wear in the steering system including the steering box. Check the condition of the shock absorbers and examine the rear springs, too, bearing in mind that broken springs are often caused by worn out shock absorbers. A word of warning here; when buying shock absorbers and hydraulic components such as master cylinders, etc. beware of unused but old stock which has been on the shelf for years. Such stock is quite likely to have deteriorated during storage and there have been instances when shock absorbers have lasted only three months on a car for this reason. There is no need to buy old stock; genuine new components are available.

The P4 rolls quite a bit if cornered hard,, but the ride should be good in all other respects. Later 80 and 100 models had lower geared steering.

Brakes

Brake servos were fitted to all cars with front wheel disc brakes, and to some late 1950s models that still had drum brakes all round. Servos tend to have problems which can't be anticipated or easily detected in the early stages. Typically, fluid will leak into the vacuum chamber and the whereabouts of the lost fluid remains a mystery. One day after much pedal pumping the lost fluid makes its way into the engine and the fellow behind finds himself driving into a big cloud of whitish-grey smoke. Renovation of the braking system could cost around £700 (a servo alone costs well over £100), so examine the whole system carefully. New brake pipes may not cost a lot, but if you strip a few threads, or shear the odd union whilst removing the old pipes, don't blame inflation for the bill at the end of the day!

"Buying a Rover?" first appeared in "Practical Classics" magazine.

What to Pay

Prices vary from well over £3000 for cars which are not necessarily perfect to under £100 for potential restoration projects. It is advisable to avoid cars which require extensive restoration work, not merely because the cost of such work may well exceed the subsequent value of the car, but because on quality cars such as these restoration work is very expensive. Bear in mind that both £500 cars and £2500 cars can be described as in 'first-class condition' in the classified columns and if this reflects some misunderstanding on the part of owners as regards the true condition and value of their cars it is also a fact that there are still instances in which the cheaper car is a better buy.

Second-hand Supercars

by Ian Ward

The star attractions at Motor-fair, as at other shows around the world, are likely to fall into the 'Supercar' category – fast, sleek and seductively curvaceous and made all the more desirable by price tags that put them beyond the reach of nearly all of us! Even personally importing an example from overseas is unlikely to help a great deal: if you can't afford the list price, then you probably won't be able to scrape up the cut rate either.

By their very description, supercars are an exclusive breed, and this deliberate rarity value generates greater demand than supply. Try walking into your local Porsche dealer, for instance, and saying you'll take the red 944 Turbo if he knocks 15 per cent off the windscreen numbers; you might be lucky to get out of the showroom with your collar uncrumpled!

To an extent, this exclusiveness is also reflected in used prices. The really sought-after beasts can fetch more as second-hand buys than they go for when brand new; this premium is dependent on how effective the manufacturer's publicity machine has been in creating real desirability for his product. Increased production rates or catalogue prices could easily solve the problem, but there is nothing like a healthy used-model trade for keeping the factory order books full.

So what constitutes a supercar? As with sports cars, there can never be a hard and fast single definition which satisfies all possible parameters. To most *aficionados,* however, a candidate can be judged by its performance (it must be very fast, with sporting handling to match), its styling (it should be sleek and eye-catching), and its price (which is likely to be in the telephone number bracket). In today's terms, we are talking about price tags of from £23,000 to £80,000, a vast range indeed, but nonetheless one in a rarified atmosphere of its own.

Out of reach supercars may be, as new buys, but what of the second-hand field? Supposing you've got £10,000 burning a hole in your pocket and you have had a life-long ambition to own an Aston Martin, what can you get for your money? In this case, quite a lot.

The V8 has been around since 1972 and for four years prior to that with Aston's old straight-six engine. It is true that changes of company ownership have brought different names, the car starting life under David Brown's patronage as the DBS, but this William Towns-styled brute is fundamentally unaltered. Thus there are enough V8s around to make bargains available and prices tend to be held down by the voracious thirst of the 5.3-litre four-cam power unit, which even under a delicate right foot will only drive the Aston about 14 miles on each precious gallon of four-star.

When the Carrera name returned to the Porsche line-up in 911 guise in 1973, its lightweight body, small production run, competition background and exclusive price made it an instant collectors piece. The thinner panels, which are more rust prone, and their frequent use on the track, can make the restoration of a (genuine!) Carrera even more expensive than its high value. But beware of lookalike Carreras with bolt-on Porsche packs that are far more common than the real thing!

The V8 now retails at £55,000, but for just £10,000 you could expect to find a very good example of late 1978 vintage, or a more modest specimen about a year newer. This is particularly good news, because the earlier months of 1978 saw a succession of alterations, which were all definite improvements. Vantage and convertible Volante variants are going to be beyond reach, but the standard V8 (usually in automatic transmission) form is a mighty beast, capable of shifting two adults and two children around in real luxury and at great pace.

Of course, as with any car of this age, you could be buying a whole load of trouble. What's more, standard old car problems will cost you much more to put right on an exotic machine such as this than on a mass-production motor-car. Clutches, exhaust systems, brake parts and so on are far from cheap.

On the plus side, though, supercars, more than anything because of their high initial prices, are nearly always well cared for. Their owners tend to be discerning and thoughtful motorists who drive with at least some mechanical sympathy and have their pride and joys regularly serviced by an authorised agent.

This means that you have a good chance of getting a full service history with the car when you buy it and this will serve a dual

If the promise of 14mpg from its 5.3-litre V8 engine doesn't put you off, then the price of these Volante convertible versions of the big Aston Martin almost certainly will. Fixed-head versions, says Ian Ward, are more affordable. But check out spares and servicing prices first! (Courtesy "Thoroughbred & Classic Cars.")

purpose. It will provide a record of the jobs carried out and parts replaced and it should offer some clue as to the authenticity of the mileage reading – old MoT test certificates are useful here, too. A further plus is that the mechanics who have looked after the car are likely to be more proficient in that job than would a mass-producer's man with any given model, simply because he will only need to know about one or two types, as opposed to perhaps ten. A car like an Aston may well have been back to the factory a few times for

version. However, this is a long way from the truth. The Series 1 was not a particularly good car – judged by the impeccable standards set by the current S3 – and although the interim Series 2 car of 1978 showed improvements, it is the newest edition, based closely on the Turbo's body, chassis and running gear, which is the one to go for.

How do you spot a good supercar? Just as with any other second-hand buy, you go round it with a fine tooth-comb. If you lack the courage of your own convictions, enlist the

When they arrived on the scene in 1981, this Ferrari 308 GTSi cost £21,809 in Berlinetta (closed) form and £22,699 in the Spyder version shown here. Even the use of K-Jetronic fuel injection wouldn't keep maintenance costs below the levels of most people's mortages! (Courtesy "Thoroughbred & Classic Cars".)

On the other hand, since the days of the XK120, Jaguars have been renowned for giving you just about everything that the supercar of the day would give without quite the cachet but also without the heartache. And your wallet should only hurt half as much! Early XJSs come as cheap as only old Jaguars can. (Courtesy "Thoroughbred & Classic Cars.")

repair or overhaul, which has to be a confidence booster.

At the other end of the supercar price scale comes the dramatically fashioned Lotus Turbo Esprit. This is currently listed at a mere £23,440, a figure which has to represent real value in this league, for a projectile which will cosset you as it thrusts you unerringly towards its 150mph maximum speed, and sticks like glue to the tarmac as you hurl it through bends which would be impossible at such speeds in a machine without such a race-bred heritage.

With a new price only a fraction that of the Aston, you might expect to pick up a real bargain on the used car lots. And you *can* have a Turbo for less than the Aston, but the saving is not as great as the figures suggest it should be. For, say £9000, you will probably be able to pick up an average example from 1981, the first year that the model was in proper production, when it already cost £17,000.

It is this relative newness of the breed, together with excellent, 20 + mpg fuel economy that despite a slight prestige edge to the Aston Martin, makes the name Lotus a more attractive proposition. Add to this the fact that the Turbo has hardly changed in its six-year life and it becomes a very attractive piece of hardware.

Not so, some other supercars. An especially notable example is the 'ordinary' Esprit. Introduced back in 1975, this Lotus might have looked the same to the layman as today's

support of a professional engineer, be it from one of the motoring organisations or from a repair shop. Read up as much as possible about the type of car you are after before you go out hunting, so that you will know exactly which model you are looking at and will have some inkling as to whether all is as the designer intended.

There is no magic involved, but as with the careful servicing already mentioned, most supercars are better put together than their mass-production counterparts, and can therefore be expected to last longer. Exceptions exist – for instance Porsches, up to the mid 1970s, had a habit of rusting gently away, and Ferraris of the same period, too. But things have changed now and popular stories of Ferrari fragility are not backed up by true experiences from owners.

Body rust is never going to be a problem with the Aston Martin or the Lotus. The V8's shell is fashioned in aluminium and the Esprit's in Lotus's own blend of up-to-the-minute plastics technology. Both sit on steel chassis, but these are not particular problem areas and Lotus now provide an eight-year anti-corrosion warranty with their galvanised item.

If the car is more than superficially smart, turn to the interior. If this is tatty it could cost a small fortune to restore it to former glory. Also, such a state may give the lie to a low recorded mileage on a car without a service history.

Engines and other mechanical items should be checked over very carefully. If there is any hint of wear in the power unit, indicated by rattles and knocks, smoke from the exhaust or fumes from the breather, you could be in for a bill running into thousands of pounds before you have derived any real pleasure from the car.

Scrutinise the exhaust system from underneath and make sure that you are allowed to drive the machine quite hard so that you can check the clutch, steering, gearchange and brakes for proper function.

As important as anything is to check the state of the tyres. Supercars demand super-rubber, which comes super-priced. For instance, four new tyres for the Aston will set you back by up to £450 and those for the Lotus by £350 – £400 – and that's without a spare!

A supercar is only going to be a bargain buy if you can avoid all but the most minor maintenance bills. If all seems well, especially if the service history shows that items like brake linings, clutch and exhaust have recently been replaced, then you should have a winner. You'll probably be looking at a mileage of between 40,000 and 75,000 for the cars we've looked at. The latter seems very high, but there is no reason to suppose – as long as there is no current evidence of wear, as mentioned – that you will not be able to add another 25,000 to the total without running into trouble.

Resale value will depend on what has happened as far as production goes, since you bought the car. If the model is obsolete and thus getting rarer it will probably start gaining value quite soon. At worst, it is not likely to plummet in value.

If you want to take advantage of such a price drop in the supercar field then go for an elderly XJS Jaguar. This may be a little rusty and will certainly drink petrol like an elephant at the water hole, but it will still be quiet, fast and elegant. For about £2,500, you can have a good 1976 car to impress the neighbours, and £9,000 should buy you the latest HE version, from 1981.

So as you walk round the next Motorshow, don't despair as you take in the most mouthwatering exhibits. Take your time and spend wisely and you, too, can go supercar motoring.

"Second-hand Supercars" first appeared in the 1985 "Motorfair" catalogue.

The 1982 DeTomaso Pantera GT5: you've really got to be an out-and-out enthusiast to even consider owning an Italian supercar. Many are wonderful feats of temperamental engineering in an all-Italian, all-aesthetic skin. But what's that? You want rear vision, leg room, luggage space, too? Forget it! (Courtesy Thoroughbred & Classic Cars".)

DRIVE AID

Buying an Alpine ... or perhaps a Tiger!

Attractive sports tourers from the Rootes Group rediscovered by John Williams

Building and selling sports cars did not come naturally to the Rootes Group, and this is perhaps reflected by the fact that the original Sunbeam Alpine was really a tuned Sunbeam Talbot 90 saloon provided with an attractive open two-seater body. The second Sunbeam Alpine was outwardly rather further removed from its Hillman, Singer and Sunbeam Rapier relations, but it was still described as a sports tourer and not as a sports car.

To some extent the Alpine's lack of exotic flavour, its structural and component links with the saloons plus the fact that the Rootes Group and their dealer network were not sports car orientated, set the Alpine off to a bad start from which it never really recovered. In fact, there is still a widespread notion that it is not quite the done thing to mention the Sunbeam Alpine in the same breath as the MGs, the Triumph TRs or the Austin Healeys

because it is "a woman's car, not a real sports car."

The truth is that in the early days of the Sunbeam Alpine, Rootes had a car that was better built, had more space and comfort and performed quite well considering its weight and engine size when compared to its British rivals. It also had the advantage of being much more up-to-date in the looks department than any of its mass-produced rivals.

Despite promising showings in competition, particularly winning the Thermal Efficiency Award at Le Mans in 1961, when Austin-Healey, Triumph and particularly MG made their sports cars more civilised, the Rootes Group did not pursue performance but went several stages further in making their Alpine even better finished, better equipped and more practical than its rivals. The Rootes approach to the car as a sports tourer rather than as a sports car is best reflected by the early introduction of an optional automatic gearbox and the fact that over a nine year period, whilst the engine capacity rose from 1494cc to 1725cc, performance did not improve accordingly.

After the Alpine was dead and buried and Chrysler had taken the Rootes Group over, the same 1725cc engine was developed to give sundry saloons the sort of performance the Alpine could have done with to embarrass MGB owners; but long before that Rootes had been shown Alpines with 4.2-litre Ford V8 power units and were distracted from the Alpine by the promise of the Tiger.

By the early 1960s when the Tiger plot

This is the now fairly scarce series I Alpine which shared its tall rear fins with the series II and III cars. The aluminium hardtop was an optional extra on the series II cars as well.

was hatched, the Rootes Group was short of money and its financial problems grew steadily worse as time went on, so there was little opportunity to make the big-engined car look noticeably different to the Alpine. There is also room to argue that the typical Hillman Minx salesman was perhaps not the best person to sell a car like the Tiger. It might be added that Rootes mechanics probably did not like working in a cramped engine bay or feel at home with American carburation.

Wheels and tyres that were not big enough for the job, weight distribution, braking and cooling that had room for improvement and undergearing sold the Tiger short because it certainly had unusual potential performance which could be used to waft the car from standstill to seventy in top gear without effort, or, if used to the full,

The later styling for the rear fins was introduced with the series IV cars and is seen on this series V model. The luggage rack is not 'correct' for this car but the bootlid was designed to accept the correct accessory.

Series III, IV and V cars could be fitted with a detachable steel hardtop which (unlike its aluminium predecessor) is heavy enough to need two people to carry it.

Brief Guide to Alpine Modifications

Alpine series I: 1494cc ohv engine with twin Zenith carburettors, independent front suspension by coil springs and wishbones, half elliptic springs and telescopic dampers at the rear. Disc brakes at the front, drums at the rear. Available with or without overdrive. Aluminium hardtop an optional extra.

Alpine series II: As above except 1592cc engine.

*Alpine series III: Revised boot layout. Cars available as 'open sports' with folding hood and (optional) steel hardtop or as GT Coupe with removable hardtop but no hood.

*Alpine series IV: Single Solex carburettor. Optional Borg Warner automatic gearbox. From Autumn 1964 an all synchromesh manual box was fitted. Revised rear fins, 'Open' or GT.

*Alpine series V: 1725cc engine with five bearing crankshaft (previously three) and two Stromberg carburettors. No automatic transmission. 'Open' or GT.

*Please note that whether or not you require a hardtop the GT versions of the series III, IV and V cars are to be avoided if you require an Alpine with a folding hood.

Unlike the Tiger the Alpine has room to spare in its engine compartment although the general arrangement is extremely untidy. Various combinations of carburation and manifolding were used. Very few people have a good word to say for the twin choke Solex instrument used at one stage.

The steel hardtop also rusts, especially at its lower rear corners and around the side windows. The windows of the hardtop are perspex which ages.

Interiors are well equipped and particularly well finished. Both the Alpine and the Tiger were superior to many rival makes in this respect. This is the interior of a series I Alpine.

Considerable improvements had been made by the time the series V Alpines appeared in late 1965.

terrify the living daylights out of normal people.

Neither the Alpine nor the Tiger fitted into the plans of Chrysler, who not only chose to forget about them, but also hid the evidence of their existence by 'running out' of spares – especially body panels – suspiciously quickly.

It is now a bit late to discuss why the Alpine, and to a lesser extent the Tiger, were not a popular choice amongst classic car enthusiasts until comparatively recently, but a large number have died of neglect and advanced rust and there are still very few Alpine and Tiger specialists. Prices are still low by sports car standards and, provided you buy a sound example and protect it from rust or carry out a proper restoration on a less sound example, both cars offer excellent value. Basically, the Alpine shell is very strong and with money, time and determination the majority of the survivors *can* be saved.

The rear seats in Alpines and Tigers hardly offer enough space for one adult passenger but one or two young children could travel in reasonable comfort.

Erecting the hood is a straightforward matter of raising it and connecting the hinged side rails to the windscreen frame before fastening two securing clips at the top of the windscreen and snap fasteners at the sides of the hood. Stowing the hood can be more difficult.

Remember to check the condition of the hood and whether it can be raised and lowered satisfactorily. Replacing a damaged or ill fitting hood could be expensive.

A very fine Mk II Tiger showing all the original features – the revised grille and headlamp rims, the 'decorative' stripes and chrome trimmed wheel arches. The Mini-lite wheels were not standard but were probably the most suitable type of wider wheel to use, getting away from the under-tyred original specification. A 4.7 litre engine was fitted. The Mk II Tigers are now rare.

A Mk I Tiger shows its paces at the Practical Classics 1981 Goodwood test day. These cars had a 4.2 litre V8 American Ford engine.

What to Look For

It is hardly fair to say that Alpines and Tigers are particularly prone to rust, but genuinely sound examples are likely to be in a small minority as it is many years since production ended, and it was not until recently that owners could obtain a supply of replacement panels. The unitary bodywork is built upon a pair of chassis rails reinforced by cruciform bracing sections, the latter being the last part of the car to become seriously affected by rust. Therefore, it is probably as well to check the underside of the car first and if it is seriously rusted you should be ready to reject that particular car. Whilst under the car have a look at the forward hangers for the rear springs and then complete the chassis checks by inspecting the jacking points in turn to ensure that they will not crumble under load. Even when sound, they do not inspire confidence.

Next examine the bodywork thoroughly starting with the front valance, and especially under the sidelights where the valance is welded to the wings. The front wings themselves are prone to rust around the headlights and along their top edge adjacent to and below the edges of the bonnet. The rear section of the front wings should be examined, too, as rust frequently develops along a vertical line behind the wheel arches and in the bottoms of the wings back to the sills. Look under the wings at the panels which form the footwells. These are sealed to the wings (not welded) and there is plenty of scope for rust once the sealing compound ages or falls away. Inside the engine compart-

What to Pay

Relatively few Alpines and even fewer Tigers are advertised for sale and prices vary widely. From the limited information which is available it would be misleading to buyers and sellers alike to attempt an accurate guide to prices. There is some evidence to support the view that an average Alpine with no serious problems can be obtained for about £1000 – £1200, and that a very good example will command a price of around £2000.

Tigers are another matter, ranging in price up to £4500. Those which are advertised for sale tend to be at or near this figure, so if you are looking for a car at a lower price, or for one which actually needs some restoration work, you will probably have to enlist the aid of the club, and you will not need to be in a hurry.

The boot on series I and II cars was inadequate ...

... but this area was revised for the series III cars, the spare wheel was moved to a vertical position and single fuel tank (previously in the bottom of the boot) being replaced by twin tanks in the wings.

A severe case of rust in the scuttle usually caused by blockage of the scuttle air intake drainage channels.

ment examine the vertical panels on either side between the wheel arches, wings and bulkhead; these are very rust-prone. Sills and their closing panels should be checked and it is worth paying special attention to doors to establish how much repair work will be needed if rust is present. Rear wings rust around the wheel arches and along their lower edges from the wheel arch to the rear valance.

Inside the car carry out further checks on the footwells by looking under the carpets, and look for evidence of leaks between the windscreen frame and the scuttle. It is worth checking the security of the seatbelt anchorages on the rear wheel arches, and handbrakes have been known to pull away from the floor. Make sure that the window winder mechanisms are working (they are prone to failure) and check that the seat mountings are intact and in sound condition.

There are no particular mechanical problems associated with the Alpine but it is obviously sensible to have a test drive and check for any suspicious noises from the engine or transmission. The engines are reputed to leak oil rather than burn it, and if the overdrive (which was fitted to the majority of cars) doesn't work, it may well be due to an accumulation of dirt in the vicinity of the solenoid.

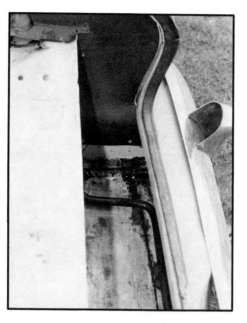

Check panels around the wheel arches at each side of the engine; these rust quickly but can be easily repaired if tackled early.

Centre left. Examine the rear wheel arches and the lower rear wings too ...

... and look for rust at the bottom rear corners of the boot. Rust here can damage the rear spring hangers, bumper mountings and jacking points.

Sills and the bottoms of doors rust and door design changed during production limiting the scope of interchangeability (the same applies to bonnets).

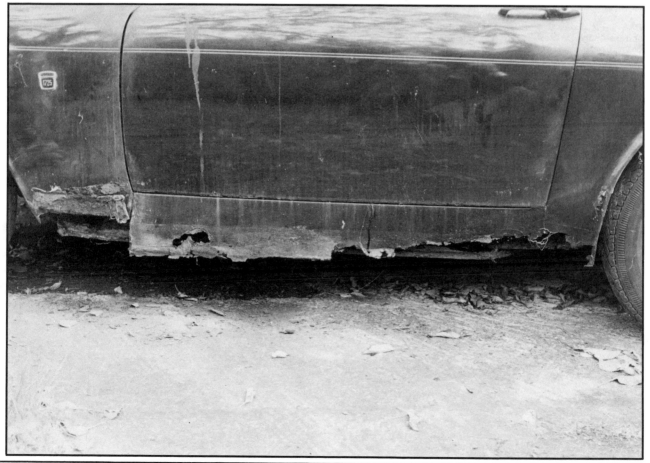

Availability of Spares

Most mechanical parts of the Alpine were used on other Rootes cars of the period and are still fairly readily available. No body panels were obtainable for these cars for some years but some reproduction panels are now being made again. The parts which are the hardest to replace are the small components which were peculiar to these cars, such as badges, chrome trim and certain rubber seals. Some of these items are available again through the clubs or spe-cialists, and no doubt the range of available parts will grow in response to increasing demand as more of these cars are restored. For the Tiger, mechanical parts are obtainable, the notable exception being the steering rack (Alpines had room for a steering box).

This article first appeared in ''Practical Classics'' magazine.
The writer wishes to thank Trevor Rogers and Kim Faulkner of the Sunbeam Alpine Owners Club for assistance in the preparation of this article.

With the approval of Rootes, Thomas Harrington Ltd of Hove produced a number of Sunbeam Harringtons based on the Alpine. Back as far as the doors this is an original Alpine, but the rest has been restyled and the fixed head coupe roof is in glass fibre. The interior is more luxuriously furnished than in 'ordinary' Alpines and there is more space, although rear leg room is still limited. The picture shows a Sunbeam Harrington Le Mans in which mechanical alterations included the addition of a brake servo and some engine tuning which enabled the maximum speed to exceed 100mph. This company also made the Harrington Alpine which was similar to the Le Mans in appearance but had prominent rear fins. This car in stage III could achieve 110mph.

Specifications and Production

	Alpine I	Alpine II	Alpine III	Alpine IV	Alpine V	Tiger 260	Tiger 289
Prod. period	Oct '59 -Oct '60	Oct '60 -Feb '63	Mar '63 -Jan '64	Jan '64 -Sep'65	Sep '65 -Jan '68	June '64 -Dec '66	Dec '66 -June '67
Prod. figures	11,904	19,956	5,863	12,406	19,122	6495	571
Bore mm	79	81.5	–	–	–	96.5	101.6
Stroke mm	76.2	–	–	–	82.55	73	73
Capacity cc	1494	1592	–	–	1725	4261	4737
Bhp	78	80	77	82	92.5	164	200
at rpm	5300	5000	–	–	5500	4400	4400
Weight cwt	18¾	–	19	20	–	22	–
0-50mph secs	10.2	9.9	10.1	10.2	9.8	6.8	6
Max. speed mph	99	99	95	93	98	117	118
Fuel con. mpg	31.5	26	25	23.5	25.5	17	16

Clubs

The clubs catering for these cars in the United Kingdom are the Sunbeam Alpine Owners Club, of which the membership secretary is Les Woodcock, 66, High Street, Newhall, Burton on Trent, Staffs. DE1 0HU, and the Sunbeam Tiger Owners Club, membership secretary Brian Postle, Beechwood, 8 Villa Real Estate, Consett, Co Durham, DH8 6BJ. Further information about the clubs can be obtained from their membership secretaries but please enclose a stamped and addressed envelope with your enquiry.

Triumph TR 4A, 5 & 6

Post-1965 TRs lost the simplicity of the early models. Jeremy Coulter investigates and helps you buy a good one

The development and history of the Triumph TRs has been too well chronicled for it to be necessary to recount it all once again. Suffice it to say that in 1965, the live-axled TR4, which was developed from the TR2, 3 and 3A was not superseded by the independently rear sprung TR4A. The independent suspension design persisted on the TR5 and TR6 until the last TR6 rolled from the production line in 1976 – to be replaced by the TR7 of totally different design. The 4A had the same basic 4-cylinder engine as the TR3 but the TR5 saw the introduction of the 6-cylinder 2500cc power unit. Those 5s and 6s sold in the UK were equipped with Lucas fuel injection but cars for export were de-toxed and had carburettors; the TR250 and TR6 carburettor respectively. Both the TR4A and the TR5 shared the same Michelotti-styled bodyshell, but the TR6 was re-styled and given a much smoother profile by Karmann. Of all the TRs, the 5 was the most powerful; the early 6s up to 1972 were only slightly less quick with 150bhp on tap, but after that the engines were de-tuned and, until their demise, the TR6 produced only some 125bhp.

The TR is a very strong and resilient car that can put up with considerable maltreatment and neglect. Unfortunately, in the past, this has been exactly the treatment meted out by many TR owners, although recently the situation has changed for the better. Often a TR will keep going when it really shouldn't and when many lesser machines have fallen by the wayside. The implications of this for the prospective TR owner are that many of the machines under consideration will be in distinctly bad condition – usually body and chassis problems rather than engine or transmission. With any TR it is the body and chassis condition that are of fundamental importance as both are time-consuming and often very expensive to repair, whereas mechanical work is usually much more straightforward. So, if you absolutely must buy a TR in imperfect condition, try hard to get one with a sound body and a suspect engine/transmission, rather than vice-versa. You will save yourself a lot of heartache and expense. When considering any car – but particularly a TR – examine it thoroughly and *then* drive it. Resist the temptation to drive it first as this is likely to blind you to the car's real faults.

The umbrella title of this article includes three TRs and there are naturally some points that apply specifically to one car; however, there are just as many areas of common ground which is not really surprising, bearing in mind the close relationship of all the models.

Body and Chassis

The wings on the 4A, 5 and 6 are all rather susceptible to rust so check these areas first. Make sure before going any further that the wings are in fact steel – indeed, at this point check the bonnet and boot as well as it's possible that a previous owner has fitted glass fibre replacements due to the unavailability or expense of the real thing. The wing tops are points to watch, as are the rear edges at each door post joint. The headlight surrounds on TR6s are vulnerable and water tends to run down the wing and start more rot both at the

joint between the front wing and the valance, and at the bottom corner of each wing.

The rear wings also tend to decay along the tops, and especially down each rear door post joint – often an indication that the door post itself is rotting. Luckily the front and rear wings are bolt-on and in theory are easily detachable, but this often is not the case as the bolts tend to rust solid. A soaking in penetrating oil sometimes does the trick, otherwise you will have to resort to drilling the bolts out or grinding off the heads. However, it is no real use bolting new outer wings to rusted inner wings, so check these sections too as closely as you can.

The 4A bonnet sometimes starts to decay along the front lip and around the hinges – the TR6 bonnet should also be checked in the latter respect, especially around the hinge mountings and these can be strained if the hinges themselves are inadequately lubricated. In the engine bay, some points to watch are the condition of the inner wings at the front, the battery box, and the surrounding bulkhead.

Doors and Roof

On all models, the doors can rot at the rear edge and along the top, adjacent to the weather strip. Blockage of the drain holes inside each door can lead to decay along the base, tending to concentrate at the rear corner. TR6s often seem to go around the keyhole which is located separately from the handle, but this is not the case on cars with the integral keyhole and handle.

Next, note the condition of the sills, especially the rearward sections, and then move inside the car and lift the carpets so that the inner sills and floorpan can be examined. The condition of the door posts should be suspected if the wings are poor; with the doors half open, examine each rear post, particularly the bottom corner, and then check the front post around the hinges and doorstop. In this position, you can also examine the leading edge of each door.

At the rear of the 4A and 5, note the condition of the boot lip – a common place for rust, especially around the handle. Inside the

Rare and fast, the TR5 has the Michelotti body and 6-cylinder engine.

A very sad TR6 door, wing and sill.

boot, on all models, check the spare wheel well, the inner wings and the wheel arches.

This really only leaves the windscreen and roof; check the screen surround for rust, particularly behind the weather seals. Although screens and surrounds can be had fairly easily, more than anything they are a pain to remove and fit so it's worth avoiding problems. At this stage, wind both windows up and down a few times to make sure that the mechanism is satisfactory and that the joint between each window and screen pillar is at least reasonable. The pillarless windows of the 4A, 5 and 6 were never particularly stable, but if you find one that rocks by an excessive amount when fully raised, it probably indicates a rotted window carrier.

The type of roof fitted to a TR depends on the model. The 4A and 5 were available with either a full soft-top or with the excellent "Surrey Top". A few TR6s are around with owner-fitted Surreys but somehow they don't look quite right. The TR6 was made with either a full hard-top or a soft-top. All models may at sometime have been fitted with a proprietary glass fibre lid. It is a matter of personal preference but on the 4A and 5, the Surrey has much to recommend it because in reasonable weather (or depending on your hardiness!) the detachable panel can quickly be unbolted and stored in the garage and the easily detachable/fitted fold-up canvas top substituted. If you buy a Surrey-topped car, make sure the canvas top is included. When considering a TR6, a good works hard-top is

The fuel injected 6-cylinder engine as fitted to the TR5 and 6.

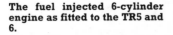

an advantage as you can always remove it at a later date and convert to a soft-top; doing it the other way round is likely to be more expensive.

Finally, a good indication that a TR has been involved in a frontal accident and subsequently repaired, is to examine the gap between the bonnet edges and the wings. This should be constant along its length and approximately the same at both sides; if it is wider at one side than at the other or if each gap is inconsistent it is quite possibly the result of accident impact, so quiz the vendor on this point.

Chassis, Suspension, Steering and Brakes

Luckily the chassis is very strong but it can suffer from rust in certain places, particularly the rear outrigger extensions which are open box sections. Also examine the rear chassis bridge on which the differential is mounted. The diff mountings can in some cases be wrenched from the bridge mountings and it has been known for owners/repairers to weld the mountings to the bridge – *not* recommended, so check closely even though the whole assembly is rather difficult to reach and see. A test you can carry out when the car is back on the ground which may reveal defective differential mountings is to drive forwards, then briskly select reverse and drive backwards, listening as you do for an ominous 'knock' from the area of the differential which may well indicate problems with the mountings.

A second bridge piece, in front of that just mentioned, acts as an upper bracket for the rear springs. It is possible for the upper ends of this bridge to distort upwards or even break off, so if the rear of the car is lopsided or sits low, this might be the trouble. Also examine the trailing arm mountings which can fracture and then finally test the condition of the links between the hydraulic damper units and each hub assembly.

At the front of the car, although the

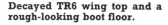
Seriously rotted rear door post and wing edge.

Decayed TR6 wing top and a rough-looking boot floor.

TR6 headlamp surrounds and valance are vulnerable as they are water traps.

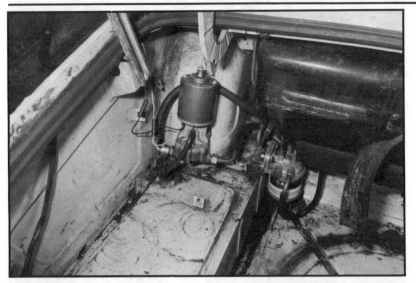

along each chassis member for evidence of rust damage. This is unlikely to occur at the front of the frame which is usually protected by accumulated engine or gear lubricant but the rearward members might be affected.

The steering components present few problems but the usual checks should be made for wear and play. It is important that the rubber gaiters at each end of the steering rack are in good condition, to prevent the ingress of damaging dirt and grit particles. The brakes are a powerful combination of front discs and rear drums with servo-assistance and no problems should be encountered.

Finally to the wheels. Wires, especially chrome, often look good but are difficult to keep clean and it is essential to check and maintain the spoke condition and tension regularly. Steel wheels may not be so

On fuel-injected cars, the fuel pump is located in the near-side corner of the boot.

TR6 cockpit – the fascia surround often gets very ragged.

suspension is basically the same as the TR4, the wishbone mountings were changed when the TR4A was introduced and these revised mountings are just not as good as the earlier ones. In fact they can break completely and cause a total collapse of one side of the front suspension, especially if the car is braked hard in reverse – so pay particular attention to the tightness of the fixing bolts and the state of the bracket welds. On the TR5 and 6, the single lower bolt was replaced by twin bolts but the problem still persists to a degree. As well as the checks mentioned above, look

attractive but they are certainly stronger; the type of wheel you opt for is entirely a matter of personal preference.

Engine, Transmission and Gearbox

The carburated 4-cylinder Vanguard-based engine fitted to the TR4A is extremely rugged and in many cases will run to a 6-figure mileage without the need for major attention. However, drops of oil on the ground under the rear of the engine could indicate a defective rear crankshaft oil seal. Keep an eye on the oil pressure as anything less than 35/40psi at 2000rpm with the engine hot should cause a little concern.

The 6-cylinder engine fitted to the TR5 and 6 lost much of the simplicity of the earlier 4-cylinder unit, the fuel-injected versions particularly so. However, if correctly adjusted and maintained, the Lucas fuel injection can operate reliably and (reasonably) economically for a long time. On the other hand, if it is neglected and, for example, the fuel tank is allowed to run almost dry, allowing dirt to be sucked into the injectors, it will become unreliable and thirsty. A simple check to make on the PI system is on the richness of the mixture. With the engine cold and without choke or throttle, operate the starter. If the engine starts first time and runs without trouble, it is likely that the system is badly adjusted. Asking to see a receipt for a recent PI service might not go amiss unless a DIY vendor looks as if he knows what he's doing. Naturally, versions of the 6-cylinder engine fitted with carburettors will not suffer from these problems, although you will pay a considerable horsepower penalty.

The bottom end of the 6-cylinder engine is not as strong as it might be. It is a very long

stroke power unit with rather narrow bearings and thin thrust washers. Any stray knocks or rattles should be worrying as it may point to thrust washer or bearing wear, but apart from this the engine is reliable.

On any TR, an overdrive gearbox is most desirable as it adds so much versatility to the normal gearing, particularly the early overdrive which operates on 2nd, 3rd and 4th, giving a ratio for every eventuality. If the overdrive doesn't work, the cause may well be a low gearbox oil level. On the other hand it may be dirt particles inside the unit – possibly the result of bearing or cog damage in the gearbox itself. Incorrect linkage adjustment or an electrical fault may also be to blame for the non-operation, so as you can see, a dead overdrive is a bit of a gamble. The 4A gearbox itself is very reliable and should seldom play up; the differential too is strong. Worn UJ spiders (there are six) on the propshaft and drive-shafts may cause some take-up knock in the transmission and it's worth testing this wear by hand if you can.

The TR5 and 6 gearbox is completely different from the unit fitted to the TR4A. Overdrive fitted to pre '73 5s and 6s operated on 2nd, 3rd and 4th but on later cars the J-type Laycock unit was replaced by the A-type which operated only on 3rd and 4th. The

From the front cover of "Thoroughbred & Classic Cars", April 1981, when this article first appeared, showing TR6s during and after extensive restoration.

gearbox layshaft roller bearings are fragile
and can break up causing a whine in all gears
but this can be difficult to detect.

Interior

Unfortunately, it is very easy for the interior of
a TR to start looking very scruffy. The door
trim pieces and front and rear inner wing
trims can get kicked inadvertently by driver
and passenger when clambering in and out.
Likewise, the carpets can wear badly at the
front if not protected by mats. The fascia and
door top trim sections often crack to reveal
foam filling underneath, particularly the door
top trims which are very vulnerable and can
fall away completely. Trim parts for TRs are
among the most difficult to obtain new or
second hand, so take note. Carpets on the
other hand are still obtainable.

TR production Figures

	UK	Export	Total
TR4A	3,075	25,390	28,465
TR5	1,161	1,786	2,947
TR250	–	8,484	8,484
TR6	8,370	86,249	94,619

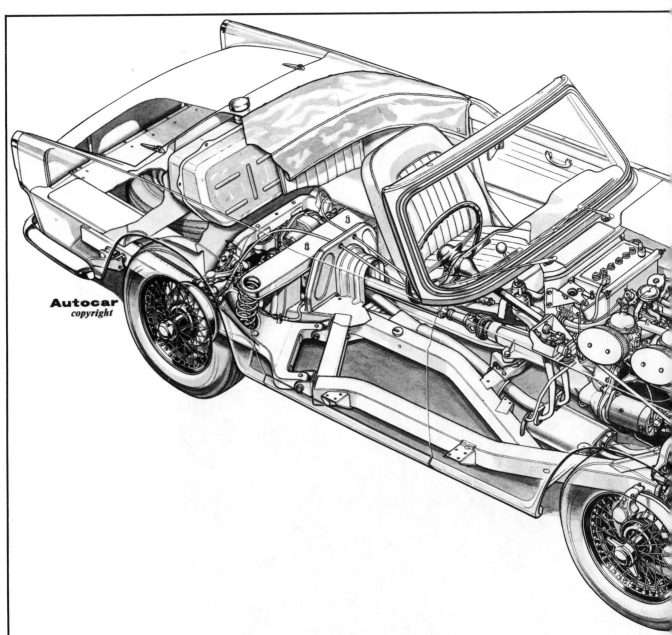

**Cutaway of a TR4A revealing
the sturdy chassis and the
major components of the
independent rear end as well
as the 4-cylinder engine.**

Autocar
copyright

220

Spares and Clubs

The spares situation for owners of TRs is much healthier than for many other marques. Some BL dealers may still hold a few parts, mainly for TR6s, which are quite 'young' cars, but generally you'll have to deal through a specialist. Foremost in the field is Cox and Buckles of Manor Road, Richmond, Surrey (tel. 01 948 6666); there are few parts they cannot supply, either new or re-manufactured and they will do their best to help you get the parts you need, if they do not actually have them in their recently acquired spacious warehouse premises in Richmond. Cox and Buckles have a second branch in the Midlands who are Peter Cox Sports Cars at 89 Fairfax Road, West Heath, Birmingham 31 (tel. 021 447 7966). TR improvements is another TR specialist, dealing in a wide range of new and second hand TR bits and pieces; they will also service your TR for you and the firm resides at 19 Carnavon Road, South Woodford, London E18 (tel 01 505 3017). A third specialist in TRs is the TR Shop at 16 Chiswick High Road, London W4 (tel. 01 995 6621) which holds stocks of new and second hand hard-to-find items for all TRs.

If you have a TR that needs restoration but maybe don't have the time to carry out the work yourself, you may like to get in touch with a company such as Racetorations which is a business associated with well known TR racer Daryl Uprichard. This firm specialises in TR spares, restoration and race preparation and their address is Unit 3b. Thornton Street, Gainsborough, Lincs. Tel: 0427 616565.

Another firm in the field of TR restoration is based near Luton and run by Kevin Kennedy. Called Classic Cars Lilley, Kevin's firm specialises in TR6s and TR5s and, as well as rebuilding customers' cars, CCL will obtain and rebuild a TR6 exactly to a customer's specifications and to an agreed budget and also hand-build TR5s and TR6s to as-new condition. Kevin can be reached on 046 276 542.

For the owner of any TR, membership of the TR Register is essential. Newsletters including detailed spares news, local groups, events and other happenings are all organised regularly and to get more information you should contact the Membership Secretary, Val Simpson, at 271 High Street, Berkhamsted, Herts HP4 1AA, tel: 04427 5906. The other TR club is the TR Drivers Club, who can be contacted through Peter Gange, 8 Benton Drive, Chinnor, Oxfordshire.

This article first appeared in "Thoroughbred & Classic Cars" magazine.

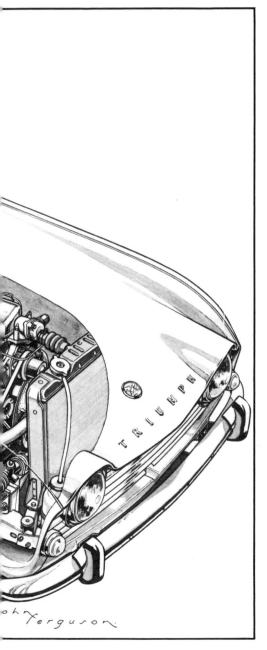

Triumph GT6

Graham Robson looks at what's involved in buying a Triumph GT6.

It was one of the most intriguing 'parts-bin engineering' jobs of the 1960s. Triumph's technical chief Harry Webster surveyed his developing range of models, slotted the forthcoming Vitesse 2-litre engine transmission into a Spitfire body/chassis unit, asked Michelotti to style a fastback roof derivative and – *voila* – the GT6 was born.

The know-alls, of course, suggested that Triumph were trying to fight back at the MGB GT, but – as so often – the know-alls were wrong. The first GT6 prototype had been built in 1963, the roof shape had been seen at Le Mans in 1964, and in any case the weld of mechanical components was so much more adventurous than that of the MG.

The GT6 had a relatively short life – seven years – and made both friends and enemies. Because it was so obviously based on other Triumph models it must have been a profit-maker for Triumph/British Leyland, yet it was not a best-seller. As far as today's sporting car enthusiasts are concerned, however, it had a great deal of character, and an unmistakable image.

Even so, there are good GT6s, and not so-good types. Here's why:

The Choice of GT6s

The GT6 story really starts with the birth of the Triumph Herald in 1956. This was the separate-chassis/built-up body/all-independent suspension model with which Standard-Triumph hoped to expand into the '60s. There were early build quality problems, and the handling soon became a cause for criticism, but the Herald went on to sell well for more than ten years.

By slotting a straight six-cylinder engine into the Herald's structure, the Vitesse 6 was born, at first in 1.6-litre form, and went on sale in mid-1962. Then, in the autumn of the same year, Triumph introduced the Spitfire 4, which (though it had a new frame) was really a short-chassis version of the Herald, clad in a smart sports car two-seater style by Michelotti. The range already described was improved, and further developed, but like most British firms in the 1960s, Standard-Triumph had the urge to make their cars faster, with larger engines. Accordingly, for launch in October 1966, the Vitesse 6 was up-graded, from 1.6-litres to 2.0-litres, fitted with a new all synchromesh gearbox, and renamed Vitesse 2-litre.

At the same time, the GT6 made its bow, and a quick look at its specification showed exactly how it had been developed. The basic 'building block' was the 6ft 11in wheelbase backbone-style Spitfire chassis frame, complete with all-independent suspension – coil springs and wishbones at the front, transverse leaf spring and swing axles at the rear. There was rack and pinion steering, and a quite phenomenal (24 foot turning circle) steering lock.

The engine chosen was the 1,998cc/95bhp/twin Zenith-Stromberg carburettor unit of the Vitesse 2-litre, allied to the new all-synchromesh gearbox, with an optional overdrive.

The engine was a snug fit, in the same way as it was to make the Vitesse out of the Herald, but there were never any overheating or accessibility problems. Unavoidably, though, it made the car a bit nose heavy (weight distribution, as measured by *Autocar's* road testers, was 57.4/42.6 per cent, biased to the front).

The basic body shell was Triumph Spitfire, complete with a lift-up bonnet/front wings/wheel arches sub-assembly. For the GT6, however, there was a fixed, fastback style, top, complete with a lift-up hatchback,

figure-hugging seats, and a new facia style, with a wooden board. It was, in some ways, a 'mini-E-Type' in its looks, though not in its performance, or its charisma. Compared with the Spitfire, the GT6 had a softer ride, and a much smoother torque delivery, plus a 105/110mph top speed – but the original car had all the usual Herald-chassis handling faults, heavy understeer which turned into flick oversteer at the limit, and a penchant for tucking its outside rear wheels under the body if pressed. In that respect, if in no other, the MGB GT left it far behind.

The result, speedily-developed, was the GT6 Mk 2 of October 1968, in which there was clever 'lower-wishbone' type of rear suspension, which cured the handling problem at a stroke. At the same time, engine revisions saw peak power raised to 104bhp, and for a time the 3.27:1 final drive ratio also became standard with overdrive as well as with non-overdrive transmission. There were also facia panel revisions, and new 'dummy-Rostyle' wheel trims, plus the latest 'bone-in-the-teeth' front bumper position. Extra cooling louvres in the front wheel arches, and the rear

quarters, did something to improve the under-bonnet and passenger compartment ventilation, respectively.

It was now a 110mph car without any doubt, and was a very quick little machine, selling well in the USA as well as in the UK.

The GT6 Mk 3 nose, with more subtle styling, but the same basic proportions.

However, in October 1970, after only two years, the car benefited from the complete reskin and chopped-tail restyle for the Spitfire, and became GT6 Mk 3, complete with a more integrated rear end shape, nicer detail lines all around, recessed door handles, and yet more slight changes to the interior. The overdrive final drive ratio, incidentally, went back to 3.89:1, but there was no change to the power output, or the performance. In the next three years, the GT6's engine power output actually crept slowly downwards, as a variety of exhaust emission regulations (mostly USA-derived) hit hard, such that the final cars only had 95bhp again! For the 1973 season, only, the GT6 Mk 3 lost its lower wishbone rear suspension, in favour of the simple, but very effective, swing-spring, swing-axle layout which had been introduced for the Spitfire Mk IV. There was no discernible loss of roadholding capability.

The GT6 was dropped at the end of 1973, really because it was no longer thought worth modifying the design to keep it 'road legal' in the USA, where the majority of sales had been made. A total of 40,926 cars were built.

The Triumph GT6 today. Where and How to Look

Only about 9,000 GT6s, of all types, were sold in the UK when the model was current. Since the last of these was made 12 years ago – and after allowing for accidents, general deterioration, and the acknowledged private export of some examples, I doubt if even 5,000 are

still left. One interesting statistic is that the one-make club, the Triumph Sports Six Club, had 1,200 GT6s on its books at the beginning of this year.

The good news, of course, is that the chassis are robust, such that the cars do not rust into the ground. The bodies, however, are by no means rust-proof, which means that a high proportion of the cars have been, or need to be, restored!

Before you even go out to find a car, read the road tests, and assess the amount of space the car offers inside. It was a deceptive style – the fact is that the GT6 was only ever a pure two-seater, with limited luggage accommodation. It was a slim car – overall width 4ft 9in – not one in which you could carry too much impedimenta.

Chassis Frame

The main structural members of the frame are very solid, and should still be in good shape today; it is the hang-on bits, outriggers, and suspension towers, plus bonnet supports, which may have suffered.

Start by checking around the front suspension towers, for any sign of twisting, chafing, or accident damage. Then check up on the outriggers, front and rear, where they are welded to the main backbone. (Outriggers, incidentally, can be purchased – there is no need to look for a complete frame). Be sure that there is no problem with the bracketry supporting the final drive, the rear lower wishbones, and the bonnet supports.

The chassis-based construction concept as used for the Triumph Herald and adapted for the Spitfire, proved so successful that it was used again for the GT6, this from a Mk 1.

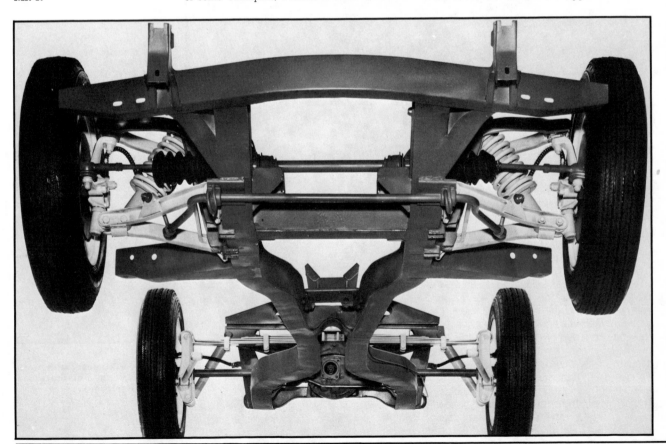

Accident damage to the GT6 frame is usually confined to the front end (a high proportion have had front-end shunts) ...), so be absolutely convinced that the suspension alignment is still sound. That advice also applies to the steering rack mountings.

Bodyshell

The GT6 rusts, quite badly, and it is much less simple to take apart than the Spitfire, to make repairs. However, because of the way the shell is built up, start an inspection by checking out all the panel fits – bonnet to frame, bonnet to scuttle, doors in apertures, and so on.

Then look long and hard (with the assistance of the versatile magnet and screwdriver – the restorer's first diagnostic tools!), at the inner and outer sills, for these provide much of the body's beam strength. The Herald/Vitesse had outer chassis longitudi-

Ventilation was aided by the opening rear quarter lights.

The GT6 was distinguished by a long, sweeping, fastback, with an opening hatch. The shape had already been seen, two years earlier, on the Spitfire race and rally cars.

Access to the somewhat restricted rear luggage bay was via a 'lift-up' rear door, with the spare wheel hidden in the depths.

nals, but this function was carried out by body sills in the sports cars. Other major problems may be concentrated in the underside, and the tail. Look at undersides of rear wings, crown lines close to panel joints (or under chrome strips), below the rear bumpers, in the spare wheel well, and where the inner wheel arches meet the other panels. There could have been water leaks, which may have affected the floor footwells, and even the door hinge areas.

The bottom edges of doors, and of the big lift-up front section, may also show rust, as may the metal areas around the headlamp/ side lamp/indicator cut-outs, along with panel joints, or the edges of recesses for bumpers and over-riders. Check up, too, the condition of the rear suspension radius arm mounts, behind the seats in the floorpan.

All in all, anywhere that water – particularly salty water – could splash, is a potential trouble spot. There is now a proportion of GT6s which have been well-restored, and are in better-than-new condition – but you'll have to pay accordingly.

The GT6 engine bay scarcely changed throughout but the Mk 3 also had cold air trunking for the air cleaner running to the nose alongside the radiator block.

Power Train

Engines, particularly the later 104 bhp variety (which have an entirely different cylinder head casting) are generally robust, and only show old age via clattery valve gear, and oil burning.

Be sure that the carburettors are properly balanced (that's not too difficult an operation, assuming that spindles are not worn, and diaphragms are in good shape).

You can get all the replacement valve gear items, even today, but an engine shouldn't need a rebuild before 70,000/80,000 miles. Be sure the oil pressure is adequate (40 psi was about normal), and that there is no suspicion of water or oil loss (some cylinder head cracking is known). In general, though, this is not a highly stressed engine, and if well watered and lubricated it should be long-lasting.

It's a nice little gearbox, with strong synchromesh and a rather notchy change. Noises, when they develop, will mostly be connected with faulty or worn bearings, particularly between the input shaft from the clutch, and the mainshaft.

Most of the GT6s have overdrives, which should not be leaking oil, and which should have a crisp change (and should work on third and top gear). Such o/ds can be rebuilt, but old-age problems are usually confined to faulty electric solenoids, and dirty oil. Remember that a transmission change means that the box has to come out through the passenger compartment (not by dropping downwards) – can you face that?

The final drives should be OK (the weak diffs were in the early four-cylinder Heralds), but check up for clonky drive-on/drive-off behaviour, and look for signs of oil leakage from seals, at the pinion entrance from the propshaft, and around the casing fixings. While you are in that area, check up on the condition of the rubber 'doughnuts' in the rear drive shafts on 'lower-wishbone' suspension cars. Replacements are still available, but they're not cheap.

Suspension, Steering and Brakes

Although the suspension layout is simplicity itself, it is also a fact that all manner of bushes, trunnions, and ball joints, can – and do – wear out. Accordingly, in the ramp inspection, and the road test that you will surely make, check out cheap-to-replace items like front suspension wishbone bushes, front suspension trunnions and the upper ball joint, and the condition of the hub bearings.

At the rear, not only the rubber 'doughnuts' of the drive shafts, but the other (inner) drive shaft U/Js wear, as do the bushes at the front end of the radius arms. Note that on 'lower-wishbone' cars the rear dampers have uppermountings way up in the wheel arches – are these bushes, too, in need of renewal?

The springs themselves should still be in good condition, but the dampers had a life of perhaps not more than 30,000/40,000 miles

time. Have a look at the handbrake cables, and the adjustment, and of course the condition of the flexible hoses.

Trim and Furnishing

Although most soft trim is still available (all parts have now been remanufactured), our advice would always be to make sure that any car you are considering buying is mechanically and bodily complete, so that you don't have a long and frustrating wait for parts.

Many of these cars have had extra switches or instruments fitted, then perhaps removed, so it is always wise to check that the wood in the facia/instrument panel is in good condition. You can still get all the glass – fortunately the screen is common with the Spitfire, and readily available.

Carpets were of no more than so-so quality, and it is possible they may need

Parts Supply

Mechanically, most parts can still be found through the Unipart network, though it helps to have a friendly, once long-established Standard-Triumph dealer, and you *must* know the old part number, even to stand a chance. The last GT6 was built, after all, before BL was even nationalised, and there have been all manner of upheavals since then!

Bodywise, some panels are becoming scarce, though much of the shell, if not the same as the equivalent Spitfire, could certainly be modified from a Spitfire panel.

There is no one particular GT6 specialist, though more and more expertise is being developed by companies known to, and encouraged by, the one-make club.

Don't whisper it too loud in the presence of Vitesse fans in the one-make club, but much of the running gear from the equivalent Vitesse 2-litre will not only fit a GT6, but is actually the same. Spitfires of the period, in general, had slightly different parts (particularly in the transmission), but compare part numbers in the invaluable Parts Books, and you might find more recent Spitfire parts (more easily available) to do the job.

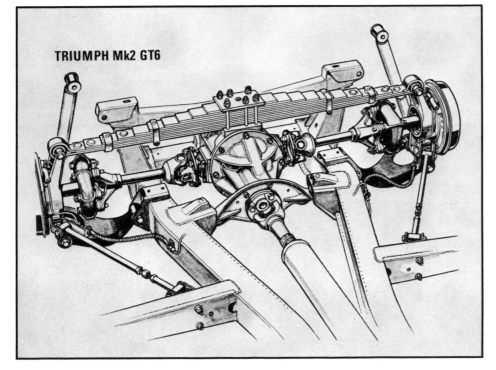

TRIUMPH Mk2 GT6

This is the suspension layout which was virtually unchanged throughout until, in its last year, the GT6 Mk 3 had a simplified 'swing spring' type of rear suspension, like that of the Mk IV Spitfire.

when new, and they may have gone soft. Road test the car and you'll soon know!

Apart from being sure that the steering ball joints are in good shape, you should also look at the rubber pad mountings between the rack and the chassis frame. If these get oil soaked, they lose their effectiveness, and the steering will feel vague.

If the car is fitted with centre-lock wire-spoke wheels, check that there are no missing, or broken, spokes, for although you can get wheels rebuilt, these days it isn't cheap or easy. Don't forget to look at the spare.

The brakes on this car – Girling front discs, and rear drums – have quite an easy time. It is a simple installation, but it may need some routine attention and rebuilding by this

renewing. Perhaps not original, but re-manufactured, supplies, can be found. In this, and other respects of restoration, the one-make club, and the specialists they recommend, can be very useful.

Be sure that all the brightwork is on the car you intend to buy. The supply of electrical items like side lamps and indicators – even the Mk 3 tail-lamp clusters – is assured, but the special items like badging are no longer easy. It is, after all, many years since British Leyland stopped building the GT6 – you can't expect them to be interested in the car any more.

One way or another, however (the one-make club recommended specialists being the advisable route) you should always be able to bring a GT6 back to its former glory.

GT6 on the Road

The basic advice we give is what everyone gives – forget about the 1966-1968 Mk 1 cars, which have evil handling when pressed, but be assured that the handling of the later models, whether lower wishbone or swing-spring (1973 only), is perfectly acceptable.

You'll find that a good GT6 has a sweet and silky torque delivery, and makes very pleasing noises (not for nothing was it dubbed a 'mini E-Type'); the engines are happiest when revving between 3,000 and 5,000rpm, but smooth throughout. Gearboxes are a pleasure to use once the initial notchiness has worn away, though you might get irritated by the general clonkiness of the drive line – there seemed to be a build up of tolerances between the clutch face and the driven wheels.

Become used to sitting low, and being in what might feel to be a slightly claustrophobic interior. The cars always seemed to be quite prone to getting muggy, and misting up internally – though the ventilation efficiency improved progressively from model to model.

There's quite firm understeer much of the time, with the Mk 2 and Mk 3 models then transferring to a rather tyre-juddery neutral stance towards the limit. The Mk 1s tuck under

The original GT6 of 1966 had a cosy, some say cramped, passenger compartment, in which a polished wood fascia was a feature.

The GT6 Mk 2's fascia differed from the original by having a matt wood panel, and a padded steering wheel.

their wheels, oversteer viciously, and are generally not nice. In all cases the ride is quite firm, and jolty – a well-worn GT6 never lets you forget that some of its bushes are worn, and even good ones can squeak and generally sound 'busy'.

The steering properly maintained and set up, can be crisp and delightful – just so long as those mounting pads are not weakened. Efforts are low, of course, but if you use all of that phenomenal lock there is quite a lot of front tyre scrub when the efforts are higher.

In outright terms, a GT6 should be good for 0-60mph in around 10 seconds, have a natural cruising speed of more than 80mph (more than 90mph, if overdrive is fitted), the flat-out top speed of about 110mph. Fuel economy? Well, naturally it all depends on the way you drive, but *Autocar's* Mk2 recorded 25.2, and its Mk 3 27.6mpg – with a relaxed approach to high-speed cruising, you might notch up 30mpg on longer runs.

Best Buys and Values

There's no doubt in our minds on this point – the best GT6s were the last ones – so the Mk 3 is the most desirable, the Mk 2 next, and the original Mk 1 least of all.

The *very* best have overdrive (a high proportion did ....), and most people say they look better with centre-lock wire wheels, in spite of the well-known old-age problems.

Our 'best buy' therefore, would be a re-skinned, overdrive and wire-wheels model built before 1973 (and the arrival of swing-spring rear suspension). As to the Mk 2's, those built after October 1969 (and chassis no. 75031) were best of all, for they had the seat recline adjustment, and other cosmetic improvements.

Values? They vary a lot, because the conditon of cars coming up for sale also vary, but GT6s are 'coming up' (as they say in the real estate and antiques business!). Reckon on spending £1,000 for a Mk 1 (but haggle ...), perhaps £1,500 for a Mk 2, and up to £2,000 for a good Mk 3, which is still cheap by almost any

modern standards. A new Fiat 126, after all, costs around £2,400 ...

Where Built

Final assembly was always at the Triumph factory at Canley, Coventry, with the engine, and all the transmissions being machined in the city. Chassis frames came from Sankeys, while bodies came together at the Forward Radiator Co (a Triumph subsidiary) in Birmingham, but were painted and trimmed in Coventry. Front suspension and steering came from Alford & Alder in Hemel Hempstead (another Triumph subsidiary).

Join the Club?

There's no doubt at all about this one – you *must* join the Triumph Sports Six Club, which has been one of the most notable success stories on the one-make club scene in the early 1980s.

The TSSC started from nothing in 1977, passed the thousand member mark three years later, and at the time of writing has over 6,000 members and climbing fast. TSSC covers all cars in what are known as the 'Herald Chassis family', but the latest census of members showed nearly 7,000 individual cars registered, of which no fewer than 1,200 were GT6s.

The club offers everything – fellowship, social events, concours, speed events, and of course a spares, restoration, and technical advisory service. They have a 'mole' at the old Coventry factory who keeps an eye on the parts situation for items becoming scarce, and a fine monthly magazine which carries much advertising from the acknowledged specialists.

To get involved send an SAE to: 121B, St. Mary's Road, Market Harborough, Leics. LE16 7DT. (tel: 0858 34424).

This article first appeared in "Sporting Cars" magazine.

Production Changes

October 1966: GT6 announced, using modified Spitfire chassis and suspension, but 2-litre 6-cyl. engine (95bhp), all-synchro. box, and fastback/hatchback two-seater style based on that of Spitfire. Swing-axle back end retained.

October 1968: GT6 Mk 2 launched, basically as before, but with much better lower-wishbone type of independent rear suspension, plus 104bhp, and restyled nose, with raised bumper.

October 1969: Cosmetic changes included fitment of reclining front seats.

October 1970. Mk 2 discontinued in favour of Mk 3, with reskinned body shell, of same general lines, but with cut-off tail, recessed door handles, no bonnet louvres.

February 1973: Mk 3 given slightly wider wheel tracks but, most important, given swing-spring swing-axle, rear suspension instead of lower-wishbone design. Nett result was very similar, though costs were considerably reduced.

December 1973: GT6 withdrawn from production.

(Note: Spitfire, on which GT6 was based in so many ways, continued in production until 1980).

GT6 Production 1966 to 1973

GT6 Mk 1 (66-68):	15,818
GT6 Mk 2 (68-70):	12,066
GT6 Mk 3 (70-73):	13,042*
Total	40,926

* This figure includes 4,218 1973-model 'swing-spring' cars.

Note: About 80 per cent (32,000) GT6s were sold for export, of which 22,658 went to the United States. Only about 9,000 GT6s were sold in the UK when new, and some of these cars have inevitably been exported since then.

Buying a Volkswagen Beetle

by Robin Wager

It was a wise man who said 'There's enough free trouble in the world without paying good money for more!' – and this was never more true than in relation to the secondhand car.

When it comes to the Beetle, its reputation goes before it to the extent that some people believe it to be unbreakable, totally reliable, and rot-proof. Of course, the truth falls somewhat short of the legend. However, I wouldn't be editing and publishing a successful Volkswagen (and Audi) magazine today if the Beetle – on which it was founded and built up its circulation – hadn't proved to be something very special among cars.

No-one has ever really succeeded in putting into words exactly what the magic attraction is, and why so many owners over the years have become hooked on it to the total exclusion of any other model; however, I believe the three main areas of appeal are (a) simplicity (b) reliability and (c) character.

Because the People's Car was envisaged by Adolf Hitler as a means of mass mobility, and because that concept was brought to

reality by the engineering genius of Ferdinand Porsche, the Beetle is cleverly uncomplicated.

A separate floorpan/chassis, carrying the engine and transaxle in a fork at the rear, supports the bolt-on body, to which in turn are bolted the four wings. The main control linkages run inside the central 'backbone' tunnel, while the air-cooled, flat-four engine is removed and installed in next to no time for maintenance. Everything is enclosed and well protected – Beetles even float!

With so little to go wrong, the Beetle's reliability is assured, but that doesn't mean mechanical failures never occur. Likewise, its shape and construction make it pretty rust-resistant, but that's not to say that Beetles never fail the MoT test through corrosion.

So how can you be sure of buying a good example secondhand? Well, in an article of this length I can't give an inch-by-inch instruction course – but the Haynes Publishing Group will soon be publishing a book that *will* do so, entitled *VW Beetle (and Transporter) – Guide to Purchase & DIY Restoration* and which is heartily recommended, especially since not only does it include a full catalogue of Specifications and production changes, but also a detailed section by Yours Truly on buying a Beetle!

The first essential is to decide which model you are after. 'But surely, 'I hear you say, 'a Beetle is a Beetle?' In appearance this may be true, yet in everything but the basic shape the car has changed so much over its 40 years of production that it would be just about

Right up to this Beetle, the last one built in Europe, the car retained its familiar outline and structure: though, beneath the skin, many, many changes took place. (Courtesy Volkswagen).

Over the years there have been so many types of interior that it is almost impossible to detail what should or shouldn't be there for originality. The best approach is to go to one of the large national club events and see what other cars in original condition and of the same age and type are fitted with. The presence of standard fixtures and fittings is a distinct plus and the absence of extra knobs, dials and gauges is also to be welcomed, unless they are contemporary and useful.

The engine, this one shown removed from the car and viewed from the front, is very easy to take out and put in, but is complex to overhaul which makes an engine rebuild relatively expensive.

impossible to detail every difference. Bear in mind, though, the following important points:

(1) The earliest Beetles (up to 1953) had two small triangular windows at the rear ('split window'); this model is now virtually unobtainable and is much sought after by collectors. From 1953 to 1957 the rear window was oval, and from then on it became more or less the shape and size it is today (yes, Beetles are still made, well into the 21st million, in South America).

(2) Up to 1967 all Beetles had 6V electrics, which can be problematical.

(3) Virtually the only departure from the 'standard' Beetle shape occurred with the 'Super Beetle' – the 1302 series – in 1970. This had what was called a 'pregnant' front end that was more bulbous, increasing luggage space and involving a change in the front suspension from the traditional torsion bars to MacPherson struts, which proved somewhat more trouble-prone. The 1302 was eventually restyled further, becoming the 1303 with its markedly curved windscreen (and, incidentally, an 'S' after either of these model designations indicates a 1.6 litre engine).

(4) Standard power unit for the Beetle was traditionally the '1200' (1192cc) with a later option of a '1300' (1285cc) and a '1500' (1493cc), the latter considered by many to have been the nicest of the standard engines. Further stretching to 1600 (1584cc) brought with it some problems, not least a thirst for fuel.

(5) From 1970 all 1300 and 1600 units were 'twin port', i.e. possessed two separate induction manifolds serving separate ports in each cylinder head. This type of engine is readily identified from a glance at the engine

compartment, and whilst offering slightly improved breathing it did tend to suffer an increased incidence of cylinder head cracking.

(6) 1500 and 1600 engined models were usually equipped with front disc brakes, the rest having drums all round (though these work extremely well).

(7) There have been many 'special editions' over the years, most of them identifiable by special wheels and/or trim.

(8) Remember that the Beetle was also produced in convertible form. The Cabriolets were not directly produced by Volkswagen and tend to be more corrosion-prone. Much rarer than the saloons, they are very sought after and command high prices in good condition (sometimes, for the unwary, in bad condition too!)

(9) Caution! The foregoing are guidelines only. Because of the interchangeability of

Beetle components, and the fact that the model has sold in over 100 markets worldwide, there are many 'mongrel' cars in the UK. Check on points like engine capacity by serial number – don't rely on the bootlid badge.

Having decided on a likely model, where do you start looking? Personal recommendation to a seller is difficult to beat, but if you can't find a car this way the obvious next step has got to be to get the latest issue of *VW Motoring,* which you should find at most main newsagents, and turn to the Classified section. Our advertisers are our readers, therefore enthusiasts, and the cars offered are likely to be well looked after and genuine. It's most unlikely that you will fail to find a suitable car by this means. An invaluable aid when vetting a prospective vehicle is a knowledgeable VW enthusiast. Your local VW club (again, listed in *VW Motoring*) will probably be able to assist

here if you don't know anyone suitable.

For the purpose of this article it must be assumed that the prospective purchaser is familiar with the more common mechanical aspects of checking out a used car – things such as bounce-testing the shock absorbers, and checking for serious oil leaks. Do all these tests as a matter of course, but be mindful of the differences between a Beetle and a mere car; for example, Beetles *never* have a leaking radiator!

Another example concerns engine noise. While one normally tends to be suspicious of a

Running boards are easy to renew. German ones are well built but South American running boards are too flimsy to stand on. You can easily check for type by attempting to flex them with your thumb.

Front and rear wings are of the bolt-on type which makes them fairly easy to change and at the same time they are cheap and readily available just like the lights, bumpers and other fixtures and fittings.

At the upper end of the expense scale is a replacement soft top for the cabriolet.

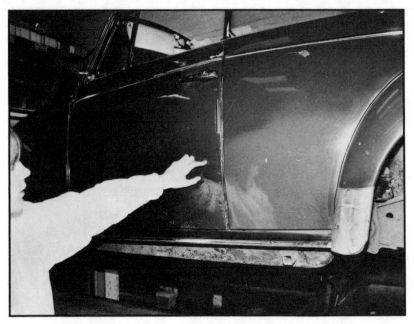

You may not think so to look at it but this was a very badly corroded car. Filler had been used so cleverly that the only way to check for it was by using a magnet. In the event, every body panel of this car had to be replaced, so be warned!

noisy engine, a Beetle's engine is *always* noisy, at least from outside the car. It's the *kind* of noise that is important; healthy tappet noise is a good sign (Beetle tappets should always be slightly loose) but beware loud metallic tapping or heavy thumping.

Similarly, a puff of smoke on starting up is not necessarily a bad omen, since the horizontal cylinders can allow oil to seep into the combustion chambers whilst the engine is stopped. If the oil smoke continues during normal running, however, that's a different matter.

If there are any significant oil leaks from the engine, try to identify the source. Sump plate or drain plug leaks are seldom a problem; pushrod tube leaks (common) are

more costly to rectify; and crankcase or oil cooler leaks could be very expensive. When test driving the car check that, with the engine thoroughly warm, the oil pressure light stays out (slight flickering at idle speed may be just a worn sender unit).

Operate the heater controls and check not only for heat, but also for any smell of exhaust fumes inside the car. Heat exchangers can and do corrode, and are pricey to renew.

The normal Beetle ride can be described as firm but bouncy. Any sensation of wandering can be attributable to the car having crossply tyres (the biggest single improvement for a Beetle, in my opinion, is to change from crossplys to radials), but may also indicate worn steering or dampers.

Check the steering itself. There should be about $3/4$in free play in the straight-ahead position at the rim of the steering wheel, with up to 4in on full lock. Anything more may mean simple adjustment, but could indicate a new steering box (pricey) or balljoints (check for wear by inspection and levering).

Do the normal clutch and gearbox tests, but remember that you are not dealing with a Ford Popular. Renewal of the transaxle unit is very expensive, so if you are at all suspicious of a fault here, such as a bad whine or jumping out of gear, take this fact into account. Make the usual brake checks. With disc brakes, be wary of a car that pulls to one side or makes noises on braking. Calipers can seize, and replacements (usually involving discs as well) are expensive.

As with the mechanical side; when it comes to checking out the bodywork we must assume some degree of knowledge. Rippled areas, of course, indicate damage repairs, as does resprayed paintwork – unless the entire car has been resprayed for cosmetic reasons.

A favourite Beetle corrosion spot is beneath the rear seat and in the rear wheel arch area. Check carefully before buying. Here repair panels are being fitted.

Externally, Beetles exhibit corrosion in certain common places, such as the base of the front and rear quarter panels, and the bottoms of the doors. When this sort of rust is readily apparent it is a fair assumption that there is more serious rot in hidden areas, so check carefully the following:

(1) Spare wheel well (under front hood – lift wheel out). The base of this can rot right away in severe cases.

(2) Base of door hinge pillars, usually accompanied by rotting of the sill channels. The best way to check the latter is to lift the rear seat cushion, which may reveal a pretty horrific sight! (While you're under there, check that the battery isn't about to drop through the floor – it can corrode its housing).

(3) The jacking points – especially if (2) reveals problems. Chances are you can't jack the car up safely using the standard jack.

(4) Around the shock absorber top mountings (and especially the MacPherson strut top housings of Super Beetles).

(5) Around the frame head at the front end of the floorpan.

In spite of what you may have found during the foregoing checks, there are very few Beetle maladies which are truly terminal. Any Beetle can be repaired, even to the extent of a new body or floorpan (or even both, rather like the proverbial broom that lasts forever with only the occasional new head or handle!) But with a badly neglected car this may be possible only at an unacceptable cost in money and/or time. The individual purchaser must also consider his or her own situation in terms of available resources, technical skills and spare time.

I have seen enough cases of enthusiasts, particularly younger ones who have spent their entire savings on a first car, suffer the disappointment of learning at the first MoT test that their Beetle needs hundreds of pounds' worth of work just to make it roadworthy. Don't fall into this trap; spend time checking out your prospective purchase, rather than money later; that way you should enjoy many thousands of miles of motoring in a car that's well built, reliable, satisfying to own and, above all, *different*. (That is, if you don't count the other 20-million-plus that have been made to date, and the hundreds that will be made tomorrow ...!)

"Buying a Volkswagen Beetle" was specially written for this book by Robin Wager, the editor of "VW Motoring" magazine.